Books in the Contemporary World Issues series address vital issues in today's society, such as genetic engineering, pollution, and biodiversity. Written by professional writers, scholars, and nonacademic experts, these books are authoritative, clearly written, up-to-date, and objective. They provide a good starting point for research by high school and college students, scholars, and general readers as well as by legislators, businesspeople, activists, and others.

Each book, carefully organized and easy to use, contains an overview of the subject, a detailed chronology, biographical sketches, facts and data and/or documents and other primary-source material, a directory of organizations and agencies, annotated lists of print and nonprint resources, and an index.

Readers of books in the Contemporary World Issues series will find the information they need to have a better understanding of the social, political, environmental, and economic issues facing the world today.

GLOBAL ORGANIZED CRIME

A Reference Handbook

Mitchel P. Roth, PhD

CONTEMPORARY
WORLD ISSUES

 ABC-CLIO

Santa Barbara, California • Denver, Colorado • Oxford, England

Library of Congress Cataloging-in-Publication Data
Roth, Mitchel P., 1953–
   Global organized crime : a reference handbook / Mitchel P. Roth.
     p. cm. — (Contemporary world issues)
   Includes index.
   ISBN 978-1-59884-332-3 (print : alk. paper) —
ISBN 978-1-59884-333-0 (ebook) 1. Organized crime—Handbooks, manuals, etc. 2. Transnational crime—Handbooks, manuals, etc.
I. Title.
   HV6441.R678   2010
   364.106—dc22   2010000107

14 13 12 11 10   1 2 3 4 5

This book is also available on the World Wide Web as an eBook.
Visit www.abc-clio.com for details.

ABC-CLIO, LLC
130 Cremona Drive, P.O. Box 1911
Santa Barbara, California 93116-1911

This book is printed on acid-free paper ∞™

Manufactured in the United States of America

Contents

List of Tables

Preface

Over the last 20 years the world's organized crime groups have adapted to the changing forces of globalization, the rise of the Internet, the collapse of the Soviet Union, the dismantlement of Yugoslavia, and the end of apartheid—events that were unimaginable at the beginning of the 1990s. This book was written with the intent of moving beyond the outdated explanations and histories of organized crime and to place these groups within the context of the 21st century. After the attacks on September 11, 2001, America's law enforcement agencies at every level of government transferred most of their resources and attention toward fighting a "war on terror." As a result most organized crime activity since 9/11 has continued virtually unimpeded. What's more, the distinctions between terrorist groups and organized crime networks have become increasingly blurred as each form of criminality borrows strategies from the other. With many terrorist groups losing their state sponsors in the aftermath of the collapse of the Soviet Union, they have turned toward criminal activities to finance their operations and in many cases have begun to look more and more like traditional organized crime groups.

Like the legitimate global economies that they mimic, a parallel illicit underground economy has developed, taking advantage of the same opportunities as its legitimate counterparts. Although global organized crime seems to be a rather new phenomenon, a brief history of this criminality in Chapter 1 demonstrates that pirates in the 17th century and slave traders even earlier were actually their forefathers in spirit and nature. Global organized crime has not manifested itself in a vacuum, but is the result of many different forces that challenge governments, police forces, and populations.

It has been more than eight years since I became a monthly instructor at the International Law Enforcement Academy (ILEA) in Roswell, New Mexico. During that time I have taught class modules on transnational organized crime and the challenges it presents to police organizations. My students are usually high-ranking police executives, who come from such disparate parts of the world as Central Asia, Sub-Saharan Africa, China, Indonesia, and Latin America. What have become increasingly clear in these classes are the participants' growing concerns over global organized crime issues. What was once mainly a domestic issue has morphed into a hydra-headed problem that now seems insurmountable to police forces hampered by jurisdictional restraints and other barriers. This book was written with many of their concerns in mind by offering a research guide to those seeking to learn more about the process of globalization and its concomitant impact on organized crime.

Chapter 1 provides an introduction into the history of global organized crime. It examines two of the oldest examples of this phenomenon, slavery and sea piracy. This chapter traces the economic factors that led to the problem of piracy on the high seas and then contrasts piracy today with times past. It also seeks to define organized crime, transnational crime, and globalization, while examining the various structures of organized crime groups. Finally, it discusses major global organized activities such as human trafficking, drug trafficking, the illicit weapons trade, and the differences between human smuggling and trafficking.

Chapter 2 examines various problems and controversies related to global organized crime. It first looks at the circumstances and conditions that create failed states and how these states provide safe havens for crime networks. It also examines the problems of corruption at various levels of government and within police forces. In addition it looks at the nexus between terrorism and organized crime. Among the topics covered related to this issue are how the groups borrow tactics from each other and how many global organized crime groups have begun to resemble hybrid organizations. Both types of groups also engage in similar criminal activities, including diamond smuggling, counterfeiting, and even narcoterrorism. Other types of criminal activities discussed include money laundering, high-tech crimes, advance fee fraud, music piracy, and the problems presented by offshore banking and shell corporations. Also in the chapter is coverage of various organization structures including the Russian Mafiya, drug cartels, prison gangs and street gangs, and activity on the Mexican-American border. Finally, it looks at the law enforcement response including such themes as problems of cooperation between countries, jurisdictional conflicts, and barriers to law enforcement and policing cyberspace.

Chapter 3 examines a variety of organized crime groups whose activities are global or transnational in scope. Distinctions are made between the American and Italian versions of the Mafia. Italian groups examined also include the 'Ndrangheta and the Camorra. Russian organized crime, the Corsicans, Mexican drug cartels, MS-13, Jamaican posses, Chinese Triads, Tongs and street gangs, Nigerian gangs, the Japanese Yakuza, and Hells Angels all get their due as well.

Chapter 4 is a chronology of the key events surrounding the history of global organized crime. Chapter 5 offers a series of biographical portraits divided into three groups: global organized crime figures, crime fighters, and researchers. Chapter 6 is devoted to documents, facts, statistics, and government documents related to global organized crime.

Chapter 7 provides information on a wide range of organizations devoted to organized crime issues, particularly on the transnational level. Chapter 8 offers a guide to print and electronic resources including book and journal article reviews, journals devoted to global organized crime issues, reviews of movies and documentaries that illustrate the subject, and a number of helpful Web sites devoted to organized crime. Finally, the book concludes with a glossary of key terms used in the book.

Although the author puts words to paper, in the end no one writes a book alone, for there is typically an editorial process to ensure that the objectives have been met. I am indebted to Mim Vasan for bringing me into this process and to my former editor Lauren Thomas, as well as my current one, Jane Messah. Finally, without the support of my wife, Ines Papandrea, and daughter, Erica, I would not have been able to lock myself away for hours on end in order to finish this project, and it is to them that I dedicate this book.

1

Global Organized Crime: A Brief History

Introduction

It has been more than a decade since former FBI Director Louis J. Freeh targeted global organized crime as a priority threat to national security, defining it as "a continuing criminal conspiracy having a firm organizational structure, a conspiracy fed by fear and corruption" (Freeh 1996). As trade and travel restrictions between countries disappear and world economies become increasingly interdependent, so do international crime syndicates. In the clamor attributable to globalization, cyberspace, and the information super-highway, organized crime continues to defy definition. Organized crime groups, according to a variety of theories and definitions, come in all shapes and sizes. What has become increasingly clear from the global perspective is that today's groups do not conform to the traditional paradigm exemplified by the Italian Mafia. Rather, organized crime groups have evolved into amorphous enterprises, shifting from one activity to another, depending on geopolitics and changing markets—both legitimate and illegitimate in nature. The 1990s witnessed a global transformation in political and economic life as well as the ascendance of revolutionary technologies that were now in the hands of ordinary civilians. In the post-Cold War world technologies, such as the Worldwide Web, and advances in telecommunications and transportation erased once-secure borders in most regions of the world.

Organized criminal activity can be found throughout most of the historical record. Preindustrial societies in China, Italy, and Japan

1

gave rise to groups such as the Triads, Yakuza, the 'Ndrangheta, and the Sicilian Mafia. Organized piracy, highway robbery, and banditry were some of the most obvious precursors to today's global organized crime problems. Sea piracy and the trade in humans, usually in the form of slaves, are the earliest examples of organized crime on a multinational or global scale; in fact the slave trade has been described as the "world's oldest trade" and can be traced back to the third millennium, and the trafficking in women at least to the beginning of the Christian era (Chanda 2007).

Piracy

History

As long as seafarers have engaged in commerce on the high seas, groups have existed who desired to steal their goods by any means necessary. Phoenicians, Vikings, and pirates, like today's Somalian pirates off the coast of East Africa, have ranged the oceans since the Roman era. In the enormous archives of such lore, these men have been referred to as *pirates, privateers, corsairs,* and *freebooters,* to name only a few. The quantity of names is not unlike the modern attempts to affix a proper name to organized crime groups using nomenclature such as *mafia, syndicate, cartel, mob, rackets,* and *gangs.*

By the Middle Ages piracy was already an ancient occupation for some men (and a few women). As oceanic trade increased over the centuries, so did the volume of piracy. With the expansion of global markets during the commercial expansion of the 16th and 17th centuries, pirates, too, expanded their trade routes, following the plunder trail from the Old World to the New. Sometimes European competition for trade monopolies led to war between nations on the high seas as the British, French, Dutch, and Spanish carved out empires in the Americas. These wars were often marked by unconventional warfare and the use of piracy (Karraker 1953).

The tendency by recent scholars has been to divide the halcyon years of piracy, or the "Golden Age of Piracy," into three distinct eras lasting from 1650 and 1730. Most pirates between 1650 and the 1680s were Protestant "sea dogs" from England, northern France, and the Netherlands, who typically targeted ships from Catholic Spain. Beginning in the 1690s, Captain William Kidd and others moved their base of operations into the Indian Ocean and built a pirate enclave on the island of Madagascar. The third and most familiar era, however, was the 10 years between 1716 and 1726, an age filled with larger-than-life characters such as Edward Teach and Bartholomew Roberts (Rediker 2004). This is the era that is so entrenched in the popular culture, featuring Long John Silver of *Treasure Island*, the black flag of the *Jolly Roger*, and the notorious Blackbeard. During this decade there were an estimated 2,000 to 4,000 pirates representing a host of ethnicities and races. Together and separately they disrupted trade in what was then considered a "strategic zone of capital accumulation," referring to the West Indies, North America, and West Africa (Rediker 2004).

An examination of piracy's so-called Golden Age between 1650 and 1730 offers up some striking parallels with global organized crime activities in the 21st century. Both pirates and slave traders exhibited a number of the characteristics consistent with modern organized crime, including the use and threat of violence, having a hierarchical structure, the use of strict rules and regulations, engaging in entrepreneurial activities, the corruption of officials, and profit motivation. Other criteria, however, such as monopolization of a particular criminal activity, longevity, racketeering and infiltration of legitimate business, restricted membership, and self-perpetuating leadership reflect more complex and urbanized societies.

Geographically, piracy took place on a global scale. Illegal pirates as well as state-sponsored ones, called privateers, had vast economic incentives to participate in the looting of cargoes of gold, jewels, grain, and even wine and drugs. The import and export market for such items was usually heavily restricted; thus in order for the smuggling system to flourish, it needed the willing participation of corrupt officials and greedy merchants, especially when it came time for the pirates to launder their ill-gotten lucre.

Economic Factors

Between 1651 and 1696, the English Parliament passed a series of Navigation Acts. These were designed to control what goods were allowed into the English colonies in North America. By stipulating that no goods could be imported into England or her colonies unless on British ships manned by British subjects, it meant a number of luxury items from other countries were now prohibited. Organized gangs of smugglers, pirates, and black marketeers were only too happy to challenge these barriers for the right price. The Navigation Acts were to 17th-century organized piracy and smuggling what alcohol and drug prohibition was to the 20th century. Colonial Americans resented the British monopoly on both shipping and trade and had no compunction about trading with pirates, establishing in effect with them an unrestricted market for cheaper goods, undercutting legitimate markets in the process. One Navigation Act in 1663 mandated that virtually all European products bound for the colonies must be landed in England first and then reloaded on English ships for the conclusion of the voyage. Ultimately added customs duties pushed up prices on a number of essentials. Portuguese salt, Irish and Scottish horses and linens, and wines from the Madeira and the Azores were just some of the products that were marked up and in the process created a healthy smuggling economy (Hoffer 2000). During alcohol Prohibition in America between 1920 and 1933, politicians and officials alike were either unwilling or unable to enforce the 18th Amendment prohibiting the manufacture and sale of alcoholic beverages. Likewise colonial officials and entrepreneurs in the New World were drawn into the orbit of the smuggling system. So, although colonial governors were expected to enforce the Navigation Acts, more often than not they participated in the smuggling and corruption behaviors that exemplified organized crime more than 200 years later. By the 18th century, smuggling and black markets were a way of life in America. One estimate suggested that five-sixths of the tea consumed in most colonies had been smuggled in (Williams 1961).

Definition

Similar to attempts to define organized crime, an exact definition of piracy universally accepted over time and between places has eluded academics, government officials, and law enforcement over the centuries. During the preindustrial era most pirate organizations lasted only as long as their captains, with few demonstrating any pattern of leadership continuity. They did share, however, a number of attributes with modern international syndicates—corrupting officials, operating sometimes with state support, and selling stolen lucre to legitimate businessmen in a type of premodern money laundering system.

During the last several decades a broad definition of piracy has emerged that equates it with the taking of property with violence on the high seas. In 2005, the International Maritime Bureau, which is a clearinghouse for piracy data, defined piracy as: "Any act of boarding or attempting to board any ship with the apparent intent to commit theft or any other crime and with the apparent intent or capability to use force in the furtherance of that act" (Walters 2007, 10).

Piracy in the 21st Century

No form of global organized crime illustrates the continuum of organized crime past and present like the ancient crime of piracy. Few observers would disagree that we are in a new "golden age" of piracy; however, technology has changed many of the pirate's tactics and strategies. During the first decade of the 21st century, pirate syndicates received millions of dollars in ransom for crews and ships. In contrast to their ancient forebears, today's pirates have access to high technology, bases in failed nation states, potential alliances with transnational terrorists, and a global economy dependent on secure commercial shipping. When the world's news organizations focused on the Indian Ocean face-off between an $800 million U.S. Navy destroyer and a handful of pirates in a lifeboat in April 2009, it became apparent that even the world's superpower had few options when confronted with low-tech pirates on the high seas (Mazzetti 2009). This incident was the first time in 200 years that pirates had captured a U.S. vessel for ransom (Gettleman 2009). In the infancy of the American republic, President Thomas Jefferson sent Marines to the shores of Tripoli to free sailors taken hostage by the Barbary pirates (today's Morocco, Tunisia, Algeria, and Libya).

Most suggestions for countering piracy have revolved around sea marshals, SEAL snipers, and punitive expeditions to destroy pirate strongholds. In 2009, however, U.S. Secretary of Defense Robert Gates explained that what created the pirate business off the coast of Somalia was a malfunctioning government faced with anarchy. Although the country has a national government, the Transitional National Government, it controls little territory. For centuries pirate networks have exploited ungoverned voids. Three hundred years ago, however, nation states operated without the restrictions that accentuate complex international law. Nation states and their navies were unimpeded in their hunt for pirates while today's world is a tangled mess hampered by jurisdictional and sovereignty issues, and human rights laws.

Ocean-going piracy is most prevalent on the fringes and coasts of the world's failed and failing states. Somalia, on the east coast of Africa, has not had a stable government for more than 20 years. In 2008, more than 90 vessels were attacked, more than one-third successfully. Ransoms have harvested millions and millions of dollars.

Each year some 20,000 merchant ships opt for the shortest route from Asia to Europe by taking the Suez Canal (Meyer 2008). Unfortunately for them at some juncture of a round trip through the canal, they will have to pass through the most active pirate freebooters who ply the waters of the Gulf of Aden between Yemen and Somalia (Keath and Quinn 2008).

In December 2008, Somali pirates accepted a ransom for a Ukrainian ship bearing tanks and other heavy weapons. In that year alone pirate attacks off the coast of Africa had risen 75 percent over the previous year (Gutterman 2008). Although there have been no substantiated connections between pirates and Islamic militants in Somalia, what worries Western nations most is that this plundered cargo in the form of weapons might be removed and sold to hard-line Islamic extremists. Fears of the Talibanization of the region by armed groups, where no stable government has ruled for more than 20 years, is a constant concern.

Piracy is considered the biggest moneymaker in Somalia, which *The Economist* referred to as Africa's most failed state in 2008, when pirates plundered an estimated $30 million of cargo for ransom (*Economist*, Nov. 22, 2008). The impact on global world trade has been felt in a number of ways. Ransoms mean higher insurance premiums and delays for customers as more ships opt for the longer path around the Cape of Good Hope. This in turn means lower revenues for the Suez Canal and another variable to be taken into account by the oil exporting nations and their markets.

In a failed state such as Somalia, there is no lack of recruits for pirate life. Armed with rifles and rocket-propelled grenades, small groups of pirates have been able to hijack sophisticated sea craft the size of multiple football fields and carrying cargoes in the tens of billions of dollars.

What distinguishes today's pirates from earlier incarnations is that they use minimal violence against hostages and rarely steal cargoes, preferring to wait for ransoms. The hijacking of the Saudi-owned tanker the Sirius Star—as long as an aircraft carrier—exemplifies the global transnational scale of modern shipping and piracy. Built in South Korea, flying the Liberian flag, and with a multinational crew counting citizens from Great Britain, Poland, Croatia, Saudi Arabia, and the Philippines, the tanker carried $100 million worth of crude oil when it was captured in November 2008. Spurred by the world oil markets, it was still an audacious attack that was noteworthy for several reasons. It was the largest ship ever attacked and officials were notably surprised that such low-tech pirates could operate so far out at sea. Typically working within 200 miles of the coast of East Africa, this attack took place 450 nautical miles from the port of Mombasa, Kenya. By all accounts it was a highly organized attack in which several high-speed inflatable rafts containing four to six gunmen were launched from a mother vessel (Daraghi and Sanders 2008). When the pirates reached the ship, it seemed like a scene out of Hollywood as they threw ladders with grappling hooks onto the ship's rails before making a beeline for the bridge in order to capture the vessel's nerve center and engine room. But instead of swords and pistols they carried modern automatic weapons.

As for the pirates themselves, they are much less organized than in previous eras. Their access to modern communications technology, however, is probably more important than sheer numbers and structure. Experts assert that the pirates were merely "foot soldiers" who were paid a previously agreed on fixed amount. Ransom negotiations were conducted by middlemen conversant in English who have access to satellite phones. In case a ship is held for a long period, the middlemen may put together a group of investors who raise cash for supplies and other costs that will be recouped with interest once the ransom is paid (Houreld 2008).

Despite all attempts to tar all pirates with the same brush, as disorganized and amateurish, this still belies the fact that a sophisticated criminal network operates somewhere behind the army of poorly trained buccaneers. One Kenyan maritime official has even compared the pirates to an incarnation of the American Mafia, as some extensive and wealthy organization buttressed by high-level informants inside various East African governments (Axe 2009).

Piracy Then and Now

One of the most obvious characteristics of organized crime groups today is the willingness to use violence in pursuit of their operations. Pirates played a role in creating their sinister image by the way they dressed, sometimes treated prisoners, and flew the skull and crossbones (but there is no evidence anyone was ever forced to walk the plank!).

What few original pirate rules and regulations that survive reveal a number of parallels with modern organized crime groups. Pirates, for example, described how to divide up plunder, choose officers, and enforce discipline, as well as what behavior would be tolerated (Rediker 1987). By agreeing to these rules, new members cemented their loyalty to the pirate subculture. Rules that most closely parallel the rules of traditional organized crime groups are intended to preserve harmony in the pirate crews and confederations by specifically detailing how to resolve quarrels and by prohibiting gambling, cowardice, desertion, drunkenness, and certain disrespect to female hostages. In like fashion modern criminal syndicates from the Mexican Mafia and the Aryan Brotherhood to the Chinese Triads, Russian syndicates, and the Italian Mafia adhere to distinct rules and regulations, with well-understood prohibitions against substance abuse and mistreating women. Some modern crack houses in America's inner cities even post rules and potential punishments on their walls. In other organizations there are often unwritten rules that are meant to maintain discipline, such as not fighting among themselves. In some pirate crews, new members were expected to swear an oath over a Bible to obey the rules, not unlike the initiation ceremonies of the Neapolitan Camorra, the Calabrian 'Ndrangheta, and the Sicilian Mafia.

Piracy flourished for decades in the New World because of the complicity of colonial politicians, business merchants, and the colonies themselves. Modern criminologists have asserted that for piracy to flourish it needed the corruption of officials, customs agents, and the merchant class (Mueller and Adler 1985). In fact corruption sometimes existed at every level of the fledgling colonial economies. Merchants dined with pirate captains, governors sold special government commissions to pirates that allowed them to plunder enemy ships, customs officers were bribed, and leading citizens sold pirates rum, weapons, and provisions. One observer even commented on how politicians and merchants in 1699 obstructed the efforts of honest officials along the Atlantic seaboard. Others point out that the "pirate industry" was the foundation for the economic prosperity in some colonies. In 2009, corruption continues to flourish, facilitating the growth of global and international crime syndicates. This is just the latest chapter in a continuing saga that has been playing out around the world for centuries.

Background

Globalization

One leading authority suggests that since the word *globalization* first appeared in the dictionary "its meaning has undergone a massive transformation" (Chanda 2007). In reality globalization is a process that has been at play for hundreds if not thousands of years. By most accounts it refers to the trend of increasing integration and interdependence of the world's nation-states. The reality of a shrinking world dates back at least to 1519 when the Portuguese explorer Ferdinand Magellan became the first person to circumnavigate the world and establish the first global linkages, initiating trading on a global scale. In previous eras continental trade was conducted by transportation relay chains using camel caravans, mule packs, and small boats. Magellan's voyage, however, confirmed, if not demonstrated, the vast potential of linking continents and trading powers more quickly and profitably by larger and faster ships. The development of oceangoing transportation had been a work in progress for centuries. The Phoenicians on the east coast of the Mediterranean (present-day Lebanon) were among the first merchants whose seafaring skills facilitated the expansion of a trading network across the Persian Gulf and the Mediterranean. Subsequently, Greek merchants during the first millennium BCE established settlements throughout the eastern Mediterranean and Black Sea coasts in such numbers that the island of Sicily and southern Italy became known as "Magna Graecia" or Greater Greece, and by the first century CE, the Roman Empire had reached the Red Sea, opening the door to trading with India (Chanda 2007).

In the wake of Magellan's circumnavigation, other innovations followed, cutting sailing times even further. The rise of steam power at the end of the 18th century provided the next big jump in oceangoing technology. Although the invention of the first reliable maritime chronometer was a huge step forward (telling navigators where they were in open sea), it was not until the introduction of steamships in 1780 that there was any great noticeable reduction in time and increased speed after 1,700 years. Shortening sailing time intensified contact and produced higher trading volume. Over the next century, vessels became larger and their turnaround times diminished. It was only natural that legitimate and illicit entrepreneurs would make their fortunes at each step of globalization—sea pirates, slave traders, and human traffickers—and contraband smuggling would join more legitimate business factions in the rush for wealth created by the new global economies.

Until the 20th century, global organized crime was mostly centered on the same activities of the previous centuries. When it came to global communication and transportation, few significant innovations before the 20th century would have stimulated new opportunities for international organized crime outside of simple cross-border criminal activities that involved myriad smuggling operations. What set the stage for global innovation was the passage of new legislation in the 1910s and 1920s, particularly in the United States. The passage of the Harrison Narcotic Act in 1914 was the culmination of years of crusading against opiates by mostly Western powers. As international regulations were put into place to police the supply of opiates, organized drug trafficking syndicates emerged to supply whichever drug just happened to be in demand. As more countries jumped on the drug prohibition bandwagon, such as Great Britain in 1920, with the passage of the Dangerous Drugs Act, drug trafficking became even more global in scope. By the 1920s, American gangsters such as Arnold Rothstein were sending agents to Europe and Asia to purchase opium to smuggle back to the United States. The period of alcohol prohibition (1920–1933) in America also stimulated the growth of international liquor smuggling operations including the illegal importation of alcoholic beverages from England by sea, rum-runners from the Caribbean, and cross-border smuggling from Mexico and Canada.

By the 1980s, globalization was making its impact on the evolution of crime syndicates as many began to take advantage of the incredible advances in communication technologies. Together with easier international travel and expanded world trade, criminal organizations in developing nations (as well as developed ones) found it easier to branch out of local and regional crime to target international victims and develop criminal networks with more prosperous countries. During the past two decades, global organized crime has been one of the main beneficiaries of the advances occasioned by globalization, which has found its expression in the numerous transnational smuggling networks ranging from human trafficking and smuggling and weapons and drug trafficking to computer crime and counterfeiting operations.

Defining Organized Crime

To create laws to effectively combat organized crime on national and international levels, it is necessary to have a mutually accepted definition that distinguishes organized crime from other forms of criminality. The lack of consensus has hindered international law enforcement for generations. Indeed, for more than a century, academics, journalists, government officials, and criminal justicians have debated the meaning of "organized crime." Attempts at arriving at a definition can seem like "tilting at windmills," as no definition can simultaneously address present and future forms of criminality. For American policymakers, the findings of the President's Commission on Organized Crime in 1986 during the Reagan administration marked a major step toward moving away from the traditional Italian model of organized crime. Scholars, journalists, and public officials were forced to reevaluate their understanding of organized crime in the United States as a host of emerging crime groups received prominence in the federal report, ranging from Jamaican Posses, Asian gangs, and Russian Mafiya to outlaw motorcycle gangs and prison gangs.

Before the 21st century organized crime definitions revolved around a number of central characteristics such as the nature of the offenses committed, the numbers of individuals involved, and the longevity of the criminal enterprise. During the 1990s, the transnational aspects of organized crime became more broadly emphasized as global organized crime syndicates emerged as one of the most challenging issues facing law enforcement before the September 11, 2001, terrorist attacks.

Before the 1990s, most organized crime definitions revolved around central characteristics such as the nature and severity of offenses committed, the numbers of individuals involved, and the enduring nature of the enterprise. A major step forward was taken in 2000 when the United Nations Convention against Transnational Organized Crime (Article 2) defined organized crime broadly "as a structured group of three or more persons existing for a period of time and acting in concert with the aim of committing one or more serious crimes or offenses in accordance with this Convention in order to obtain, directly or indirectly, a financial or material benefit" (United Nations Office on Drugs and Crime 2000). International representatives at the 2000 meeting, however, could not arrive at a consensus on a definition or a list of criminal acts, but decided to adopt a broad definition of organized criminal groups and not limit its attention to hierarchically structured "mafia-type organizations." Reflecting the changing nature of global organized crime activity, officials began to focus more attention on loosely organized criminal groups who committed serious crimes that were transnational in nature (United Nations Office on Drugs and Crime, Sept. 2002, 4–5).

In September 2003, the United Nations Convention against Transnational Organized Crime was signed into law three years after first being introduced. Over the years most countries had developed their own definitions as to what constituted transnational organized crime. For the first time, however, the new Convention offered a singular legal definition that was acceptable to most countries (Fijnaut and Paoli 2004).

Transnational Crime: Definitions and Types

Transnational crime has blurred the distinctions between domestic and foreign affairs because criminals exert global impact today. Operating from countries around the world they have been able to create international ties including in the United States. According to the 2000 United Nations Convention on Transnational Organized Crime, transnational refers to offenses that involve at least two countries. This can occur in a variety of combinations. For example it would be considered transnational in nature if the criminal acts were committed in more than one country or if much of the planning and supervision of the activity comes from one country but the crime itself is committed in another one. It would also fit the rubric if the crime was committed in one country but it had an impact on at least one other country as well (United Nations Office on Drugs and Crime 2000).

The United Nations has identified 18 categories of transnational offenses typically involving actors and activities affecting more than one country. These categories include money laundering, terrorist activities, theft of intellectual property, art and cultural objects, illicit arms trafficking, aircraft hijacking, sea piracy, insurance fraud, computer and environmental crime, trafficking in persons and human body parts, illegal drug trafficking, fraudulent bankruptcy, infiltration of legal business, and corruption and bribery of public or party officials (UNODC 2000).

Mafia

The term *mafia* has been used to describe a number of different forms of international organized crime, such as in the case of the so-called Russian, Sicilian, Asian, and Albanian mafias. In most cases there has been a tendency to view these groups as the products of underdeveloped and disordered social systems. More recent academic investigations suggest that groups like the Italian Mafia are produced by societies on the brink of modernization and embroiled in economic transformation and turmoil. At the same time, however, these developing societies have not quite arrived at the point where they have created a legal apparatus capable of protecting individual property rights and settling business disputes between its citizens. The notion that mafias materialize during times of "rapid but flawed transitions to [a] market economy" has been supported by recent studies on Japanese and post-Soviet organized crime groups (Varese 2006, 411–412; Gambetta 1993).

Scholars and officials have long grappled with trying to explain the public's identification of the Italian people with the mafia and organized crime. The term *mafia* has been bandied about so much it has lost most of its original meaning. Words such as mafia, syndicate, cartel, mob, rackets, gang, and so forth have been used interchangeably over the past century and have only obscured the meaning of the term *mafia*. One historian noted that "Mafia is the only word in the Sicilian dialect to be incorporated into all of the world's languages" (Smith 1995, 7). Perhaps no other five-letter word conjures up more images, misconceptions, and misguided ethnic stereotypes than the Italian word *mafia*. Any discussion of the etymology of the word begins on the island of Sicily, strategically located at the crossroads of Mediterranean civilization. The island has been ruled by a succession of conquerors over the past millennia. Arab, Roman, Byzantine, Norman, Catalan, French, Greek, Austrian, and Spanish armies have all targeted the island for its commercial and military opportunities.

The word *mafia* has not been found in an Italian dictionary before the 1860s (Fentress 2000). There is no agreed upon or simple definition for the word or a consensus as to its murky origins. But this has not stopped it from being routinely applied to a wide range of criminal behaviors and enterprises. Organized crime scholars use the term to refer to traditional organized crime groups that originated on the island of Sicily and then imported certain traditions to America during a wave of late 19th-century and early 20th-century immigration. Over time two variations of the Italian Mafia evolved according to the different social and economic conditions of the Old and New Worlds. The American and Sicilian versions of the Mafia remain distinct, with members linked on occasion by personal relationships and associations. Although both permutations share some tendencies, the American version has long operated mostly in the underworld, on the periphery of society, while its Sicilian counterpart has inextricable links with the region's up-perworld (see Chapter 3).

Structures of Organized Crime Groups

If there is any international agreement on the structure of orga-nized crime in the 21st century, it is that organized crime groups are adaptable and flexible in nature, capable of assuming chameleon-like qualities to take advantage of whatever opportunities exist to make money. In the United States beginning in the 1950s, a number of organized crime hearings were conducted at the federal level to grasp the true nature of this criminal enterprise. Both the Kefau-ver Hearings (1950–1951) and the McClellan Committee Hearings (1963–1964) contributed to the stereotypical view of the modern Mafia in which organized crime operated as a hierarchical structure. Other conferences and committees on organized crime brought to-gether America's leading authorities throughout the 1960s and 1970s. The President's Commission on Organized Crime in 1986, how-ever, diverged from previous investigations by expanding the defi-nition well beyond the well-worn Italian Mafia stereotypes. The Commission broadened the government's interpretation of the of the organized crime problem by moving beyond the parameters set by the earlier investigations. Moving beyond the parochial view of the Italian Mafia as synonymous with organized crime, it expanded its emphasis to include outlaw motorcycle gangs; prison gangs; and Chinese, Vietnamese, Japanese, Cuban, Colombian, Irish, Russian, and Canadian criminal networks.

Organized crime groups, according to myriad theories and definitions, come in all shapes and sizes. It is clear that one shape does not fit all, and today's groups are much more fluid, flexible, and pragmatic than past examples, with few regards to restricting membership by ethnicity and other criteria. According to a 2002 report by the United Nations Office on Drugs and Crime, the global investigation of organized crime is seriously hampered by a pen-chant for focusing on the "more visible and prominent groups" such as the Russian gangs and the Italian Mafia, while often ignoring the less traditional organized crime networks that are more adaptable to the world of globalization, such as Nigerian fraud rings, high-tech crime rings, or Eastern European sex trafficking networks (United Nations Office on Drugs and Crime, September 2002, 6). These groups are often amorphous, with an ever-changing cast of actors and structures that are less recognizable and more dynamic in organization.

One survey of 40 selected organized crime groups in 16 countries in 2002 has contributed to a better understanding of the changing nature and structure of 21st-century organized crime. The survey revealed five types of structures exhibited by prominent groups. At the most basic level are smaller groups or *rigid hierarchies* of up to 20 members with one boss, who engages in one main criminal activity and confines its operations to only one or two countries. These groups apparently use less violence and corruption and have made little inroads in infiltrating the legitimate economy. Next in ascending order are *devolved hierarchies,* with up to 50 members and a hierarchical command structure. They are often engaged in two or more types of activities in from three to four countries. These gangs might occasionally use violence and corruption, have some political influence at the lowest levels of government, and have some investments in the legitimate marketplace. Unlike rigid hierarchies, the devolved hierarchy sometimes cooperates with other criminal syndicates in its home country. Moving up the food chain of structure is a third type, which is referred to as a *hierarchical conglomerate.* Groups at this level have from 50 to 100 members, operate extensively internationally, have political influence in higher corridors of power, and operate in conjunction with crime syndicates in other countries. Its structure is more sophisticated and runs the gamut from an "association of organized crime groups" often under the leadership of a central hierarchy. Violence and corruption are considered essential ingredients in their criminal operations and there is an extensive overlapping of legitimate and illicit activities while operating in at least five different countries. What also distinguishes this model is that its organization is ethnic, or family-based, with core membership coming from the same ethnic group, region, or country. *Core criminal groups* typically have more than 100 members and have some of the same features as the hierarchical conglomerate. What differentiates them are their higher involvement in international geopolitics, particularly their ability to influence politicians in foreign countries. The highest form of structure is referred to as an *organized criminal network.* It is more difficult to describe this type of network, which is its strength. It is defined by the activities of its main players who often collaborate on criminal schemes in different types of alliances depending on the job and the required skill-sets. An individual in this structure achieves one's position according to one's skills and ability to earn (UNODC 2002, 19).

Major Global Organized Crime Activities

International crime syndicates have long counted drug trafficking, human smuggling and trafficking, and weapons smuggling among their most lucrative activities. In the 21st century counterfeiting technologies, the Internet and cyberspace have become mainstays as well. The process of globalization has opened and expanded markets that have reshaped and revolutionized the business of organized crime. Organized crime groups in India and South America, for example, have been connected to human organ trafficking, whereas others have found profits in smuggling endangered species, forged airplane parts, fake pharmaceuticals, and various counterfeit consumer products. New illicit global networks have emerged in recent years dealing in such niche products as human organs, endangered species, hazardous wastes, and stolen art all operated with the same method used in better known rackets such as stolen cars, illegal logging, and cigarette smuggling, but without the same scrutiny and media coverage.

By most accounts some of these groups have been shifting their attention from the mainstays of drugs and arms trafficking toward human smuggling and trafficking, activities with high profits but less risk of draconian punishment as in the case of weapons and drugs. Most crime experts assert that what is most attractive about the human trade is the fact that there is an unquenchable thirst for immigration around the world, leading to a continuous flow of profit. Globalization is often blamed for influencing the movement of people from poorer countries to richer ones. Poverty, despair, war, and civil crisis continue to play a central role, as do the economic dislocations that have followed the collapse of communism.

Slavery and Human Trafficking

Ancient Athens and Rome were known for their slave markets. In antiquity no less a figure than the Greek philosopher Aristotle defended the practice, commenting "humanity is divided into two:

the masters and the slaves" (Chanda 2007, 215). Although slavery is an ancient tradition that probably predates the written record, by the 15th century it had become a global enterprise, albeit a legal one. Slavery had for the most part disappeared from the European continent for almost a millennium before reemerging in the 16th century. What increased the demand was the tremendous demand for slaves in the New World. Spain was the first European power to permit the transfer of slaves, but was quickly followed by Portuguese, Dutch, French, and British slave traders. In 1672, the King of England granted a charter to the Royal African Company permitting it to sell slaves; by the end of that century the slave trade was regarded as a legal and desirable branch of commerce.

By the mid-1800s, no branch of the contraband trade was as widespread as the international trafficking of African slaves. Although the legal traffic had been abolished by Great Britain in 1807, there was still an enormous demand for slaves in the United States, Brazil, Cuba, India, and the Arab world, and the trade continued. There seemed to be no end to the supply of slaves, with more being exported from Africa in the 1830s by either illegal British traders or non-English vessels after the trade was banned by British authorities than in the average years of the previous centuries (Chanda 2007).

In the aftermath of the emancipation of slaves in the 1860s, the United States attracted the largest number of legal immigrants during what historians call "the first golden age of globalization" in the 19th century (Ruggie 2000). By the late 19th century, slavery was outlawed in most places in the world, but middlemen found no shortage of hopeful and vulnerable would-be migrants to prey on for profit. The emergence of inexpensive and faster mass travel in the 1970s brought new opportunities for human traffickers to deliver cheap and often bonded laborers to employers in countries thousands of miles away (Picarelli 2007).

Over four centuries close to 12 million slaves were forcibly extracted from Africa and taken to the Americas (Ashcroft 2001, 70). Modern estimates suggest that this figure pales when compared to the modern trafficking of humans. It has been estimated that over the past decade, almost 30 million women and children were trafficked in Southeast Asia alone (Naim 2005, 88). Most international governments concur that the number of people illegally crossing borders today, often in coerced conditions, has no precedent in human history. Moises Naim cites one United Nations study that suggests 4 million people are trafficked and smuggled each year for a value of between $7 and $10 billion. Other figures suggest this is only the tip of the iceberg. The FBI now estimates Mexican human traffickers are earning between $6 and $9 billion each year (Naim 2005).

Today, the smuggling and trafficking of humans generates huge profits for global organized crime groups and is one of the unforeseen results of the process of globalization. Although it is not yet as profitable as the global drug trade, according to Moises Naim in some cases it is "the fastest growing" illicit trade (Naim 2005). Values and prices are gauged by the migrant's wealth and nationality, as well as the incumbent risks of the journey, the degree of professionalism of the service providers, and the attractiveness of the destination country.

Highly populated countries such as China and India emerged as the major sources for unfree migration during the 1800s, regions where population pressures compounded by the necessity of finding work and food led to an inexhaustible supply of migrants. Chinese laborers were sometimes kidnapped, seduced by dreams of riches abroad and sold by unscrupulous traffickers. The peak of Chinese migration was between 1842 and 1900, when 400,000 reached the United States, Australia, and Canada; another 400,000 ended up in the Caribbean and Latin America, and 1.5 million in British Malaya, Burma, the Philippines, and Indonesia. These patterns began to change in 1882 when the U.S. Congress passed the Chinese Exclusion Act restricting immigration from China. During the first two decades of the 20th century, a number of European countries, including Great Britain, France, Italy, Russia, Austria, and Germany, began introducing similar onerous legislation restricting and regulating who could immigrate to their countries (Chanda 2007, 167).

Compared to the landowners immersed in the earlier slave trade in the New World, their modern European and American incarnations have turned to illegal immigrant trafficking to cut labor costs. In former times slaves were kidnapped from villages and sold overseas. Today, willing immigrants in many parts of the world pay exorbitant fees to illegally enter Western Europe and the United States. By most accounts, what has most contributed to the increase in human smuggling and trafficking has been the tightening of border controls and points of entry in various parts of the world. This has increasingly forced refugees into the hands of smugglers (Karrstrand 2007).

One recent case exemplifies the interconnectedness of global cultures and human trafficking. In May 2009, Spanish police announced they had broken up a smuggling operation that forced Nigerian women into prostitution by threatening them with voodoo curses. Traffickers had used the common modern ruse of luring the women to Europe with promises of opportunities and better living conditions, but first they were brought to a voodoo (juju) priest. The women were then smuggled from Nigeria to Spain. Once at their destination, the victims were forced to prostitute themselves to repay debts accrued in the journey or "face the wrath of voodoo spirits." A growing number of observers have noted the increasing use of this type of intimidation by traffickers. The ringleaders used family members in Nigeria to recruit women who were then transported to Libya by way of Benin and Niger and then shipped by boat to Italy and finally Spain. According to the victims, they were informed they owed the traffickers $70,000 upon reaching Spain (Burnett 2009).

According to the most recent estimates of the Department of Homeland Security, the five countries where most illegal immigrants in the United States come from and the percentage increase of their population from 2000 were Mexico with 6.9 million (+49%), El Salvador with 540,000 (+26%), followed by Guatemala with 500,000 (+74%), the Philippines with 290,000 (+47%), and China with 290,000 (+49%) (Hoefer, Rytina, and Baker 2008).

Structures of Human Trafficking Operations

Although on the face of it, human smuggling is a simple process, to be successful and achieve longevity it requires the assistance of a number of specialized and skilled individuals. Among the requirements are individuals to arrange transportation and proper (often counterfeited) documents and travel guides for border crossings and to act as chaperones on the journey. Others provide logistical support, providing crucial information at different stages of the overland journey—bribing guards and officials or providing directions. Once they reach their destinations, these people often act as bodyguards to intimidate victims and ensure they do not run away or report the crime; others provide accommodations and food at safe houses.

Human Trafficking versus Human Smuggling

The difference between human smuggling and trafficking cases is often blurred. The main distinction is based on the level of coercion and consent. Some human trafficking cases begin as simple smuggling operations, but some time during the process the journey might take an unexpected turn when a victim/customer might be expected to work forced labor or prostitute themselves to pay hidden costs or unforeseen debts.

In 2005, at the Third Summit of Heads of State and Government, the Council of Europe Convention on Action against Trafficking in Human Beings made a distinction between human smuggling and trafficking. Human trafficking is characterized by a number of schemes and strategies ranging from recruitment of potential victims to the transportation and harboring as well as receiving individuals by participants in the trafficking networks. Some times victims are coerced through threats or violence to be trafficked; other times they are deceived by fraud and even abducted. Once victims are caught in the web of the human traffickers, they become vulnerable and usually exploited. Exploitation can include prostitution, forced labor, forced removal of organs, and practices similar to slavery (Council of Europe 2005).

The United Nationals Protocol against the Smuggling of Migrants by Land, Sea and Air identifies *human smuggling* as "the procurement, in order to obtain directly or indirectly, a financial or other material benefit, of the illegal entry of a person into a State Party of which the person is not a national or permanent resident" (Surtees 2008, 42–43). It is estimated that of the more than 130 million international migrants, close to one-fourth of them are illegal or "irregular" migrants, and that at any time at least 4 million are on the move (Ghosh 2000; Council of Europe 2005, 37). In the 21st century, Western Europe is considered one of their more attractive destinations because of its high living standards and job opportunities, particularly today, as fertility levels are considered below the replacement level as the region's population ages.

The tightening of border controls and points of entry in the European Union has been a boon for organized smuggling networks. Illegal migrants must rely on these operations to reach their destinations. The price is steep. Those from Hungary and Russia heading into Western Europe pay between 8,000 and 10,000 euros each, while traveling from China to Italy can cost as much as $13,000 (Council of Europe 2005, 39). Recent antitrafficking efforts have changed patterns of movement, especially speedboat routes on the Adriatic. As a result, most immigration takes place overland, taking advantage of open borders offered by the Schengen Agreement in Europe and the North American Free Trade Agreement on the Mexican-American border.

Coyotes

Coyotes are the Mexican permutation of the human smuggler. Smugglers have participated in the illegal smuggling of immigrants, often desperate refugees from Mexico and Central America, into the southwestern United States for generations. In Arizona alone, this black market business is estimated to bring in between $1 and $2 billion each year. In 2005, Arizona officials estimated that 1 million illegal immigrants passed through the state, with daily rates approaching 3,000 and 4,000. In 2006, Phoenix area investigators placed the number of coyotes in the region at more than 1,000 (Wagner 2006). In earlier years it was relatively easy for someone to cross the border illegally without much assistance into Texas and Arizona. This all changed, however, in the 1990s as officials took notice and clamped down on illegal immigration. This in turn drove prices up and attracted professional criminals to the business. Various operations became streamlined and professionalized, creating veritable crime syndicates that adopted modern surveillance and communications systems. Prospective customers are known as *goats, furniture,* and *pollo,* or chicken (Wagner 2006). Costs have risen to between $1,200 and $2,500 to be guided across the border (Wagner 2006). The new breed of organizations have scared off the small time "mom-and pop" smuggling operations. Today, most of the smugglers are Mexican nationals. Each smuggling ring has members responsible for specific duties—recruiters, guides, drivers, drophouse managers, cooks, and guards; others are document specialists and money collectors. After undocumented immigrants arrive on American soil, they are usually brought to drophouses while the coyotes collect the cash, arrange transportation, and fend off other smugglers who would steal their clients for ransom. In recent years the coyotaje business has undergone a facelift, as increasingly more women have risen to the top of smuggling operations. In 2006 alone, more than 3,400 women coyotes where arrested for smuggling undocumented workers along the southwestern American border (Nunez 2007). Prospective smugglers looking for a criminal career will often select humans over drugs and weapons because the penalties in the United States are lighter.

Snakeheads

The Chinese use the term *snakehead* or *shetou* to denote those who specialize in human smuggling. When it comes to human smuggling, the Chinese have a distinct tradition from other countries (Keefe 2006). Unlike forced migration or human tracking, human smuggling is considered a voluntary but usually illegal activity. A significant number smuggled abroad come from a tiny patch of southern China about the size of Delaware. It is estimated that of the 55 million Chinese who relocated overseas, 85 percent originated from the Fujian province (Keefe 2006). Although Chinese immigrants have traveled to the United State since the mid-19th century, the modern snakeheads emerged in the 1960s and 1970s, when citizens fled the mainland to the British colony of Honk Kong for a number of reasons including "push" factors such as political repression and Chinese policies of sterilization and forced abortion, as well as "pull" factors of American capitalism. As a result of this migration, New York's Chinatown increased 10-fold by the 1980s, from 20,000 to 200,000. Sometimes the new migrants were called "$18,000 men," signifying the costs of that era (Keefe 2006). The period between 1988 and 1993 saw "the largest influx of illegal Chinese in the country's history" into America. One study suggests that snakeheads earned $3.5 billion in the mid-1990s from this trade (Keefe 2006). Further demonstrating the global orientation of organized crime today is one curious syndicate made up of Fujianese and Mohawk Indians who smuggled thousands of refugees through the sovereign reservation that lies between the United States and Canada. According to Patrick R. Keefe, the network brought in $175 million in one two-year period (Keefe 2006).

Illicit Drug Trafficking

Individuals have used narcotics for medicinal, recreational, and religious purposes for millennia. As early as the 18th century, Spanish officials were taxing and selling the coca leaf to pay for New World expansion; however, the global drug trade can be traced back at least to the 1840s. When it comes to global narcotrafficking networks, few today could approach the power of Great Britain in that era. In 1773, the British East India Company gained control of India's Bengal opium fields. Although the British were eager to trade for Chinese tea, silk, rice, and other commodities to feed the growing demand for the products at home, the Chinese found few products that they were interested in purchasing in return. There were few reports of opium addiction in China before 1800. When China attempted to ban the trade of opium, the British went to war, insisting on exporting it to China from its colonial possessions in India, to pay for tea and silk, sparking the Opium Wars, the first war of globalization. Over the next century the British inundated China with opium, creating a serious problem among users with little if any familiarity with the drug. China's subsequent defeat by the British in the 1842 Opium War forced the country to accept free trade of opium within its borders.

The passage of the Harrison Narcotics Act in 1914 criminalized the nonmedical use of opium, morphine, and coca derivatives in the United States. Other international treaties followed, putting in place restrictions and regulations. But almost as soon this new system was in place, organized drug trafficking syndicates emerged to supply whichever drug happened to be in demand. By the 1920s, one U.S Treasury Department commented that "the peddlers appeared to have established a national organization, smuggling in drugs through the Canadian and Mexican borders" (quoted in Lunde 2004, 28). Other countries soon followed the United States onto the drug prohibition bandwagon. In 1920, Great Britain passed the Dangerous Drugs Act, which targeted access to cocaine, morphine, opium, codeine, hashish, and barbiturates for nonmedical purposes. This was followed by the criminalization of cannabis in 1928, almost a decade before the United States followed suit in 1937.

The passage of the U.S. Opium Exclusion Act in 1909 opened up new opportunities for global organized crime trafficking. By most accounts it was the Jewish gangsters who first saw the potential and soon organized a smuggling network from the leading supplier of the day, China; this was followed by the building of laboratories to dilute and package the narcotics for resale and forming distribution networks to get the product to addicts. The profits could be enormous. For example in 1923, a kilo (2.2 lbs) of pure heroin cost $3,000 at its Chinese source. Once it was cut and divided into 15,500 multigrain capsules, it returned a profit of $300,000 (Volkman 1998). In the 1920s, mobster extraordinaire Arnold Rothstein moved into the narcotics racket. The profits were irresistible at a time when a pound of raw opium could be bought for $1,000 and refined to earn 150 times that amount (Volkman 1998). Rothstein was soon sending his agents to Europe and Asia to purchase opium and smuggle it into the United States.

World drug production and consumption increased in the 1960s, fueled by the rise of international drug trafficking and facilitated by growing globalization and world trade and improved means of transportation and communication. Further facilitating its growth were the combined "demand pull" of youth populations from developed nations and the "supply push" provided by the economic difficulties of a number of source countries and the discovery of the lucrative drug trade by various warlords, insurgency groups, and organized crime groups (Chawla and Pietschmann 2005).

Nothing illustrates the transnational or global nature of organized crime in the 21st century more than the drug war on the Mexican border with the United States. Drug trafficking in Mexico is estimated to employ 150,000 people (Booth and Fainaru 2009). A number of drug gangs—what some have branded as cartels—battle for dominance of the trade routes into the United States from border towns adjacent to California, Arizona, and Texas. Most have diversified their organized crime activities to include kidnapping, weapons and human trafficking, and smuggling. U.S. officials face the Herculean task of stopping the flow of weapons and bulk currency south of the border; Mexico faces an uphill battle trying to stem the flow of drugs and humans smuggled into the United States. According to the most recent National Drug Threat Assessment Report, Mexican drug trafficking networks represented "the greatest organized crime threat to the United States" while linking the Mexican cartels to drug trafficking operations in close to 230 American cities (NDIC 2009, 45). What worries U.S. officials most is the drug violence on the Mexican border crossing into the Southwestern border states as the bloody drug war continues with rival gangs battling for dominance and to expand operations.

Officials assert that cocaine trafficking is the leading drug menace to the United States. While the availability of cocaine fluctuates, as does its price, the demand remains strong throughout the world, and new markets continue to open as living standards and incomes rise in developing countries. Despite a number of international efforts and strategies and cooperative efforts between North and Latin America, the drug gangs are quick to adapt to rapidly changing conditions and barriers. The gangs closest to the United States on the Mexican border are in the best position to react to changing conditions. Many of these conditions are elucidated in the aforementioned 2009 National Drug Intelligence Center report, including the impact of coca eradication programs in the Andes, violence between competing drug cartels, improved border controls, large seizures of cocaine, and the opening of new markets overseas (NDIC 2009, 1). Some observers have even suggested that foreign markets offer the most potential as a result of the shrinking value of the U.S. dollar.

The opium poppy has been used for at least 4,000 years. The Sumerians of the Fertile Crescent referred to it as did Homer in the *Iliad*. The poppy probably came to China from the Middle East sometime in the 7th or 8th centuries, but it was not until the 18th century that opium smoking became endemic in parts of the Far East and China.

Heroin is produced in four major source areas located in South America, Mexico, Southeast Asia (the Golden Triangle), and Southwest Asia (the Golden Crescent). Most global heroin production takes place in Southwest Asia, especially in Afghanistan; however, only a small portion reaches the United States. Most of the heroin coming out of Afghanistan or Pakistan is destined for markets in Europe and Asia.

The trafficking of refined heroin to U.S. ports involved an elaborate organizational web of transportation routes, couriers, and payoffs. In the years leading up to World War II and the Communist revolution in China (1949), American gangsters brought heroin in from Shanghai; however, the outbreak of war made this untenable. The Maoist Revolution was most successful in eradicating the scourge from China with draconian suppression. Many drug syndicates moved their bases of operation from Shanghai to Hong Kong. But the Far East heroin market was shattered by the war and its "revolutionary aftermath" and would not return until the 1950s and 1960s emergence of Southeast Asia's Golden Triangle. The lack of Asian narcotics during this era "reinvigorated" Middle East and Mediterranean drug operations. Most of the heroin business was concentrated in the hands of independent operators based in France and operating in conjunction with Corsican gangs located in Marseilles. This arrangement began in the 1930s. The so-called French Connection was at the epicenter of the heroin drug trade for years. Between World War II and the 1960s, Hong Kong and Marseilles were the heroin refining capitals of the world; later this activity became more dispersed as opium-heroin trafficking networks from Southeast Asia and Europe were reestablished.

According to the National Drug Intelligence Center, heroin distribution by Mexican drug trafficking gangs has expanded, fueled by rising heroin production in Mexico and decreasing heroin production in Colombia. In Southwest Asia its distribution and availability are less reliable. Some Nigerian criminal networks, however, are now distributing Southwest Asian heroin and maneuvering to increase their influence on the heroin distribution market. Southeast heroin has become increasingly less available in the United States. Today most southwest Asian heroin is smuggled into the United States by couriers on commercial flights from Europe, Africa, or Asia. Nonetheless the two primary sources of heroin in the United States are Mexico and Colombia.

Southwest Asian heroin reaches the United States smuggled on commercial flights by couriers from Asian countries including India, Pakistan, and Turkey and transits through West African countries such as Nigeria and Ghana. By most accounts the couriers usually enter the United States through cities such as Baltimore, Chicago, Houston, Los Angeles, New York City, Philadelphia, and Washington, D.C. It also reaches the United States through the southwestern region, especially through Los Angeles, by Afghan, Iranian, Pakistani, and Turkish traffickers before being transported to drug markets in the eastern states, where the demand is greatest. It is also not unheard of for couriers to bring it in on cruise ships, through package delivery services, and hidden in containerized cargo.

During the 1990s, the New Jersey State Commission of Investigation revealed Nigerian involvement in the global heroin trade. The so-called African Connection has become increasingly interconnected in the international drug trade as Nigeria emerged as a major transshipment point for Southeast Asian heroin heading to Europe and the United States. Today, the Drug Enforcement Administration regards Nigeria as an indispensable juncture in the heroin trade and Africa's most prominent transshipment point. According to one leading observer of the global crime scene, Nigeria now operates heroin labs that process opium brought in from Afghanistan and Myanmar and has also transited through Pakistan, Uzbekistan, Thailand, or China.

Compared to heroin and cocaine, which are products of plants grown throughout parts of Asia and Latin America, methamphetamine is a "purpose-made" drug, created in laboratories from chemicals found in popular cough and cold remedies. Unlike other drug traffickers, meth dealers are subject to government pressure and

Chomsky, Noam. 2006 *Failed States: The Abuse of Power and the Assault on Democracy.* New York: Henry Holt.

Council of Europe. 2005, December. "Organized Crime Situation Report 2005: Focus on the Threat of Economic Crime," Strasbourg, France: Department of Crime Problems.

Curtis, Glen E., and Tara Karacan. 2002, December. "The Nexus Among Terrorists, Narcotics Traffickers, Weapons Proliferators, and Organized Crime networks in Western Europe," Federal Research Division, Washington, D.C.: Library of Congress: 1–68.

Daraghi, Borzou, and Edmund Sanders. 2008, November 18. "Pirates Seize Supertanker in Brazen Open-Sea Attack." *Houston Chronicle:* A1, A12.

Economist. 2008, November 22. "Ahoy There!": 60.

Felsen, David, and Akis Kalaitzidis. 2005. "A Historical Overview of Transnational Crime." In *Handbook of Transnational Crime and Justice,* ed. Phil Reichel, 3–19. Thousand Oaks, CA: Sage, pp. 3–19.

Fentress, James. 2000. *Rebels and Mafiosi: Death in a Sicilian Landscape.* New York: Cornell University Press.

Fijnaut, Cyrille, and Letizia Paoli, eds. 2004. *Organized Crime in Europe: Concepts, Patterns and Control Policies in the European Union and Beyond.* Norwell, MA: Springer.

Freeh, Louis. 1996, April 30. "Testimony before House Committee on International Relations." Hearing on Russian Organized Crime. Available at http://www.globalsecurity.org/security/library/congress/1996_h/h960430f.htm. Accessed September 5, 2009.

Gambetta, Diego. 1993. *The Sicilian Mafia: The Business of Private Protection.* Cambridge, MA: Harvard University Press.

Gettleman, Jeffrey. 2006, November 10. "Chased by Gang Violence, Residents Flee Kenyan Slum." *New York Times International:* A4.

Gettleman, Jeffrey. 2009, April 12. "What Tho. Jefferson Knew about Pirates." *New York Times:* 4.

Gettleman, Jeffrey. 2009, May 9. "For Somalia's Pirates, Worst Enemy May Be Waiting Back on Shore." *New York Times:* A1, A9.

Ghosh, Bimal, ed. 2000. *Managing Migration: Time for a New International Regime?* Oxford: Oxford University Press.

Gutterman, Steve. 2008, December 1. "Ransom Discussion Nears Deal." *Houston Chronicle:* A15.

Hagedorn, John M., ed. 2007. *Gangs in the Global City: Alternatives to Traditional Criminology.* Urbana: University of Illinois Press.

Hess, Henner. 1973. *Mafia and Mafiosi: The Structure of Power.* Lexington, MA: Lexington Books.

Hoefer, Michael, Nancy Rytina, and Bryan C. Baker. 2007, January. "Estimate of Unauthorized Immigrant Population Residing in the United States." Available at http://www.dhs.gov/xlibrary/assets/statistics/publications/ois_ill_pe_2007.pdf. Accessed September 3, 2009.

Hoffer, Peter Charles. 2000. *The Brave New World: A History of Early America.* Boston: Houghton Mifflin.

Houreld, Katherine. 2008, December 5. "For Filipino Captives, a Kind Pirate Isn't an Oxymoron." *Houston Chronicle:* A19.

Kaplan, Robert D. 2009, April 12. "Anarchy on Land Means Piracy at Sea." *New York Times:* 9.

Karraker, Cyrus H. 1953. *Piracy Was a Business.* Rindge, NH: Richard R. Smith.

Karrstrand, Klas. 2007, May 9–10. "Countering Narcotics and Organized Crime in the Baltic Sea Region." Report from the Silk Road Studies Program Workshop, Talinn, Estonia. Available at http://www.silkroadstudies.org.

Keath, Lee, and Jennifer Quinn. 2008, November 19. "Wanted: Some Hearties to Police the High Seas." *Houston Chronicle:* A3.

Keefe, Patrick Radden. 2006, April 24. "The Snakehead." *The New Yorker* 82 (10). Available at http://www.newyorker.com/archive/2006/04/24/060424fa_fact6.

Langewiesche, William. 2004. *The Outlaw Sea: A World of Freedom, Chaos, and Crime.* New York: North Point Press.

Langton, Jerry. 2007. *Iced: Crystal Meth, the Biography of North America's Deadliest New Plague.* New York: North Point Press.

Lee, Maggy, ed. 2007. *Human Trafficking.* Devon, UK: Willan Publishing.

Lunde, Paul. 2004. *Organized Crime: An Inside Guide to the World's Most Successful Industry.* New York: DK Publishing.

Mazzetti, Mark. 2009, April 10. "Navy's Standoff with Pirates Shows U.S. Power Has Limits." *New York Times:* A1, A15.

Meiners, Stephen. 2009, March 26. "Central America: An Emerging Role in the Drug Trade." *STRATFOR.* Available at http://www.stratfor.com/weekly/200090326_central_america_emerging_role_drug_trade. Accessed March 27, 2009.

Meyer, Bill. 2008, November 11. "Tanker capture raises alarm over Somali piracy." Available at http://www.cleveland.com/world/index.ssf/2008/11/tanker_capture_raises_alarm_ov.html.Accessed October 9, 2009.

Mueller, Gerhard O. W., and Freda Adler. 1985. *Outlaws of the Ocean: The Complete Book of Contemporary Crime on the High Seas.* New York: Hearst Marine Books.

Naim, Moises. 2006. *Illicit: How Smugglers, Traffickers, and Copycats Are Hijacking the Global Economy.* New York: Anchor Books.

National Drug Intelligence Center. 2009. *National Drug Threat Assessment.* Washington, D.C.: U.S. Department of Justice.

Nunez, Claudia. 2007, December 27. "Women Are the New Coyotes." *New American Media.* Available at http://arizonasportsfan.com/vb/showthread.php?t=104452. Accessed January 15, 2008.

O'Neill, Siobhan.2007, May 24. "Terrorist Precursor Crimes: Issues and Options for Congress." Washington, D.C.: Congressional Research Service.

Owen, Frank. 2007. *No Speed Limit: The Highs and Lows of Meth.* New York: St. Martin's Press.

Picarelli, John T. 2007. "Historical Approaches to the Trade in Human Beings." In *Human Trafficking,* ed. Maggy Lee. 26–48. Devon: UK: Willan Publishing.

Powell, Stewart M., and Clay Robison. 2009, March 19. "U.S. Going on Offense at Border." *Houston Chronicle:* A1, A6.

Rediker, Marcus. 1987. *Between the Devil and the Deep Blue Sea: Merchant Seamen, Pirates and Anglo-Americans.* Cambridge, UK: Cambridge University Press.

Rediker, Marcus. 2004. *Villains of All Nations: Atlantic Pirates in the Golden Age.* Boston: Beacon Press.

Roth, Mitchel P. 2009. *Organized Crime.* Upper Saddle River, NJ: Pearson.

Ruggie, John G. 2000. "Weaving the Global Compact: Sustaining the Single Global Economic Space." Available at http://www.un.org/Pubs/chronicle/2000/issue2/0200p36.htm.

Smith, Denis Mack. 1995, November 30. "The Ruling Class." *New York Times Book Review:* 7.

Surtees, Rebecca. 2008. "Traffickers and Trafficking in Southern and Eastern Europe." *European Journal of Criminology* 5 (1): 39–68.

Turley, Hans. 1999. *Rum, Sodomy and the Lash: Piracy, Sexuality and Masculine Identity.* New York: New York University Press.

United Nations Office on Drugs and Crime (UNODC). 2000. *United Nations Convention on Transnational Organized Crime.* Available at http://www.unodc.org/unodc/en/treaties/CTOC/index.html. Accessed September 3, 2009.

United Nations Office on Drugs and Crime (UNODC). 2002, September. *Global Programme against Transnational Organized Crime: Results of a Pilot Survey of Forty Selected Organized Criminal Groups in Sixteen Countries.* Vienna: UNDOC.

United Nations Office on Drugs and Crime, Vienna. 2005. *Transnational Organized Crime in the West African Region.* New York: United Nations.

Varese, Federico. 2006. "How Mafias Migrate: The Case of the 'Ndrangheta in Northern Italy." *Law and Society Review* 40 (2): 411–444.

Volkman, Ernest. 1998. *Gangbusters: The Destruction of America's Last Great Mafia Dynasty.* Boston: Faber and Faber.

Wagner, Denise. 2006, July 23. "Human Trafficking Profits Spur Horrors." Available at http://www.azcentral.com/arizonarepublic/news/articles/0723drophouse-main2.html. Accessed January 15, 2008.

Walters, Stephen. 2007, February. "Contemporary Maritime Piracy." *Crime and Justice International:* 10–16.

Will, George. 2009, March 19. "Drug War in Mexico Is Taking a Toll on Border States." *Houston Chronicle:* B9.

Williams, Neville. 1961. *Contraband Cargoes: Seven Centuries of Smuggling.* Hamden, CT: Shoe String Press.

2

Problems, Controversies, and Solutions

Introduction

Among the most challenging problems for law enforcement in the 21st century are the globalization of terrorism and crime and the rise in information technology-related crime. Constant war and conflicts in regions characterized by failed and failing states have only contributed to the problem as law enforcement becomes overwhelmed on all fronts. One of the biggest challenges today is cooperation between police agencies and government officials across borders. There are so many barriers to cooperation among international police forces that at times the challenges seem insurmountable, particularly when it comes to variations in technological know-how, languages, cultures, criminal justice systems, and historical experiences. In past years any examination of organized crime was conducted along the lines of specific groups and structures, usually confined to one or two countries, and in some case revolving around transnational criminal networks. In the 21st century, the interconnectedness of the world's national economies has only complicated the understanding of global criminal syndicates. This chapter examines the impact of failed states, terrorism, tribalism and ethnicity, civil wars, the end of the Cold War, and other issues to offer a foundation for a better understanding of the roots of global organized crime and the challenges in controlling it.

Circumstances and Conditions

Failed States

Defining a Failed State

A *failed state* is typically a nation-state characterized by high levels of crime and violence, endemic corruption, the inability of its leader to exercise sovereignty without brutal force, absence of consent of the governed, and an unremitting atmosphere of uncertainty and instability. Many failed and failing states, plagued by various warlords, criminal groups, and competing governments, become havens for international organized crime networks, who take advantage of areas outside the government's control. Some observers suggest globalization has created pockets in the world where failed or weak states are left to govern with little economic or political power, giving rise to domestic organized crime groups who operate their own underground economies, providing some form of political stability in the region because they are strong enough to resist the state. As a result of the economic vacuums created by globalization, shell states form fueling the growth of the global underground economy by offering the refuge of illegal trade routes for drugs, arms smugglers, contraband dealers, and human traffic (Napoleoni 2003).

Failed states appear in a variety of incarnations ranging from "high state functioning to complete state failure" (Sung 2004). An argument can indeed be made that no state has ever been in complete control of its jurisdiction, for crime and abuse of state authority exist in every society to some degree. For example, the most advanced Western nations with prosperous economies have flourishing drug markets in impoverished urban centers. When the aspect of economic failure raises its head or when there is an unequal distribution of basic goods and services for subsistence, however, the result is often the rise of an alternative or *underground economy*. When the government is unable to ensure the availability of goods and services, a black market usually emerges. A black market entails activities hidden from fiscal authorities and involves illicit trade in goods and services contrary to government regulations. Its very existence predisposes citizens to illegality by training (and conditioning) large numbers of citizens in illegal transactions. Most critical to the underground economy are the vice industries and trafficking of illegal goods.

Failed States and Global Organized Crime

The absence of a strong central government or an effective law enforcement apparatus often serves as an open invitation for the relocation of international criminal enterprises. What's more, organized crime groups find sanctuary in countries that are without sustainable economic development. And with the absence of central authority, there is little to prevent syndicates from taking advantage of the opportunities awaiting them. Close to 50 countries today can be considered failed or failing states. Among the most prominent are Afghanistan, Iraq, and Somalia, which was recently branded "Africa's most utterly failed state" (*Economist* 2009). Although each is distinct from the other, they share some common ingredients ranging from political and economic instability, poverty, and rampant organized crime activity to civil disorder, terrorism, human trafficking, ethnic conflict, disease, and genocide. Lack of leadership is often one of the greatest barriers to fixing failed states. Noam Chomsky (2006) defined failed states as those that are unable or unwilling "to protect their citizens from violence and perhaps even destruction." Often these same states "regard themselves as beyond the reach of domestic or international law" (Chomsky 2006). States fall into the status of failed states when their central governments "cease to offer freedoms, civil rights, criminal and civil justice, personal safety, and collective security in an efficient and just manner" (Chomsky 2006).

Corruption

Political Officials

Organized crime at every level in society has flourished thanks to its contacts with legitimate politicians, government officials, and business entrepreneurs. In countries from the United States to Colombia, from Liberia to Russia, leading politicians, oligarchs, police officers, city political bosses, and military personnel have been tied to corruption and organized crime activities. More than 25 years ago, one leading expert on corruption noted "presidents, vice presidents, congressmen, senators, governors, and racketeers are implicated in a ubiquitous system of payoffs and favors, back-scratching, stealing, illegal campaign contributions, and personal aggrandizements" (Chambliss 1988). At the highest office in the United States,

President Ulysses S. Grant's second term in office set the bar for corruption and fraud in the corridors of power. One scandal during his administration, known as the Whiskey Tax Evasion conspiracy, involved a plot to defraud the government out of millions of dollars in tax revenue on distilled spirits in order to raise money to pay for the campaign for Grant's second term in 1872.

When it comes to links between organized crime and the urban metropolis, no city is as prominent as Chicago, which as early as the 1860s was regarded as America's "wickedest city." Chicago "businessman" Michael "Big Mike" McDonald was regarded as "the first true crime lord" and among the first to recognize the importance of the political fix by supporting winning candidates for mayor and other offices during the 1870s (Russo 2001). Chicago's tradition of political corruption continued into the 20th and 21st centuries. No city in America is so linked to corruption (although several others come close). Although Chicago's political hierarchy has not been directly connected to any global crime rings, the city is a destination and transit point for many international crime networks today.

Latin America has its version of the political boss as well—the *Coronelismo* in Brazil and the *cacique* in Mexico. In 2007, the Washington Office on Latin America released a report describing selected bribes paid by Vladimiro Montesinos of the Peruvian Congress. Formerly a captain in the army, he was fired for various criminal activities in the 1970s. He later reinvented himself as an expensive defense attorney for drug traffickers, politicians, and military officers facing fraud charges. One expert reported that while Peru was under President Fujimori, individuals such as Montesinos helped turn the country into a "mafia state" (WOLA 2007). Fujimori was sentenced to 25 years in prison in 2009 for human rights charges involving mass murder and kidnappings committed under his administration in the early 1990s. Investigators have documented how Montesinos, despite ties to drug traffickers, served as Fujimori's right-hand man and spymaster while sharing spoils on a range of trafficking schemes with top-ranking Peruvian military officers, including multimillion kickback profits from various weapons purchases and related procurements, while sharing funds from the military pension fund with his cabal (Conaghan 2006, 119).

Any discussion of organized crime in Russia must take into account the persistence of the *krysha,* or "roof," which operationally speaking refers to an organization or individual that can provide protection and patronage that is necessary to carry on business or government practices (think Boss Tweed of New York City). This system dates back to the organized crime practices of the former Soviet Union, when the "state itself started to sell private protection" (Varese 2001). In the late 1980s, the Soviet Interior Ministry issued an order that allowed Soviet policemen to enter into contracts with various industrial concerns, collective farms, and ministries to provide security services for commercial establishments. Things had gotten so bad for gangsters that one Moscow boss complained: "It's gotten impossible to work; one place the cops are providing roofs; somewhere else it's the KGB" (CSIS 1997). As communism collapsed in the wake of Perestroika in 1991, the *kryshas* filled an organizational void, leading in effect to one variant of corrupt patronage replacing another. Few would argue that the Soviet system, particularly in its last decades, was being run by a "kleptocracy" of Communist bureaucrats. Some observers even began to use the word *mafiya* when referring to the Communist Party and the State. Industrial and agricultural managers were considered part of the country's most powerful mafia networks, as were the directors of any business that controlled the exploitation of the nation's natural resources as the distribution and production of goods. Few doubted that bribery and corruption were required to move up the Russian economic ladder to wealth (Lintner 2003).

Police

Corruption plagues Mexico's criminal justice system at every level. It is one thing to arrest crime syndicate leaders. It is a greater challenge to keep them behind bars because of corruption and payoffs. In May 2009, for example, 53 prisoners, including at least 11 gunmen from the Gulf Cartel, escaped from a prison in Zacatecas. Attention immediately focused on the prison's warden, two ranking police officers, and 40 jailers, who were subsequently arrested for questioning. That same week federal prosecutors in Mexico ordered the arrest of the former police chief and former public security director of Morelos, a state south of Mexico City. They were among those sought for providing protection to the Beltran Leyva drug trafficking organization (Althaus 2009).

One cannot look at the current drug war on the Mexican-American border without acknowledging the central role played by corruption. According to one recent estimate, 62 percent of Mexican law enforcement was on the payroll of drug gangs (Schaan 2009); however, no country is immune to police corruption. One recent case in the United States illustrates how one corrupt officer can ruin an investigation. In 2002, former FBI Special Agent John Connolly was convicted of racketeering, obstructing justice, and making false statements to federal investigators. Evidence was introduced in a long trial that proved the agent had leaked the proceedings of a grand jury investigation to Boston crime boss James "Whitey" Bulger, who was able to escape one step ahead of the law and is now on the FBI Most Wanted List. In another related case, a Massachusetts state trooper was convicted of obstructing justice after passing on surveillance information to Bulger associates (Nardini 2006).

A more recent case, however, probably has more parallels for the current situation in Mexico, where it has become almost impossible to tell the good guys from the bad. In 2005, two highly decorated former New York Police Department detectives were indicted for moonlighting as hit men for the mob, one of the most sensational police corruption cases in department history. They were convicted for their roles in eight murders committed between 1986 and 1990. According to the prosecution, the two were paid $4,000 a month to help the Lucchese crime family (and more if they performed a hit themselves). They were accused of committing at least two murders themselves after pulling over targeted drivers for traffic stops. They were tried and convicted of Racketeer Influenced and Corrupt Organizations Act (RICO) charges that included racketeering conspiracy, witness tampering, witness retaliation, and obstruction of justice. Because of legal technicalities in the conspiracy case, however, a judge threw out the case and the defendants were acquitted (McGrath 2006, McShane 2006).

Tribalism and Ethnicity

In certain regions of the world, a high premium is placed on an individual's tribal or ethnic background. In Africa, for example, it is common for criminal gangs and organized crime syndicates to be bound together by these natural affinities. Not surprisingly, criminal gangs and organized crime groups are often bound together by these same built-in loyalties. In the same way, conflict arises between these gangs that often can be traced back to events that occurred during or even long before colonialism and the members' living memories. For example in November 2006, at least 10 people were killed and hundreds of homes torched in a bout of gang violence between Kenyan gangs precipitated by a bootlegging dispute exacerbated by tribal rivalries between the Mungiki from the Kikuyu tribe, one of the nation's largest, and the Taliban from Luo, another important tribe (Gettleman 2006). One resident publicly suggested that the conflict was more about tribal rivalries than criminal rackets, issues that are too often ignored by foreign observers.

In the new millennium, transnational crime syndicates have taken advantage of the artificial colonial borders that divide ethnic groups in most African nations. According to one study there are at least 177 ethnic culture areas in Africa divided by national borders. For example, the Nigerian-Cameroon boundary divides 14 tribes, whereas that of Burkina-Faso divides 21 tribes (Reader 1998, 575–576). In most of these regions one's national identity usually is second place to kinship, ethnic, and tribal links.

Transnational crime is facilitated by the migration of populations across borders and in the process becomes a factor in a transportation and migration process that transfers illicit and stolen merchandise across borders. With the rise in globalization, most countries now host immigrant communities within their borders. Organized crime syndicates have used this process by creating new legal commerce networks to shield deep-rooted trafficking networks that control the trafficking of illegal goods between various African host nations and their homes abroad. Such relationships have been well documented among Chinese, Indian, Nigerian, and Russian communities in southern Africa, and likewise among Indian and Middle Eastern groups in East and West Africa.

Civil Wars, Political Transitions, Regional Conflicts

As recently as the 1980s, it was a Soviet tradition to downplay the existence of organized crime and little effort was directed at fighting it. After the collapse of the Soviet Union, hundreds if not thousands of new criminal groups emerged in Russia to take advantage of the latest opportunities offered by the democratization process. Scholars trace organized crime in Russia back to the birth of the Soviet system itself. By the 1960s, modern syndicates had emerged, thanks in part to the state apparatus that "encouraged, facilitated and protected it" (Wright 2006, 148). During the Brezhnev regime in the 1970s and 1980s, it became clear to an increasingly dissatisfied public that the country was being run by a "kleptocracy" of Communist bureaucrats. It became fashionable to brand the corruption "Mafiya." But rather than referring to a monolithic hierarchy, the term referred to the daily inequities of life in the Soviet Union exemplified by the power structure and the incumbent corruption that persisted under the Communist system, where those who controlled certain services or commodities—retail sales managers, mechanics, doctors, prostitutes, butchers and so forth—were as likely as anyone to be branded "Mafiya." Many viewed the Communist Party and State as "Mafiya." Industrial and agricultural managers were considered part of the country's most powerful "mafia networks," as were the directors of large state ministries and factories—any enterprise that controlled the exploitation of its natural resources and the production and distribution of goods. Few argued that bribery and corruption were required to move up the economic ladder.

In the final decades of the 20th century, journalists used the term to refer to the emerging crime syndicates and gangs taking advantage of the release of price controls that marked the former Soviet economy. In 1991, Yeltsin banned the Communist Party. Out of the rubble of the Soviet Union emerged 15 new republics. This development facilitated the expansion of Russian organized crime syndicates who took advantage of the confused state of affairs and the shortage of goods as they created a black market that would eventually spread to Western Europe and America. As early as 1994, the FBI identified Russian gangs operating in a number of major U.S. cities. Journalist Robert I. Friedman perhaps put it best when he said they "didn't come here to enjoy the American dream, they came here to steal it" (Friedman 2000, xix).

Organized crime spreads rapidly in times of political transition and violence. Prominent examples include the fall of the Soviet Union, the Yugoslavian conflicts, and the end of apartheid in South Africa, all of which took place in the early 1990s. Likewise, since the end of the Cold War in the 1990s, there has been a noticeable increase in the overlapping of politically inspired violence and organized crime activity in Latin America, Asia, and Africa. Poorer countries in Africa and Central Asia lost Cold War sponsors and many then collapsed into low-intensity civil conflicts. Where U.S. and Soviets once competed for dominance bestowing weapons on friendly governments, weapons traffickers have stepped in to fill the vacuum.

In 1994, South Africa replaced the policy of apartheid with a constitutional democracy. Before this time, the authoritarian nature of what was essentially a police state stemmed the expansion into the country by global crime syndicates, although homegrown groups flourished. While the security apparatus focused its investigations on political opposition, indigenous organized crime groups expanded throughout the country; and in the face of stringent border controls, organized crime increased significantly by trickling over the borders into neighboring countries. As South Africa became more tourist-friendly, its open border and new trading partners offered new links for criminal syndicates (Gastrow 1999).

More than 75,000 people died during El Salvador's violent civil war in the early 1980s. More than a million El Salvadorans fled to the United States seeking sanctuary, many settling in Hispanic-friendly communities in southern California (USAID 2006). Some of the immigrants had served in the paramilitary Farabundo Marti National Liberation Front (FMNL) during the conflict and were well versed in military weaponry and tactics and the concomitant brutality that often went along with it. FMNL and civilian refugees eventually banded together to protect themselves from myriad Los Angeles gangs, evolving into Mara Salvatrucha, better known as MS-13.

According to a number of observers, there were almost 100,000 private security guards in Guatemala as of 2009, outnumbering the police and the army. Most are poorly educated and badly paid. It is unknown how many of them turned to crime (O'Connor 2009). In 1996, after a 36-year civil war that left thousands dead, Guatemala is awash in guns. This combined high unemployment and poverty have contributed to the growing drug trade, organized crime, and violent crime. With more than 6,000 murders in a country of 13 million, murder is the leading cause of death for young males (Washington Office on Latin America October 2007).

The Vietnam War was one of the seminal events of the 1960s and mid-1970s. In its aftermath thousands of Asian refugees, mostly Vietnamese, immigrated to the United States. Among the émigrés were many who had ties to the former South Vietnamese government and the U.S. military. Others consisted of corrupt officials, former military officers, and black market profiteers who had made a fortune during the decade long conflict. The first wave of immigrants came to the United States directly after the war, with successive waves heading for Canada, Australia, England, France, and Germany. Recent scholarship suggests that among the unintended consequences of this emigration was the transmittal of ancient conflicts between the Vietnamese and Chinese to the United States. Violence resulted as gangs went to war with each other in several major cities, most notably Toronto and Boston. In one of the most prominent examples, members of the Chinese Ghost Shadows unleashed a barrage of bullets on Vietnamese mourners at the funeral of one gang kingpin.

A number of African countries suffered through violent civil conflicts since the 1980s. In regions such as West Africa, particularly in Sierra Leone and Liberia, military forces have been forced to turn to organized crime activities to fund their armies. Both countries are considered failed states, where "chaos is the norm and war is away of life." As a result, the region became a welcoming beacon to "non-state actors" such as drug syndicates, criminal organizations, and terrorist groups (Farah 2004). Warfare between the Popular Movement for the Liberation of Angola (MPLA) and the National Union for the Total Independence of Angola (UNITA) in Angola, the northern Nilotics and southern Bantu tribes in Uganda, the Liberian civil war, northern Arabs and southern Africans in Sudan, Moslems and Christians in northern Nigeria, and the Mozambican National Resistance (RENAMO) and the Liberation Front of Mozambique (FRELIMO) in Mozambique, just to name some of the most prominent. These conflicts often facilitated a growing weapons and drug trade. According to a 2005 United Nations study, wherever there was civil warfare it is difficult to distinguish between organized crime and political violence, and armed conflict has actually encouraged certain forms of organized crime to flourish under the guise of political struggle. The main debate, however, is whether these cliques can be considered actual organized crime groups. By most accounts few of these groups are hierarchically structured, and most seem to be highly flexible and individualistic in their methods.

After the death of its leader, Marshal Tito, in 1980, Yugoslavia suffered a series of conflicts that would lead to the country's disintegration in the 1990s and into the emergence of the new countries of Serbia, Croatia, Bosnia-Herzegovina, Slovenia, and Kosovo. Many Yugoslavian gangsters who had fled the country during the Tito years moved back to become involved in the wartime rackets. The end of the Yugoslavian conflict and humanitarian crisis in 1999 had the unanticipated consequence of stimulating the growth in organized crime activity, including gambling, money laundering, drug trafficking, human smuggling, extortion, robbery, and murder. The region encompassing the former Yugoslavia, as well as other Balkan nations, contains the countries of Albania, Bosnia-Herzegovina, Croatia, Kosovo, Macedonia, Serbia, Montenegro, Bulgaria, Greece, and Romania, a region that has been called "the soft underbelly of the European narcotics market" (Michaletos 2007). Balkan organized crime groups can be traced back to the traditional clans of the 15th century. Each clan established itself in the different territories and controlled most activities in that region. Modern-day organized crime in the Balkans is built in part on the structure of the earlier family clans and ethnic solidarity (FBI, 2008). In the 21st century, Balkan syndicates have transformed themselves from a hierarchical model toward more loosely organized networks. By 2007, most European investigators acknowledged that Serbian and ethnic Albanian clans controlled the heroin coming north out of Afghanistan, weapons smuggled through the Balkans, and prostitutes trafficked from Africa to Copenhagen (Fleishman 2006).

Until the Yugoslavian conflicts, most of the European drug market was supplied with narcotics being brought in through the Balkan route, which began in Pakistan, Iran, and Turkey, where the narcotics were processed. The road led through Greece; Bulgaria; the former Yugoslavian republics of Serbia, Slovenia, and Croatia; Romania; Hungary; the Czech Republic; and Slovakia, until reaching final destinations in Austria, Italy, Switzerland, and the rest of Western Europe. The outbreak of war in the region led Albanian syndicates to blaze new paths to Europe in order to avoid the warfare. A southern route was inaugurated from Turkey and then through Bulgaria, former Yugoslavian republics, Kosovo and Albania, to Italy and other countries. The northern route went from Turkey through Bulgaria, Romania, and Hungary to the Czech Republic, Slovakia, and Western Europe. Once the war ended, the old Balkan route was reestablished; however, the new route for drug trafficking stayed and the entire network was expanded by Kosovan Albanians and Turkish groups (BIA 2003).

Organized Crime and Terrorism

Before the end of the Cold War in the 1990s, the labels *terrorist* and *criminal* were generally clear-cut. Since then the distinction has become less clear. Globalization and the collapse of the Soviet Union are among the factors that have increased the links between organized crime and terrorist groups. With the decline in state sponsorship of terrorism, a number of groups have turned to a variety of criminal enterprises that were formerly the domain of organized crime syndicates to finance their activities. Scholars began linking these two phenomena in the 1970s and 1980s, an era when leftist terrorist groups in Latin America forged relationships with drug cartels. These relationships were sometimes referred to as narcoterrorism. But in the 1990s, Western law enforcement reported that terrorist groups were increasingly involved in criminal activity around the world. For example, as early as 1993, French authorities uncovered evidence that illegal drug sales in Muslim slum areas were under the direction of Afghanistan War veterans with ties to Algerian terrorist groups.

Most international organized crime and terrorist groups operate secretly and usually take sanctuary in an underground network. Both use intimidation, ruthlessness, and violence against mostly civilian targets. They use similar tactics such as kidnapping assassination and extortion. In both types of organizations, the control of the group over the individual is strong. Both use front operations such as legitimate businesses or charities to obscure their activities and launder money. In any case both types of criminals have to use underground economies and networks to move people, goods, weapons, contraband, and, most important, money. Terrorists use existing criminal networks for logistics, including financing activities (Carter 2004). Some terrorist groups even run banks and create phony (shell) companies to launder money, whereas others engage in secret arrangements and form alliances with organized crime groups (Ehrenfeld 2003).

By the beginning of the 21st century, one study reported that at least 30 terrorist campaigns were financed by organized drug trafficking groups. For example, Islamic extremist groups such as Hezbollah and Hamas have been widely cited for participation in complex money-laundering schemes, arms and drug trafficking, and intellectual property piracy. A wide range of terrorist groups have resorted to global organized crime to finance their activities, but its adoption by Muslim extremists has been troubling to most devout Muslims.

In 2003, one investigation examined countries in Africa, the former Soviet Union and Eastern Europe, South Asia, Western Europe and Italy, and the Western Hemisphere, and in each region researchers discovered examples of the confluence of terrorism and organized crime. The investigators noted that beginning in the mid-1990s, it had become clear that both types of organizations had "globalized and diversified their operations" (Berry, Curtis, Hudson, Karacan, Kollars, and Miro 2003). Little had changed by 2007 when a report by Siobhan O'Neil of the Congressional Research Service asserted terrorists have turned more and more to crime to fund their activities. Explanations have varied, but most agree that it is a response to dwindling state sponsorship and the rising number of amateurs creating "small, semi-autonomous terrorist cells" (O'Neil 2007). Authorities have cited the cocaine, hashish, and heroin drug trade; but nothing is out of the question including counterfeiting, bootlegging Viagra, and stealing and cutting infant formula.

Over the past decade the ideological motives of once doctrinaire extremist groups have eroded to the point of blurring their distinction from organized crime groups. It has become de rigueur for researchers to discuss the process by which international terrorists and criminals adopt each others' methods and strategies. Researchers such as Louise Shelley insist the "merger of transnational crime, terrorism and corruption is profound," (Shelley 2003) but others such as Raphael Perl of the Library of Congress's Congressional Research Center insist "it is important to recognize that we are dealing with two distinct and separate phenomena" (Perl 2003). Nonetheless, terrorist groups have become increasingly pragmatic when it comes to financing their organizations using drug smuggling, money laundering, and organized fraud.

Both groups continue to adapt to the changing geopolitical climate. Because both need safe havens to operate from, a failed or failing state is especially seductive. Once upon a time terrorists went jurisdiction shopping to see which targets were most vulnerable when it came to security. Now they are just as likely to look for countries from which they can base their criminal operations outside the parameters of terrorism. All of these groups share the need for a country offering maximum opportunities for survival and expansion for their criminal networks.

Researchers across the spectrum have increasingly turned their attention to the process by which organized crime syndicates and international terrorists adopt each others' organizational and operational characteristics. Global terrorist groups have become intimately involved in weapons and drug trafficking networks, illegal immigrant smuggling, and money laundering—staples of most global organized crime groups. While the debate continues over the so-called terrorism-crime relationship, more recently Shelley and Picarelli (2005) devised a multistage process to explain this metamorphosis. In the first stage the two groups begin to actively buy and sell services from each other, borrowing each other's methods in a process of "activity appropriation." Both groups in the next stage will begin to work more closely together in a symbiotic relationship once they mutually recognize their shared methodologies and motivations. In some regions such as the Tri-Border area of Paraguay, Brazil, and Argentina, there is so much overlapping of activities it is impossible to distinguish one behavior from the other. What is most likely occurring is that both global organized crime groups and terrorist groups are using overlapping networks and often cooperating in various enterprises. According to a 2006 FBI study for the Pentagon, this phenomenon is growing because "terrorists and organized criminals use similar approaches to promote their operations" (quoted in Milton 2006). Both rely on an underworld of black markets and laundered money, both rely on shifting networks and secret cells to accomplish objectives, and both need weapons, false documents, and safe hiding places.

The amount of money required for a terrorist operation demonstrates the financial resources required. One report suggested that Iran's attempt to establish a "Hezbollah-like network of cells" in Iraq costs between $750,000 and $3 million a month for one unit of Iran's Revolutionary Guards (Hennessy-Fiske and Susman 2007). Although in this case they have the sponsorship of the Iranian government, most groups do not have this luxury and must rely on crime strategies. What is most clear about the convergence of these two groups is that terrorists support their activities through whatever avenues are convenient and profitable, and can include any combination of the following: legal employment, accepting voluntary donations, social assistance, or using criminal activities. The goals of both often dovetail when it comes to raising money. For example, it is easier to traffic drugs through zones of civil conflict, and various extremists have discovered that drug trafficking is an important source for purchasing weapons, organizing terrorist attacks, and maintaining armed terrorist cells.

Borrowed Tactics

Organized crime in South Asia runs the spectrum from drug and arms trafficking to extortion, money laundering, and kidnapping. More recently the links between organized crime and terrorism have become better documented, particularly in the region's urban centers in India and Pakistan. Since the early 1990s, there have been an alarming number of terrorist attacks launched with the participation of crime syndicates. In 2003, the U.S. Treasury Department designated Dawood Ibrahim a "global terrorist" for allowing al Qaeda to use his smuggling routes, supporting jihadists in Pakistan, and participating in the Mumbai attacks of 1993.

Dawood Ibrahim was placed on the list of drug kingpins in the U.S. Kingpin Act in 2000. Ibrahim built Mumbai's most formidable criminal syndicate by smuggling black market gold and other commodities into India's closed economy, while steamrolling his way into the nation's Bollywood industry (Kaplan, Fang, and Sangwan 2005). During the 1980s and 1990s, he was the acknowledged leader of the Mumbai underworld, directing a multibillion dollar vice empire involving prostitution, drugs, and gambling. His connection to Bollywood ensured no star would refuse his request to appear in one of his films. Ibrahim is one of the rare players on the international stage who is regarded as both a crime kingpin and a terrorist leader. His syndicate was identified as being involved in the March 12, 1993 attacks in Mumbai that left 257 dead and more than 700 injured. The planning and carrying out of the attacks is a graphic example of how terrorists and organized criminals cooperate. Ibrahim and another South Asian syndicate boss, Tiger Memon, recruited members to be trained for attacks in Pakistan. They were tutored in the use of variety of weapons, including a potent explosive additive known as RDX (Zaidi 2003). With the collusion of corrupt customs officials, the weapons were landed in ports near the target center.

The Sicilian Mafia has taken pages from the terrorist playbook as well. In 1982, Italy passed a law that would allow authorities to confiscate Mafia wealth. Although various threats were made to wage war on the Italian state itself, it was not until 1991 that any type of agreement could be reached—a decision to strike at the nation's cultural heritage, such as museums and churches. It was the first time in its history that the Sicilian Mafia took such measures to cause economic damage by ruining the tourist industry (Dickie 2004). The explosion of a car bomb outside Florence's famed Uffizi gallery on May 27, 1993 launched the campaign, killing five and wounding dozens. This bombing was followed in the summer by bombings of two Roman churches and a modern art gallery (Bohlen 1995). Unlike terrorist groups, which typically claim responsibility for their actions, the Mafia does not. Links between the attacks and the Mafia, however, were apparent from the beginning when it was discovered that the device used in the Uffizi bombing was similar to others used in Sicily (as well as from information provided by a legion of informers, or *pentiti*). The bombings ceased as the government backed off from its campaign to confiscate Mafia wealth. Sicilian crime boss Bernardo Provenzano has been credited by most scholars for ordering his followers to desist from attacking civilians, policemen, and politicians, and in the process bringing the Mafia back from the verge of destruction (Longrigg 2009). He no doubt saw the folly of attacking these civilian targets once his predecessor, Toto Riina, was locked up for life for launching the wave of violence in the early 1990s that only precipitated a harsher crackdown by the authorities. What's more, Provenzano was well aware how these tactics hampered the Mafia's ability to make money. So in essence, an unwritten truce was called in which the Italian government would reduce its Mafia suppression efforts as long as the Mafia's rackets were conducted according to traditional standards that basically meant they would only kill each other.

Organized Crime Hybrids

During its heyday in the 1990s and the first years of the 21st century, the Revolutionary Armed Forces of Colombia (FARC) was a major player in the illicit drug trade. Founded in 1966, FARC had a membership at its zenith estimated to range in the tens of thousands. During the last four decades it has proven to be among the most durable and resourceful rebel groups in the world. Over the years it has increasingly taken on a "hybrid" appearance, toeing the line between terrorist and organized crime network. Before its recent setbacks in 2008 and 2009, its coffers were consistently replenished by a variety of traditional organized crime activities not limited to kidnapping for ransom, extortion (which they refer to as revolutionary taxes), and robbery. Drug manufacturing and trafficking, however, has been its greatest profit-maker, bringing in an estimated $300 million a year (ISVG 2003). Some estimates even placed FARC profits at $600 million a year through related protection rackets involving poppy growers and by slowly eliminating some of the cartel middlemen and organizing its own distribution network (Hanson 2009). By taking part in the most important stages of the manufacturing and distribution process, FARC ensured a steady stream of funds. In addition, the group taxes cultivators of coca plants and controls manufacturing laboratories. It has been estimated that at one time the group made a "tax for peace" profit on any Colombian citizen worth more than $1 million. During the administration of President Andres Pastrana, FARC consolidated and expanded its activities thanks to a number of concessions made by the government, which included establishing a demilitarized zone and a crackdown on the opposition paramilitary groups (ISVG 2003).

Intersecting Activities

The majority of modern terrorist groups have turned to organized crime activity in one form of another to fund their operations. Terrorist groups need money to operate. During the last 20 years, state sponsorship has virtually disappeared and terrorists now count on a variety of criminal methods to raise funds including kidnapping, extortion robbery, fraud, larceny, smuggling, dealing in contraband, forgery, and counterfeiting (Nance 2003). Terrorist groups have used criminal activity to fund their operations since at least the 1970s when various Leftist groups in Western Europe and the Americas used bank robbery, which they called "expropriation," and other forms of armed theft. Since then a number of terrorist groups have either adopted organized crime tactics on their own or set up associations with established organized crime groups. Those conforming to the association model include the Albanian mafia with the Kosovo Liberation Army (KLA), the Colombian cocaine cartels with FARC, the South Asian Dawood syndicate with al Qaeda and the Sri Lankan Tamil Tigers, and the Central Asian syndicates with the Islamic Movement of Uzbekistan.

One leading expert suggests: "The most illustrative nexus between a criminal and terrorist group—one in which a mutual relationship has proven integral to the operation of both entities"—is the relationship between the Albanian mafia and the KLA during the Kosovo conflict (Makarenko 2005, 132). The KLA emerged in 1996 out of the conflict in Yugoslavia, with the goal of winning Kosovan independence from Serbia. More than 90 percent of Kosovo's population is ethnic Albanian, so it should be no surprise that there was such an affinity between the two groups, especially considering that Albanian crime syndicates shared the KLA's concerns over pan-Albanian ideals, politics, and terrorism (Mutschke 2000). The links between the two groups, however, were forged much earlier following the democratization process that began in 1990. During this time of adjustment, the rule of law that had so characterized the formerly Communist regime gave way to an environment characterized by criminal syndicates. It was also during this period that Albanian drug traffickers were consolidating their control over the Balkan heroin-smuggling routes. By the end of the 1990s, the convergence of these groups had become a major concern for law enforcement, as the KLA and the Albanian syndicates morphed into "a well-oiled arrangement" in which millions of dollars in drug profits were funneled to the KLA to purchase weapons. This sometimes was the result of "drugs-for-arms" barter (Makarenko 2005). It is estimated that between 1996 and 1999, at least half the funds reaching Kosovo came from the drug trade. In 1998, the U.S. State Department branded the KLA a terrorist organization after reporting that it financed its campaigns with heroin profits and from support by various Islamic extremist groups. In 1998, Interpol declared the KLA a major player in the trade of drugs for weapons, was transporting US$2 billion worth of drugs into Western Europe each year (Mutschke 2000). By the summer of 1999, observers were calling Kosovo the "Colombia of Europe," as KLA supporters became prominent in the international underworld. What is most probable but rarely mentioned is that organized crime groups hoped their participation in the campaign would provide them a safe haven in the Kosovo region. Despite gaining its independence in 2008, Kosovo still is marked by a criminogenic environment characterized by high unemployment and industrial decay that have led the population to perhaps be a little more tolerant of illegal activities. By some accounts the heroin trade has even revitalized some local economies (Roth 2000).

Narcoterrorism

The term *narcoterrorism* was coined by Peruvian president Belaunde Terry in 1983 to describe violent attacks on antinarcotics police by the Shining Path (*Sendero Luminoso*) insurgents in Peru. Other Latin American countries have borrowed the term, most notably Colombia, in reference to links between drug traffickers and guerrillas. There is still a lack of consensus as to what exactly constitutes narcoterrorism, with critics suggesting that it connotes "too broad a range of activities to be definitive for a particular type of terrorism" (Kushner 2003). Some scholars suggest that it refers to all insurgent actors involved in the drug trade, whereas others argue the term only confuses the issues linking terrorism and drug trafficking. Most authorities agree, however, that it refers to a type of terrorism linked to the production of illegal drugs.

Much of the debate stems from the actors involved. Although narcoguerrillas are considered the purveyors of narcoterrorism, the question becomes whether some criminal groups are primarily criminal syndicates that masquerade as political movements. During the 1980s, Peru was plagued by communist-inspired revolutionary movements such as the Shining Path and Tupac-Amaru (MRTA) groups. There was an initial presumption that these movements were legitimate and that their involvement in the drug trade was due to their reliance on drug lords who financed their operations. Out of this relationship grew the notion, promulgated by a U.S. government report, of the "narcoguerrilla as an alliance between drug smugglers and arms dealers in support of terrorists and guerrillas" and as an extension of Soviet influence in Latin America (Clawson and Lee 1996). More recent scholarship suggests this was not the case at all, that in reality these aforementioned movements existed not as political movements but as "original, full-fledged creations of the local drug lords, who set the movements up as armed insurrection organizations to help them fight against" the drug eradication campaign set in motion by the president of Peru (Nakamura 1999, 100).

Beginning in the early 1980s, members of Colombia's Medillin cocaine cartel embarked on a campaign to obtain power and respectability through legitimate channels. Under the leadership of Pablo Escobar, however, the cartel took a more deadly turn toward violence in order to acquire some type of political legitimacy by attacking anyone who attempted to oppose it or enforce the law. Many observers link the drug lord's campaign of terror to the recriminations from the 1984 murder of justice minister Rodrigo Lara Bonilla, who had the nerve to run against Escobar for a congressional seat. Up to that time, Colombian President Belisario Betancur had been opposed to extradition. In the months leading up to the assassination, however, he began to extradite drug traffickers to the United States, a most feared destination for crime kingpins. By most accounts it was at this point that the cocaine kingpins turned to acts labeled narcoterrorism, which included public bombings and the targeted killings of judges, policemen, judges, journalists, presidential candidates, and anyone viewed as opposition to the cartel (Thoumi 2003). Others have suggested that it was just as likely that the 1984 Tranquilandia raids, which saw the destruction of more than 12 tons of cocaine and millions of dollars of investments, was the turning point, as it was just two months after this that the campaign of narcoterrorism was launched in full force (Lupsha and Cho 1999). Throughout the 1980s and into the 1990s, huge bombs were detonated in public places and monuments to government security such as police stations, leading the new administration of President Virgilio Barco to declare "an all-out war against narco-terrorists" (Thoumi 2003, 206). Today's depredations by the Mexican cartels, replete with brutal torture, beheadings, and targeted assassinations have an eerie resonance to those who covered the years of *plata o plomo* (silver or lead) in Colombia, when the Medillin cartel offered judges the choice of taking financial bribes or a bullet.

Unlike previous crackdowns on the drug syndicates, this new strategy proved more successful as the government seized Medillin cartel property and arrested and extradited its leaders. Although the cartel responded with its own declaration of "total and absolute war" and continued its campaign of terror, it also sowed the seeds for its demise, as any support of the once popular kingpin Escobar withered away and his foes began to assist the government.

Mexican drug cartels have also ratcheted up their use of terrorist activities to deter the current crackdown on drug trafficking organizations by President Felipe Calderon soon after he took office in 2006. Latin American cartels had nothing on their Mexican counterparts when it came to violence and intimidation. The Juarez cartel, for example, was known for cutting off the fingers of informants and making them eat them (Watson 2007). A number of indicators suggest the terror campaign is working, with police resignations and desertion from the military at record numbers. Even the news media has been targeted by the gangs, which has led to many papers censoring the amount of coverage they give to organized crime. Further evidence of the failure of the punitive crusade against the drug trade was the government's decision in 2009 to pass legislation decriminalizing the possession and use of small amounts of marijuana and cocaine.

Diamond Smuggling

It is estimated that three-fourths of the world's rough diamonds are mined in Africa. International syndicates from Russia, China, Italy, and Africa are among the many criminal groups taking part in this often unregulated business. The trade in untraceable diamonds intersects with organized crime activity and terrorism in a variety of ways. For example, rebel groups have turned to this trade to pay for weapons and support war plans.

In recent years crime syndicates have entered the diamond business at different levels. The Sicilian Mafia has established front companies to purchase a diamond cutting and polishing license and gained a foothold in Namibia's diamond cutting industry. Any participation in this business offers crime syndicates enormous money laundering opportunities. Because the Sicilians were laundering dirty money, they had no problem paying up to 30 percent market value for rough diamonds. Once these were cut, they would be untraceable among the millions of carats of cut diamonds traded internationally (Grobler 2007).

Al Qaeda followed in the footsteps of other savvy Middle Eastern groups, such as Hezbollah, by entering the West African diamond trade. Hezbollah had been financing its activities with diamonds thanks to the assistance of an underworld of Russian weapons traffickers, British mercenaries, retired Israeli military officers, and Western merchants all eager to play their parts in the diamond trade (Farah 2004). According to a 2003 British human rights organization report, al Qaeda spent nearly a decade illegally smuggling and trading for diamonds in western Africa (White 2009). It initially became involved in the legitimate trade to establish a base and contacts in the market. Over time, members began moving most of the trade into the underground market. Taking advantage of the weak states and regulations of Africa, al Qaeda soon established its own international trading network. Although there is still some debate about whether diamonds were used to support al Qaeda (namely by the 9/11 Commission), in 2002 Belgian investigators arrested an al Qaeda contact on charges of diamond smuggling and illegal weapons trafficking following an examination of the suspect's computer and other records that revealed tens of millions of dollars linked to the al Qaeda purchase of diamonds. What perhaps was most disturbing was evidence that this was only one part of a plot to purchase high-tech weapons in Central America from Nicaraguan army contacts, with the assistance of an Israeli weapons dealer located in Central America (Farah 2004).

Counterfeiting

The counterfeiting of various commodities is an integral part of organized crime networks that support terrorist groups. An Interpol official has even suggested that "terrorist groups who resemble organized crime groups" are drawn to counterfeiting because it is possible to "invest at the beginning of the counterfeiting cycle and extract an illicit profit at each stage of the counterfeiting process from production to sale, thus maximizing returns" (Noble 2003, 7). According to a 2000 study by the Global Anti-Counterfeiting Group in Paris, at least 11 percent of the world's clothing is counterfeit (Thomas 2007). A number of other legitimate commodities are counterfeited by organized crime groups, including DVDs, CDs, cigarettes, alcohol, and even cosmetics. On the surface this activity might seem harmless. It seems much more malignant, however, once one acknowledges that various counterfeit rackets are operated under the auspices of criminal organizations that also engage in parallel activities of drug trafficking, child prostitution, human trafficking, and terrorism. Profits from the sale of these goods have funded groups connected with Hezbollah, Northern Ireland paramilitary organizations, and Colombia's FARC, to name just a few. In fact, some terrorism experts regard counterfeiting as one of the three top sources of funding for international terrorism (Thomas 2007).

In Northern Ireland the most popular counterfeit goods are clothes, computer games, CDs, DVDs, cigarettes, currency, and vodka. Interpol estimates this activity costs the economy millions of dollars each year. Northern Ireland's police authorities reported in 2003 seizing more counterfeit goods than all other UK police forces combined, but believe this represents only 5 percent of the total market (Thompson 2003). Goods are typically sold door to door by salesmen. In one instance a man was stopped at Belfast International Airport in June 2003 after debarking a flight from Singapore with $500,000 USD in counterfeit DVDs (Thompson 2003). Counterfeit currency that originated in this region has been found throughout the world, including copies of sterling, euros, and dollars. Investigators claim the British sterling's counterfeited watermarks and foil strips are almost undetectable. Unlike legitimate trade, those that are counterfeited only have to pass limited scrutiny (by consumers), with little in the way of safety concerns. Some goods are made with harmful ingredients, including cigarettes from the Far East that contain harmful fillers along with the tobacco, as well as bogus vodka that is watered down with industrial alcohol.

By the end of the 20th century, advances in technology had revolutionized and expanded illegal counterfeit networks. For example, currency counterfeiting used to be a specialized industry, but the advent of computers, laser printers, and scanners has expanded capability to make more passable bank notes. At one time the $100 bill was the most frequently counterfeited currency in the world, and as a result global markets were awash in them. In response, the U.S. Treasury Department redesigned this bill and added a watermark and other security devices. In less than a month counterfeit $100 bills were being reproduced and used successfully in Eastern Europe thanks to high-resolution color scanners that can reproduce the watermarks and colors of fibers in the paper (Taylor, Caeti, Loper, Fritsch, and Liederbach 2006).

Asia is the epicenter for software piracy, which continues to have wide appeal for organized crime groups. Some groups have even made the transition from drug trafficking to this type of counterfeiting, as "the profits are high and the risk is very low" compared to human smuggling and drugs, where it is difficult to develop a legitimate front or cover operation (Gates 2001). A software office in Silicon Valley, however, has a certain "air of respectability" (Gates 2001).

Nuclear Smuggling

In 2007, a U.S. ambassador proclaimed that "smuggling and loose border control associated with Georgia's separatist conflicts" posed a threat "not just to Georgia, but to all the international community" (Sheets and Broad 2007, A19). What he was referring to was recent intelligence reports that indicated illicit smuggling continued unabated in this former Soviet republic as tiny separatist regions broke away to "to become lawless criminal havens" (Sheets and Broad 2007, A19). In one public opinion piece published around the same time entitled, "How Organized Crime is a Nuclear Smuggler's New Best Friend," investigators revealed a number of factors leading to a widening access to nuclear materials among criminal groups (Shelley and Orttung 2006). Among the more troubling revelations were reports tying the influx of drugs through Central Asia and Russia from Afghanistan to increased drug abuse among nuclear workers in one closed city. What makes this so troubling is the potential for narcotics kingpins associated with organized crime to take advantage of vulnerable addicts. Some news reports suggest it is possible to gain entrance into a closed city where some nuclear sites are located for as little as a $5 bribe. This might not be as alarming, except for similar claims made by other investigators. One report revealed that "More than one fifth of the 120,000 workers in Russia's former 'nuclear cities'—where more than half of all employees earn less than $50 a month—say they would be willing to work in the military complex of another country" for the right place (Naim 2003, 31) Signaling the ongoing relationship between immigration, globalization, and international crime, Russian construction companies have hired a large number of undocumented workers, some perhaps previously targeted by Islamic recruiters. According to another source, a construction foreman at one Russian project hired to protect nuclear materials was murdered for refusing to cooperate with organized crime (Shelley and Orttung 2006).

There is little doubt that the small arms market is a worldwide concern. In 1994, German police reported the arrest of a plutonium black-marketeer, the fourth such seizure that summer. The year before, Germany reported 123 known cases of illegal nuclear materials trading in that country. The 1994 arrest took place at Munich airport, where more than 11 ounces of material was confiscated, making it the largest such seizure up to that time. The substance was brought by Lufthansa jet from Moscow (Walsh and Boudreaux 1994). The illegal market for state-of-the-art weaponry, including nuclear weapons materials, increases each day as criminal syndicates, nation-states, and warlords vie for the latest tanks, radar systems, and missiles. According to the International Atomic Energy Agency, there have been more than a dozen substantiated cases (and probably many more) of smuggled nuclear-weapons-usable material since the mid-1990s.

It is unknown how much of the material is available on the black market, but there is little doubt that there is a growing demand for the products in the interconnected worlds of terrorist and organized crime groups (Naim 2003). But it would require a terrorist/criminal group to gather all of the scientists, engineers, and other required actors to produce a nuclear device capable of approaching the explosive capabilities of the weapons dropped against the Japanese in World War II. Despite a formidable number of challenges, technical and scientific in nature, it is not out of the realm of possibility that terrorists with the assistance of criminal syndicates can acquire the materials to create a nuclear explosion. Russia still remains one of the best targets for nuclear materials. It has been well chronicled how poor security conditions, combined with low salaries and morale of scientists, present strong incentives for all involved. Other scenarios include obtaining nuclear weapons through force, bribery, and theft (Kushner 2003).

Despite countless doomsday scenarios posited by everyone from academics and law enforcement to screenwriters and novelists, "there has never been a single verified case, anywhere, of the theft of any sort of nuclear weapon" (Langewiesche 2006, 83). There are a number of convincing explanations why terrorists and criminals have not succeeded in getting their hands on nuclear weapons almost 20 years after the fall of the Soviet Union. One of the more thoughtful investigators suggests the explanation is rather simple: either they are "ignorant, incompetent, and distracted," or nuclear weapons and materials are much better protected than was previously presumed (Langewiesche 2006).

Other Types of Criminal Activities

Money Laundering

Money laundering is used by organized crime groups around the world to conceal the existence of illicit income (as well as its source and use). This is often accomplished under the guise of legitimate

business fronts. According to the International Monetary Fun
tween 2 and 5 percent of the world's gross domestic product
billion) consisted of money being fraudulently laundered (Nackan
and Cooperman 2006).

Various sources have been credited with introducing the term
money laundering, but it was probably coined sometime in the late
1920s or early 1930s, when U.S. Treasury agents were tracking Al Capone. Few homes had running water let alone a washing machine
in this era, so most took their clothes to the neighborhood laundry.
Capone's syndicate apparently controlled hundreds of Chicago's
laundries. The business allowed his organization to conceal its illicit
income from bootlegging and other sources by claiming it as income from his legitimate laundry business—hence the association
between money and laundering (Lunde 2004).

The concept of modern money laundering can be traced back
at least to the Prohibition era of the 1920s, when American bootleggers flush with cash needed to disguise their profits from the tax
services. Jewish gangster icon Meyer Lansky's biographer and others credit Lansky as the pioneer of money laundering, tracing his
involvement back to his days as a "one-man think tank" for Lucky
Luciano in the early 1930s (Lacey 1992, 4–5). Using a series of shell
companies and offshore bank accounts, Lansky made it even more
sophisticated by transferring profits from New Orleans slot machines to a Swiss bank account in 1934. He followed with accounts
in the Caribbean and other lax tax havens. Lansky engineered one
scheme called the "loan-back," which exploited the liberal policies
in the Swiss banking system in the 1960s. Couriers carried cash from
the United States to Switzerland to avoid tax services. The money
was deposited in a Swiss bank account, which was identified only
by a distinct number (a practice now frowned on). Lansky then borrowed back his own money. Once safe in his coffers it was usually
safe from the taxmen.

Hawala

Parallel underground banking arrangements have operated alongside legitimate banking systems for centuries. Underground or informal banking networks have been variously referred to as alternative
remittance systems, informal funds transfer systems, and informal
value transfer systems. Different systems evolved in various parts
of the world, including *hawala* in South Asia and *fei-ch'ien* in China.
Informal networks like these continue to operate from Asia to the

Americas (McCusker 2006). Of these the most prominent is *hawala*, which originated in an era marked by substantial long-distance trade by sea and by camel caravans. This system played an important part in a merchant's security strategy. Because pirates and robbers were always a threat to commodities in transit, traders created a system of monetary transfer based solely on trust (and grounded in Islamic propriety). This allowed both travelers and traders to conduct business in foreign countries without physically carrying currency (Mabrey 2003).

Hawala is widely used throughout South Asia and the Middle East. Attempting to track funding through *hawala* has been compared to trying to catch smoke or "electronic blips as they fly through the atmosphere" (Madinger 2006, 391).

Because a *hawala* transaction leaves no paper trail, any estimates of the money exchanged in this way is meaningless. It is especially useful for transmitting funds from and for criminal and terrorist activities. These transactions have been compared to wire transfers facilitated through banks and companies such as Western Union. The *hawala* system is attractive for both its simplicity and convenience. For example, if one needs to transmit money for goods in countries hundreds or thousands of miles apart, the process begins with finding an upstanding member of the local Muslim community. The *hawala* businessman provides a chit receipt for the funds being transferred; he then telephones or faxes instructions to a party in another country, who is instructed to provide money to the intended recipient, minus his fee. In the end, this system is still simple, quick, safe, and effective, with no requirements to save documents that can easily be shredded.

Offshore Banking and Shell Corporations

Any bank located outside the United States is considered offshore. Other nations have different laws and regulations in regard to company formation, with many countries offering extensive secrecy provisions, including rules of nondisclosure of company officers, shareholders, or owners. Because of their lax requirements, the Isle of Man, Panama, Gibraltar, Bermuda, the Bahamas, the Netherlands Antilles, Hong Kong, Luxembourg, and Switzerland have been among the most popular destinations for those requiring privacy in their business dealings (Madinger 2006).

Shell corporations are considered "the mainstay of money laundering schemes." Shell corporations typically have no assets or liabilities and just require a charter to operate. Shell banks have been around since at least the 1960s, when the Internal Revenue Service discovered a pattern of shell banking institutions opening up throughout the Bahamas. Visitors to these "banks" usually found an empty office with the name of the bank on the door. Shell banks were created expressly for the purpose of concealing the names of depositors through means of secret numbered accounts. What really captured the attention of investigators was that some of these were closely associated with gambling interest, union racketeers, and underworld couriers from around the world. It did not take long before inspectors figured out that much of the money pouring into shell banks were proceeds from casino skims in Las Vegas and, more important, were out of American jurisdiction. Underworld figures used these funds to finance gambling operations in the Caribbean (Messick 1969).

Money reaches the shell banks from the United States by private planes, boats, and other means. After money is deposited in the shell banks, the funds are redeposited into more substantial English or Canadian banks located in the Bahamas. Once the funds are secreted into these accounts using the name of the depository shell bank, the funds can be either retained in Nassau or forwarded with commission to Switzerland for redeposit (Madinger 2006).

In 2001, New York's Federal Reserve Bank estimated that more than $800 billion was sitting in Grand Cayman banks (Mathers 2004). In recent years, however, much has changed. According to one observer, "today it's harder to launder money in Cayman than it is in the United States," noting that once the Financial Action Task Force (FATF) dubbed the country the world's leading noncooperative country when it came to enforcing money laundering laws, the government there responded by introducing new money laundering legislation (Mathers 2004, 159). The FATF was established by the G-7 group of industrialized countries in 1989 to fight money laundering, and in 2000 it declared 29 offshore jurisdictions to be deficient and created a list of the 15 most uncooperative countries and territories (Naim 2005).

Controlling Money Laundering

By most accounts money laundering remained a low priority for law enforcement until cash came rolling in during the cocaine trade in the 1970s. It did not even become a federal criminal offense per se in the United States until the passage of the Money Laundering

Control Act of 1986. Before that time prosecutors brought cases under a variety of taxation statutes related to defrauding the government. The first meaningful legislation dealing with money laundering was the Bank Secrecy Act in 1970, which mandated a series of reporting and record-keeping requirements designed to help track money launderers. In theory, it was based on the proposition that unusual transactions of currency at domestic financial institutions and unusual shipments of currency into or out of the United States might be related to organized crime activity (Powis 1992). Its most important requirements forced banks and other financial institutions to report currency transactions over $10,000 into or out of the country on a Customs Form 4790. Over the years the laws and penalties have been amended, and in 1990 financial institutions were required to obtain identification and maintain records on all purchases between $3,000 and $10,000, including those made with cashier's checks, bank checks and drafts, traveler's checks, and money orders (Powis 1992).

One longtime ruse to get around these requirements was through structuring, a process in which large sums are broken down into amounts under $10,000 for purposes of conducting transactions at financial institutions. During the 1980s, it became a major tool for drug traffickers. Better known as *smurfing,* it sometimes involves organizations of between 5 and 15 couriers that launder money through a series of structured transactions. Large amounts of cash are given to small groups within the smurfing organization; the groups then travel to various cities where individuals visit a number of banks buying cashiers checks and money orders for less than $10,000. This is done repeatedly until all the cash has been dispersed. The checks are then mailed back to the hub city and deposited into banking accounts. At this point it is not necessary to file cash transaction reports, as these are required by law only for cash transactions. The cash is often wired to accounts in countries with strict bank secrecy laws. Although smurfing is time consuming, labor intensive, and expensive, it is still popular (Powis 1992).

Electronic Money Laundering

The spread of electronic banking and e-payment systems has been a blessing for money launderers. Digital technology has done for money laundering what it has accomplished in the legitimate economy with online retail selling. Most researchers assert that organized crime groups are at the forefront of adopting and developing technologies to facilitate money laundering. Billions of dollars in money transfers are conducted each day through electronic impulses. This method is widely used by banks shipping money to each other, stock exchanges, brokerages, commodities dealers, credit card companies, money remitters, governments, and wealthy individuals. Currently the three major electronic funds transfer systems are CHIPS, SWIFT, and Fedwire, which combined handle about $2 trillion in transfer each day (Madinger 2006). Digital technology allows money to move across the planet at the speed of light. By using such a route, criminals have the advantage of jurisdiction shopping for countries and regions where transaction regulations are less rigorous (Grabosky 2007). Criminal networks use electronic money laundering in a variety of ways. Some use legitimate online services such as auctions, where a buyer and a seller can team up in order to transfer "phantom" items at a previously agreed on price; thus criminal proceeds are transformed into cash as the result of the sale of a legitimate commodity. Others use online gambling services to create an account with service providers using illicit income, and then eventually cashing out the account and collecting funds as winnings. Some have even set up their own telecommunications companies to commit fraud and money laundering (Grabosky 2007).

High-Tech Crimes

Almost every new technology that has been created has been quickly adapted by criminals. Organized crime groups have shown an uncanny ability to adapt and use the newest technologies that have played an integral role in the trend toward globalization.

International organized crime groups have joined the information technology revolution by recruiting computer specialists. Modern members of international crime groups are likely to monitor online chat rooms and newsgroups deciding on who would be likely recruits for their syndicates. Besides offering handsome financial incentives, there are cases where individuals have been intimidated into joining.

In April 2005, American and international law enforcement agencies cooperated in Operation Cyber Chase, which focused on an Internet pharmacy based in India that had been reportedly selling controlled drugs to thousands of online customers. At the time the only requirement for purchasing drugs was a credit card and an address. The foreign distributor sold drugs on 200 Web sites and shipped drugs in bulk to cities in the United States, where the drugs were repackaged and shipped to customers. As a result of the investigation, more than 20 individuals were arrested in the United States, Canada, and India, and $7 million from banks and almost 7 million doses of the drug were seized (McAfee 2005).

Since the 1990s, global organized crime groups have vastly benefited from advances in the worlds of information and high technology. There is a remarkable continuity between the crimes committed online today and those from earlier eras. Even if the tools are different, the goals and motivations have stayed the same. In earlier eras it was common for merchants in immigrant communities and ethnic enclaves to pay protection money to organized gangs under the threat of harm or business disruption. Today organized gangs are just as likely to threaten the disruption of online business if ransoms are not paid. Bank robbers still rob banks and security vans, but the more technologically savvy have found it safer and more profitable to hack into a bank's computer system and transfer money using electronic payment systems. Internet extortion has also proven quite profitable. Also referred to as digital extortion or cyberextortion, it involves making specific demands of an individual or group of individuals under the threat of either physical or economic harm. Although the demands are usually financial in nature, some cases involve nonfinancial considerations such as sexual favors. But the vast majority have targeted wealthy organizations and individuals.

Traditional organized crime groups have never lagged far behind innovations in technology by both law enforcement and the business world. In 1998, one Mafia family set up a business offering services to companies to prepare them for the year 2000 (Y2K) problem. The consultancy firm had its own Web site and toll-free number, and by most accounts had a great solution for the Y2K bug. As soon as the company's programmers got into a client's financial software, they adjusted it so that the company's funds were redirected to other offshore mob accounts. By the beginning of the 21st century, New York's vaunted crime families were making the transition to high-tech crime through a number of schemes ranging from telephone bill and phone card fraud to counterfeit CDs and credit card cloning. The deputy assistant director of the FBI Cyberdivision reported that the American Mafia made $360 million during a seven-year period through e-crime by using search engines to hack into secure files and pull out credit card details, or by creating algorithms to generate "legitimate" credit cards (Richards 2006).

Since the beginning of the 21st century, the FBI has been among the law enforcement agencies expanding its campaign against cyber criminals outside U.S. jurisdiction. More recently the FBI created Cyber Action Teams composed of two dozen individuals including agents, computer forensic experts, and computer code specialists. In 2005, the FBI claimed to have 150 agents dedicated to computer crime and related crimes in 56 offices around the world. In 2008, the Justice Department consolidated the headquarters and field resources of the FBI's Cyber Program into a single unit that would better facilitate the coordination and investigation of federal crimes involving the use of computer systems. But the biggest challenge to policing high-tech crime is that many of the crimes take place internationally. For example, in one case a bank reported a robbery in Sweden after customers were infected with a Trojan virus, leaving the bank with a 1 million euro loss. The subsequent investigation revealed that the Trojan was created in Russia, although this individual never personally used it; however, he did offer advice on the Web on how to use it for a fee. Individuals paid for his expertise and used it to attack the Swedish bank. This scenario would require investigators from three different countries (Weinberg 2007). Computer crime is difficult to police to begin with, but when multiple national police forces are required, the barriers to success are multiplied, as the investigation often becomes mired in international red tape.

Nigerian Advance Fee Fraud

Among the groups who have made the transition to the computer age without losing a step are the Nigerian practitioners of the 419 scam (refers to Nigerian criminal statute 419, which made the fraud illegal in 1980). They once depended on fax machines and e-mails in their advance fee fraud schemes but now are just as likely to be involved in intellectual property crimes such as pirating compact discs and computer programs. Anyone who uses the Internet and a computer has probably heard from one of these too good to be true offers that a large sum of money needs to be transferred to a Western bank account and all that is required is your bank account and other personal information. In return the recipient would receive a handsome commission. By 2006, the United States had become the most lucrative 419 market, with losses reaching $800 million a year (Chaudhuri 2007). Despite the Nigerian connection these are truly global operations. Most scams begin in Nigeria, the Netherlands, the United Kingdom, or South Africa. More recently, India has become the third fastest-growing market for the fraud. In 2006, Indian victims lost $32 million (almost 10 times the amount of the previous year) (Chaudhuri 2007).

Music Piracy

The introduction of optical discs, including such devices as the CD and DVD, has radically changed the landscape of music piracy. Like other businesses in the intellectual property sector, the music industry has proved vulnerable to global organized crime networks. According to the International Federation of the Phonographic Industry, which represents the worldwide recording industry, there is plenty of evidence linking this crime to people trafficking, money laundering, drug smuggling, terrorism, and other crimes (IFPI 2004). In 2004, it was estimated that the annual sale of pirated music was close to 2 billion units worth between US$4 and $5 billion. No region of the world has escaped this crime.

One of the unanticipated results of the Yugoslavian conflicts in the 1990s was that increased naval presence in the Adriatic interrupted the traffic in contraband cigarettes from the Balkans to Italy, an activity managed by Italian organized crime groups. In cities such as Naples, cigarette smuggling had been an important source of income for the Camorra over the years. The collapse of this trade resulted in a downturn in employment and income for organized crime groups. Ever pragmatic, adaptable, and flexible, they found profits elsewhere. This coincided with the technological development in CD counterfeiting with the introduction of faster and cheaper CD burners. The convergence of these two trends saw the Naples underworld move from trafficking cigarettes to music piracy. By the turn of the century, it was Italy's epicenter for this crime, putting out 70 percent of the country's counterfeit CDs (*Jane's Intelligence Review* 2007). In 2002, Operation Jessica (FBI investigation) revealed the existence of large-scale organized crime involvement in the counterfeiting market, with the leading role played by the Frattasio family. The investigation demonstrated the extensive involvement in the importation of the raw materials required (recordable CDs, blank music, and video cassettes) from Eastern Europe. Operation Jessica established the operational structure that ran the enterprise, featuring a pyramidal hierarchy with the Frattasio family members at the top. As the counterfeiting empire expanded, it had to create the necessary financial structure to pay for raw materials and launder profits. This required setting up a number of dummy companies and corporate structures that could be used to purchase equipment and raw materials for music duplication. As the operation expanded, it developed links outside the region into northern Italy and east to Ukraine (*Jane's Intelligence Review* 2007).

Gang Structures

Russian Mafiya

In an attempt to distinguish the post-Soviet incarnation of organized crime from the traditionally accepted Western incarnation, investigative journalist Stephen Handelman is credited with popularizing the alternate spelling of mafia, as in *mafiya*. Its use dates back to the 1970s when the expression was used to refer to corrupt Communist Party officials, but since 1991 the meaning has broadened to include prominent businessmen and oligarchs who have acquired huge fortunes in Russia (Handelman 1995). For more than a decade the term was used by officials, experts, and the media to describe Russian organized crime; but this only obscures the fact that Russian Organized Crime is composed of diverse ethnicities and cultures, including Ukrainians, Lithuanians, Georgians, Armenians, Chechens, and Dagestanis. Many use the term *Russian Mafiya* to allude to mobsters in general from the region, whereas others are under the misconception that there is some centralized organization with a rigid hierarchy that fits under the mafiya rubric. Russian mob experts are of the opinion the term is used "for convenience sake." One Russian expert rejects the term, preferring the usage of the term *violent entrepreneurs*, suggesting that the use of the label is "a convenient mechanism for putting a disproportionate amount of responsibility for the rise in criminal groups on the legacy of communism instead of blaming the ill-conceived reform policies of Gorbachev and Yeltsin" (Volkov 2002). Nonetheless, there is a growing consensus that the term *mafiya* now refers more to a method of operation rather than a group, and that its meaning can be found in the countless cases of torture, extortion, and murder by a wide range of actors in Russia, including politicians, businessmen, and gangsters (Serio 2006).

Drug Cartels

It has been fashionable to use the term *cartel* to describe mostly drug-trafficking syndicates from Latin America and Mexico. The Cali and Medillin cartels in Colombia were prominent in the 1980s and 1990s, but today's focus has shifted to various Mexican cartels on the U.S. border. Economists, criminologists, policymakers, and others continue to debate whether Latin America's drug-trafficking organizations constitute true cartels in the economic sense. The best definition of cartel refers to a group of independent organizations that collaborate to control production, pricing, and the marketing of goods by its members.

Most authorities have accepted the cartel explanation, including the U.S. Drug Enforcement Administration (DEA), as well as some criminologists who define drug cartels as "independent trafficking organizations that have pooled their resources to cooperate with each other" (Potter 2008, 184). The DEA insisted that groups such as the Medillin and Cali cartels were able to control prices, eliminate competition, and avoid arrest through the use of violence and corruption, while using criminal and legitimate businesses to launder drug profits.

One critic of the cartel theory argued that the reality behind a cocaine trade run by a "handful of massive, vertically integrated cartels that restricted production and set international prices" is a misconception and a "longstanding illusion" (Kenney 2007). By most accounts, the current view is that the cocaine business from its inception in the 1970s to the present has never been the province of a handful of drug cartels in Mexico and Colombia. In the 1970s, several independent drug-smuggling outfits in Colombia did indeed band together into what some labeled cartels (for want of a better term). The leaders of the Cali and Medillin cartels offered the drug world a vision and a business strategy. Shipments were organized so that if one or more were confiscated, others would surely get through. On the other hand, if one trafficking unit was intercepted by authorities, only those participants were apprehended. Typically they were the source of only limited information because the units, like small cells, were isolated from each other and the top kingpins. If one suggests that a cartel is "a close, corporate bond between its participants, who may engage in concerted efforts to limit the size of the market," however, the opposite is true (Fuentes and Kelly 1999). Thus, on examining the Colombian cartels, the term more appropriately alludes to a "geographically confined, loose federation or coalition of major drug trafficking organizations that have formed alliances for the self serving purpose of reducing the risky nature of the business" (Fuentes and Kelly 1999, 348). Focusing only on these two organizations in Colombia leaves the impression there were no others, when in reality there were dozens of smaller cocaine trafficking organizations at work contemporaneously alongside the Cali and Medillin syndicates.

In the end, despite the demise of the Cali and Medillin "cartels," cocaine is as cheap and plentiful as ever. If these organizations actually controlled the industry like a traditional cartel, this should have at least interrupted its availability at its destination markets. In reality, the Colombian trade was never dominated by monolithic cartels but was the result of numerous small, independent enterprises that became increasingly diffuse and decentralized after the fall of the Cali and Medillin leaders, the Rodriquez Brothers and Pablo Escobar, respectively. Subsequent interviews with imprisoned cocaine kingpins lend credence to the cartel myth. Most have debunked the notion of a cartel dominating the cocaine trade. As one Medillin associate put it, "The cartels never existed until they were created by the media and the U.S. government" (Kenney 2007, 25).

Export Syndicates

More recent scholarship examines Andean cocaine trafficking networks in terms of *export syndicates,* rather than cartels in the traditional economic sense, as they do not control raw material production and most distribution systems in their main markets; therefore these organizations "could not prevent a large increase in coca cultivation and long term decline in coca prices" (Thoumi 2003, 94). Functioning as export syndicates, these trafficking networks are created to share risks and guarantee lucrative returns on the profit for each partner. Thus, they are actually risk-minimizing structures created in lieu of the ability to plan production quotas or ensure that orders are carried out as planned through several tiers of production and distribution. The foremost interpreter of this scheme argues that the definition of *cartel* is not applicable because the main actors in the production of cocaine are those who gather coca leaves and manufacture coca paste, transport it, refine it, and distribute it to main markets "tend to be fluid [as] the structure of the industry adapts itself to changes in the business environment brought about by the activities of law enforcement agencies and other factors" (Thoumi 2003, 95). So, while there is little doubt that cocaine traffickers would like to operate like cartels and control market forces, it is really beyond their control.

Crossing the U.S.–Mexico Border

After stepping down as CIA director, General Michael Hayden asserted that "Mexico ranked alongside Iran as a top security risk to the U.S." (Hawley 2009, A2). The violence on the American border among the warring drug gangs has led the U.S. Department of Homeland Security to begin contemplating a game plan to intervene on the border to combat potential drug violence on the American side. In March 2009, however, the Obama Administration announced that despite the blueprint being worked on to deal with the violence, there was no plan to permanently militarize the border. If any troops were sent, they would probably be National Guard units; however, in the past this has been controversial. Some Texas officials claim that law enforcement agencies were poorly coordinating their efforts on the border and suggested that there be greater border security cooperation among federal agencies (Powell 2009).

U.S. Secretary of State Hillary Clinton went on record in March 2009 admitting that the United States shared the responsibility for the violent drug trade on the border citing "our insatiable demand for illegal drugs" and "our inability to prevent weapons" from falling into the hands of Mexican criminals through illegal weapons transfers (Landler 2009). This is a remarkable turnaround from the previous administration when then Secretary of State Condoleezza Rice denied any connection between the expiration of assault weapons prohibition in the United States and drug violence in 2008. Nevertheless, it took until June 2009 for President Barack Obama to sign the appropriations measure that released $420 million for the Merida Initiative in Mexico (Embassy of the United States in Mexico 2009). Mexican officials were disappointed, however, that Congress had cut funding by almost a third from the $1.4 billion originally promised for the drug countertrafficking program. Critics suggested that the United States was sending mixed signals by not following through with its promised funding.

The publication of the *National Drug Threat Assessment* by the National Drug Intelligence Center in 2009, however, put more heat on the new U.S. administration to respond to the Mexican drug trafficking organizations, which the report claimed poses "a significant threat to our nation" (NDIC 2009, iii). The report further noted the ability of the gangs to quickly respond to new law enforcement and policy initiatives developed by various counterdrug agencies. What worries many in law enforcement is the spiraling violence of urban street gangs and their increasing participation in the drug trade in collaboration with Mexican and Asian drug trafficking organizations.

Prison Gangs and Street Gangs

The years between 1946 and 1967 were formative ones for American Outlaw Motorcycle Gangs (OMGs), as larger clubs absorbed smaller ones and formal structures were put in place allowing clubs to evolve into structured, organized crime groups. A handful of OMGs operate on an international basis. Foremost among them is the Hells Angels. (The gang dispensed with the apostrophe in "Hell's" many years ago.) Originating in 1947, it opened up its first chapter under the Angels moniker in 1948. Over the past 60 years, it has opened chapters in a number of foreign countries. As recently as 2006, the Criminal Intelligence Service Canada described the gang as "the foremost organized crime group in the country." The Angels have a more prominent presence in Canada than in the United States. In Canada they have 32 active chapters and at least 500 full members; the largest chapter is in Montreal. Chapters are the foundation on which most OMGs are structured. Chapters control geographic areas where activities are conducted. Experts suggest that the Hells Angels and other OMGs slid under the Canadian radar screen, taking advantage of the vacuum in organized crime leadership left by Canada's crackdown on Mafia activities, which reduced any significant competition.

A number of observers have remarked on the operational similarities between traditional organized crime (such as the Mafia) and Hells Angels. For example, the club is divided into two factions, with Omaha, Nebraska, the dividing line. Each faction has an annually elected president, vice president, recording secretary, and treasurer. The President of the West Coast faction is responsible for chapters on the American and Canadian West Coasts, Alaska, Australia, and New Zealand. The East Coast president presides over other chapters including those in Europe and South America.

Over the past decade law enforcement has observed some groups developing international connections that provide them with access to wholesale quantities of illegal drugs. In February 2004, for example, three members of the Dutch Hells Angels were killed after the theft of $11 million in cocaine. A subsequent inquiry revealed their international ties to Colombian drug dealers. In this particular case the drugs were shipped from FARC to Amsterdam via a new Hells Angels chapter on the Caribbean island of Curacao.

The Angels have more than doubled their chapters from 45 in 1980 to more than 108, with the latest located in Manaus in the Brazilian Amazon. Some authorities regard this group as America's major crime export, tracing its membership in 2006 to at least 25 countries (Marsden and Sher 2006). Members have been linked to activities including arson, assault, corruption, gambling, forgery, pornography, international white slavery, loan sharking, and car and cycle theft, all of which have helped transform them from a domestic motorcycle gang into an international criminal enterprise.

Mara Salvatrucha (MS-13) is considered among America's most dangerous gangs. In its early days its membership was restricted to Salvadorans, but in the new century the gang boasted members from Ecuador, Guatemala, Honduras, and Mexico, as well as several African Americans. The gang is involved in a host of criminal enterprises including car theft; these cars are often traded to South American drug cartels for cash. One estimate in 2000 suggested that perhaps 80 percent of the cars driven in El Salvador had been stolen in the United States. Besides car theft they are connected to extortion, home invasion robberies, polydrug trafficking, and other rackets. MS-13 made the transition from merely another gang culture to organized criminal network in a rather short time because of its flexibility and willingness to "do any crime at any time" (Domash 2005, 2). What has made members so difficult to track are their mobility and ability to respond to new police strategies. Investigators have noticed how they move from state to state whenever they feel the heat of law enforcement. Gang members have been reported in Alaska, Oregon, Utah, Texas, Nevada, Oklahoma, Michigan, New York, Maryland, Virginia, Georgia, Florida, and the nation's capital. Likewise they gravitate from country to country in Central America. Besides keeping on the move and developing more sophisticated organizational structures, MS-13 members have responded to surveillance efforts by changing their gang colors and substituting numbers such as "67" or "76" for 13 (Domash 2005).

Law Enforcement

International Cooperation

Organized crime is a common threat to most countries in the 21st century. Any crime that transcends national borders creates a number of challenges for law enforcement around the world. International cooperative efforts in policing have been frustrated by a number of obstacles. Transnational criminal activities have stimulated cooperative efforts between international police agencies for more than a century. It was only in the years after World War I, however, that a true organization apparatus was created to further police cooperation among foreign countries with the creation of Interpol. Founded in Vienna in 1923, the International Criminal Police Organization (Interpol) was disbanded in 1938 and resuscitated at the end of World War II. It facilitates coordinative endeavors between countries, but it also is restricted. As an international organization, its charter prohibits employees to engage in investigations or coordination of a political, military, religious, or racial character.

One of the first organized crime investigations and prosecutions with international implications was the 1985–1987 Pizza Connection case, a cooperative effort by American, Italian, Swiss, Brazilian, and Spanish law enforcement agencies that shut down a major international drug trafficking and money laundering conspiracy involving American and Sicilian criminals. This case, *U.S. v. Badalamenti,* illustrates the contacts between Old World and New World Italian gangsters and what can be achieved when international police agencies work together.

In the 1970s, the Sicilian Mafia entered into an alliance with heroin suppliers in Turkey and established a network of refineries in Sicily. They also formed alliances with South American suppliers of cocaine before moving into the trade in the United States. The Sicilian Mafia came up with an ingenious distribution method known as the Pizza Connection, using a nationwide network of pizzerias to market drugs and launder money. Beginning in the 1970s, they also entered a franchise agreement with American organized crime groups and brought in thousands of their own people to work at hundreds of pizzerias. Instead of joining the domestic Mafia, however, most reported to Sicilian boss Gaetano Badalamenti. Badalamenti operated pizza parlors as fronts for heroin trafficking, establishing a multimillion dollar clandestine operation. Speaking in code and placing orders of heroin in quantities of cheese, tomato paste, and pizza dough, they distributed heroin with the help of the Bonanno family, which had the strongest ties to Sicily. Although the group was tied domestically to New York's Bonanno crime family, the actual operation was run by Sicilian immigrants, mostly in the American Midwest, who distributed drugs manufactured in Sicily.

In this case the FBI and the Italian police used informants and undercover agents such as Joe Pistone (Donnie Brasco) to infiltrate the crime syndicates involved, mostly the Sicilian Mafia and the Bonanno Family. It also was successful in recruiting high-level informants who provided critical information. Italy's Anti-Mafia unit also convinced one of Sicily's key organizers to return from South America to testify against his associates in the Mafia, and in Latin and North America. What made this a triumphant moment for international police cooperation, however, was that the many police agencies working this case shared information and resources.

The Pizza Connection trial began on September 30, 1985. By the time it ended 17 months later, it had become one of the longest and most complex criminal trials in American history. Of the 22 original defendants, 17 were convicted for taking part in the drug trafficking conspiracy, 4 pled guilty, and 1 was murdered after the trial began. The defendants were all sentenced to long prison sentences.

The record of innovative approaches to cooperative law enforcement has been mixed. Among the more successful recent international investigations was the April 2000 Budapest Project. This investigation was led by the FBI-Hungarian National Police Organized Crime Task Force, which operated out of Budapest, Hungary. Its goal was to dismantle organized crime networks that had popped up in Central Europe after the fall of the Soviet Union. Among the task force's first major coups was building a case against Ukrainian-born crime kingpin Semion Mogilevich. He was forced to flee from Budapest back to Moscow, barely eluding indictments charging him with money laundering, securities fraud, and RICO conspiracy charges. In the investigation's early stages, four FBI agents partnered with seven elite officers from the Hungarian National Police.

European Union

The European Union (EU) is a treaty-based framework that defines and manages economic and political cooperation among its member states. The internationalization of organized crime has been influenced by the strengthening of the EU, with recent steps toward lowering border controls between states. Europe is probably the most profitable market globally for the drug trade and remains the most important organized crime activity of the region's crime networks (Council of Europe 2005). The European Market was created in 1993, with the goal of increasing the region's economic integration by allowing the free movement of goods, services, people, and capital between nation states. This process was designed to create a single space of mobility for EU citizens to travel, work, and live in Europe. The unintended consequence of this policy and similar schemes such as the 1985 Schengen Agreement (named after the city in Luxembourg it was signed in), which removed a number of systematic border controls between participating countries, was to facilitate smuggling operations of criminal groups' intent on expanding their operations. Today, 27 countries have full membership status in the EU.

The European Police Office (Europol), modeled after Interpol, was established in the Maastricht Treaty on European Union in 1992. Initially its main focus was on the drug trade. Two years later its mandate was expanded to include preventing the trafficking in nuclear materials, money laundering, motor vehicle theft, and human smuggling and trafficking. Europol was ratified by European members states in 1996. Its main objective today is improving police cooperation among member states to combat terrorism and international organized crime. Like Interpol, its agents have no arrest powers, but are allowed to participate in operations with other police forces. Europol has enhanced law enforcement cooperation by entering into bilateral agreements with a number of non-EU countries and international organizations including Interpol, the World Custom Organization, and the United States. Nonetheless, a number of problems still exist that have hindered multinational cooperation. Most of these problems involve sharing information (or not) with countries that harbor terrorists or organized crime groups. Another problem is related to the compiling of statistical data, which varies from country to country. This hinders any meaningful responses to certain crime problems. Most scholars in this field have argued for a clearly defined policy governing international police cooperation, especially one dealing with the exchange of information and operational support (Haberfeld and McDonald 2005).

Barriers to International Law Enforcement

Barriers to cooperation begin at the most basic level—arriving at a legal definition of organized crime. It is important to have agreement among countries when legislating against it in bilateral or multilateral agreements. Recent attempts by the United Nations and the EU have gone a long way in this direction. Major challenges to international cooperation among police forces fighting organized crime include language barriers, variations in legal traditions among countries, disparity in technological resources, regional conflict and civil war, and sharing intelligence.

Language

Language facilitators are key ingredients in the war on terror and organized crime. Any shortage of translators and interpreters can hamper international investigations and create an insurmountable barrier to effective communication, timely interrogations, and timely translation of documents. Language barriers can also impede communications between nations and between interrogators and suspects. Using the EU as a microcosm for examining this issue explains the barrier on the regional level. Its almost two dozen member states have 20 official languages including Czech, Danish, Dutch, English, Estonian, Finnish, French, German, Greek, Hungarian, Italian, Lettish, Lithuanian, Maltese, Slovak, Slovene, Polish, Portuguese, Spanish, and Swedish. (Although official EU documents are supposed to be published in all the languages, daily routine is dominated by English, as the use of French is diminishing.) Of these languages only three are considered working languages—French, German, and English. (By comparison the United Nations uses six working languages.) As a result of so many languages, there is always the potential at any given time that hundreds of different interpreters might be required to translate all statements into all languages incorporated in the EU. For example, a meeting of the EU in 11 official languages would require 380 interpreters (Roth and Sever 2005). Currently, the EU employs at least 4,000 interpreters. Because of the requirements of the language variations, however, it can take up to a week for something to be translated into languages of all the member states. This often involves the translation first across intermediate languages because of a deficit of interpreters for some languages. This process has led to a loss of information and clarity, and even errors resulting from the inherent dangers of multiple language interpretations. (Suggestions have been made to make English the official language of the EU, or to make Esperanto a common second language.) In one country alone, such as in the case of Estonia, there are several native languages. Of the 1.4 million inhabitants, 70 percent speak Estonian and 29 percent speak Russian and a number of dialects). Switzerland, with 7.3 million people has 4.6 million German speakers, 1.4 million French speakers, and 500,000 Italian speakers (Davies 2004). In 2004, only 10 of the EU countries were able to meet the deadline for the translation of the EU's notebook into their native languages. As a result some of the laws of the EU could not be enforced in national courts, as citizens could claim they did not understand them. Malta was among the countries affected because of a lack of Maltese translators. Even larger countries such as Poland, however, could not meet the translation deadline, thereby compromising various investigations (Davies 2004).

Varying Laws and Jurisdictions

Another barrier is the variations in legal traditions and notions of criminality around the world. There is no common system of criminalization, and variations among national substantive criminal laws can create obstacles to mutual legal assistance and extradition. As it stands, what might be a crime in one nation might not be in another. For example, crimes such as blasphemy and apostasy are serious crimes under the Islamic legal tradition. This brings up the dilemma of whether a non-Islamic country can be expected to extradite an individual for these offenses. Obstacles often beckon when secular countries cooperate with more religious regimes. It is important that nations are sensitive to issues of religion and ideology at all levels, including law enforcement. Even the difference between common and civil legal traditions requires a commensurate reconciliation of disparate legal systems.

Technology

When it comes to access to modern technology, there is a wide divide between the "have" and "have not" countries; it should be a high priority that these countries enter agreements allowing for the sharing of access to modern crime-fighting technologies. One of the weaknesses in most international conventions and agreements is that they are more focused on judicial cooperation than on police cooperation. Without sound systems for regulating the exchange of operational police information, transnational crime networks will continue to hold the upper hand. Europe has developed a variety of cooperative efforts over the years, with Interpol and Europol being the most prominent. In the 21st century, it is imperative for police forces to cooperate beyond their national borders and jurisdictions. Organized criminal activities that transcend national borders will always create challenges for law enforcement. First steps have been en through bilateral and multilateral agreements such as Europe's hengen Agreement.

Policing Cyberspace

International law enforcement faces a number of challenges when responding to cybercrime, as many of the acts take place internationally. In one case a bank reported a robbery in Sweden after customers were infected with a Trojan (computer virus), leaving the bank with a loss of 1 million euros. An investigation suggested the virus was created by someone in Russia, although the individual never personally used it. He did, however, offer a Web page with advice on how to use if for a fee. Others paid the fee and attacked the Swedish bank. This scenario required investigations in three different countries (Weinberg 2007). If this case had involved the FBI, agents would not have been allowed to travel overseas unless they were asked by a particular country, and once they did, they would have no special powers of arrest, but would be available for technical and investigation support. In the cyber era, foreign police departments have noted improved interaction and reciprocity with the FBI. In one 2006 case, the FBI reported breaking up a credit card theft ring involving the United States, Poland, and Romania. During the investigation, the FBI temporarily stationed agents with their counterparts to help surveillance and information sharing. This contrasts with past practices of stationing FBI agents at U.S. consulates and embassies abroad. Although there have been a number of successful cooperative ventures, there are still cases that result in conflict and distrust, such as a 2002 case in which Russian police accused an FBI agent with computer hacking after the agent downloaded evidence from a seized computer in Russia without official approval (Bryan-Low 2006).

Conclusion

America's "First War on Organized Crime" was kick-started by the late Attorney General Robert F. Kennedy in the early 1960s when he resuscitated the Organized Crime and Racketeering Section of the Department of Justice, and the Task Force on Organized Crime of the President's Commission on Crime and Administration of Justice (1967) produced a report heralding the power and organization of organized crime in the United States. Ex-Attorney General Robert Kennedy was assassinated (in 1968), however, before these initiatives bore any fruit. Until the 1980s, organized crime was treated as a domestic problem in the United States; and the results of most federal, state, and local organized crime initiatives were rather lackluster. The Pizza Connection case (1985–1987) demonstrated the reach of global organized crime networks and was a rare victory for international law enforcement efforts. Throughout the 1990s, however, most law enforcement efforts were too narrowly focused on the usual suspects of traditional Italian and Italian American organized crime.

By the early 21st century, other international issues dominated the attention of law enforcement, most notably terrorism. It took the new U.S. Attorney General Michael Mukasey in April 2008 to turn attention from the "War on Terrorism" to the almost forgotten "War on Organized Crime." This was no doubt the result of the globalization of organized crime and the obvious links between terrorism and organized crime, as Mukasey warned of the rising threat from "a new breed of mobsters around the world [that] was infiltrating industries, providing logistical support to terrorists and becoming capable of 'creating havoc in our economic infrastructure'" (Schmitt 2008). Because of the transnational challenges of fighting these new "hybrid" organizations and networks, the new "war" has paid few dividends so far. One of the few victories has been recent extradition agreement treaties between Latin America and Mexico with the United States that have seen a number of drug kingpins transferred to the United States to face more punitive (and certain) justice. Others, however, are always waiting in the ranks to take their places.

New technologies have played a major role in the trend toward globalization. Illicit trafficking networks have reaped rewards from these alongside legitimate competitors, allowing them to lower risks, increase productivity, and streamline their business. Drug traffickers and pirates, gun runners, and human smugglers have access to technologies that aid communication with far-flung gangs around the world. Drug dealers are just as likely to arrange deals online or even from the anonymity of a cybercafé as they are on a street corner. Alternatively, they can simply use a disposable cell phone that can be tossed in the garbage after a short time.

The global nature of computer crimes and the blurring of electronic borders have led the FBI and other law enforcement agencies to reach out beyond the United States to improve cooperation with other agencies around the world. The FBI now ranks cybercrime as its third priority behind terrorism and espionage. Most authorities insist that terrorism and cybercrime are not just changing the shape of organized crime, but the way individuals organize to commit crimes as well.

References

Althaus, Dudley. 2009, May 19. "Warden, Jailers Held in Mexico Prison Escape." *Houston Chronicle:* A8.

Berry, LaVerle, Glenn E. Curtis, Rex A. Hudson, Tara Karacan, Nina A Kollars, and Ramon Miro. 2003, October. *Nations Hospitable to Organized Crime and Terrorism.* Federal Research Division, Washington, D.C.: Library of Congress: 1–252.

Berry, LaVerle, Glenn E. Curtis, Rex A. Hudson, and Nina A Kollars. 2002, May. *A Global Overview of Narcotics-Funded Terrorist and Other Extremist Groups.* Federal Research Division, Washington, D.C.: Library of Congress: 1–142.

BIA (Security Information Agency). 2003, September. "Albanian Terrorism and Organized Crime in Kosovo and Metohija." Available at http://www.kosovo.net/albterrorism.htm. Assessed February 21, 1008.

Bohlen, Celestine. 1995, April 28. "Mafia's Foes Fear Rome Is Falling." *New York Times,* http://www.nytimes.com/1995/04/28/world/mafia-s-foes-fear-rome-is-faltering.html. Accessed September 7, 2009.

Bryan-Low, Cassell. 2006, November 21."To Catch Crooks in Cyberspace, FBI Goes Global." *The Wall Street Journal:* A1, A11.

Carter, David L. 2004. *Law Enforcement Intelligence: A Guide for State, Local and Tribal Agencies,* U.S. Department of Justice. Available at http://www.cops.usdoj.gov/default.asp?Item+1404.

Chambliss, William J. 1988. *On the Take: From Petty Crooks to Presidents.* Bloomington: Indiana University Press.

Chaudhuri, Pramit Pal. 2007, March 9. "U.S. to Find Means to Stop Spread of 419 Fraud." *Hindustan Times,* http://home.rica.net/alphae/419coal/news2007.htm.

Chomsky, Noam. 2006. *Failed States: The Abuse of Power and the Assault on Democracy.* New York: Metropolitan Books.

Clawson, Patrick, and Renssalaer Lee III. 1996. *The Andean Cocaine Industry.* New York: St. Martins Press.

Clutterbuck, Lindsay. 2004. "Law Enforcement." In *Attacking Terrorism,* ed. Audrey Kurth Cronin and James M. Ludes, 140–161. Washington, D.C.: Georgetown University Press.

Conaghan, Catherine. 2006. *Fujimori's Peru: Deception in the Public Sphere.* Pittsburgh: University of Pittsburgh Press.

Connor, Anne-Marie. 2009, April 25. "More Guards but Less Security for Guatemalans." *Houston Chronicle:* A17.

Council of Europe. 2005, December. "Organized Crime Situation Report 2005: Focus on the Threat of Economic Crime." Strasbourg, France: Department of Crime Problems.

CSIS (Center for Strategic and International Studies). 1997. "Russian Organized Crime: Global Organized Crime Project." Available at http://www.csis.org. Accessed December 10, 2008.

Davies, Ruth. 2004, April 22. "New EU Member States Will Not Meet Rulebook Translation Deadline." MaltaMedia Online Network.

Dickie, John. 2004. *Cosa Nostra: A History of the Sicilian Mafia.* London: Hodder and Stoughton.

Domash, Shelly. 2005, March 1. "America's Most Dangerous Gang." *Police Magazine,* http://www.policemag.com/Articles/2005/02/America-s-Most-Dangerous-Gang.aspx. Accessed September 3, 2009.

The Economist. 2009, January 10."Back into the Abyss?" 42.

Ehrenfeld, Rachel. 2003. *Funding Evil: How Terrorism Is Financed and How to Stop It.* Chicago: Bonus Books.

Embassy of the United States in Mexico. 2009, June 25."President Obama Signs Supplemental Budget, Increasing Merida Initiative Funding for Mexico to $1.12." Press Release. Available at http://mexico.usembassy.gov/eng/releases/ep090626_merida.html. Accessed November 4, 2009.

Farah, Douglas. 2004. *Blood from Stones: The Secret Financial Network of Terror.* New York: Broadway Books.

FBI. 2008. "Balkan Organized Crime. " Available at http://www.fbi.gov/hq/cid/orgcrime/balkan.htm. Accessed December 20, 2008.

Fleishman, Jeffrey. 2006, December 10. "Midnight Sun Has a Dark Side." *Los Angeles Times,* http://articles.latimes.com/2006/dec/10/world/fg-mafia10.Accessed September 7, 2009.

Friedman, George. 2008, May 13. "Mexico: On the Road to a Failed State?" Available at http://www.strafor.com/weekly/mexico_road_failed_state. Accessed March 27, 2009.

Friedman, Robert I. 2000. *Red Mafiya: How the Russian Mob Has Invaded America.* New York: Little, Brown.

Fuentes, Joseph R., and Robert J. Kelly. 1999, November. "Drug Supply and Demand: The Dynamics of the American Drug Market and Some

Aspects of Colombian and Mexican Drug Trafficking." *Journal of Contemporary Criminal Justice* 15 (4): 328–351.

Gastrow, Peter. 1999. "Main Trends in the Development of South Africa's Organized Crime." *African Security Review* 8 (6): http://www.iss.co.za/pubs?ASR?8No6?MainTrands.html.

Gates, Dominic. 2001, August 13. "FBI Busts Four Alleged Software Pirates." *Industry Standard,* http://www.pcworld.com/printable/article/id,57883/printable.html.

Gettleman, Jeffrey. 2006, November 10. "Chased By Gang Violence, Residents Flee Kenyan Slum." *New York Times International:* A4.

Ghani, Ashraf, and Clare Lockhart. 2009. *Fixing Failed States: A Framework for Rebuilding a Fractured World.* New York: Oxford University Press.

Grabosky, Peter. 2007. *Electronic Crime.* Upper Saddle River, NJ: Pearson.

Grobler, John. 2007, March 23. "Mafia Linked to Namibian Diamonds." *The Namibian.* http://dusteye.wordpress.com/2007/03/23/mafia-linked-to-namibian-diamonds. Accessed May 26, 2008.

Haberfeld, Maria, and William H. McDonald. 2005. "International Cooperation in Policing." In *Handbook of Transnational Crime & Justice,* ed. Phil Reichel, 286–309. Thousand Oaks, CA: Sage.

Hamm, Mark S., and Cecile Van de Voorde. 2005. "Crimes Committed by Terrorist Groups: Theory, Research, and Prevention." *Trends in Organized Crime* 9 (2):18–51.

Handelman, Stephen. 1995. *Comrade Criminal: Russia's New Mafiya.* New Haven, CT: Yale University Press.

Hanson, Stephanie. 2009, August 19. "FARC, ELN: Colombia's Left Wing Guerrillas." Council on Foreign Affairs, http://www.cfr.org/publication/9272/. Accessed September 4, 2009.

Hawley, Chris. 2009, February 23. "On the Border, a Crisis Escalates." *USA TODAY:* A1, A2.

Hennessy-Fiske, Molly, and Tina Susman. 2007, July 3. "U.S. Says Iran Backs Hezbollah Militants." *Houston Chronicle:* A7.

IFPI (International Federation of the Phonographic Industry). 2004, July 1. "Music Piracy Fighters Gather in Dublin for Global Enforcement Conference." Available at http://www.ifpi.org/content/section_news/20040701.html. Accessed August 8, 2009.

ISVG (Institute for the Study of Violent Groups). 2003, March. "Revolutionary Armed Forces." *Crime and Justice International:* 29.

Jane's Intelligence Review. 2007, June 1. "Pirate Gold—Music Counterfeiting in Italy." 1–6.

Kaplan, David E., Bay Fang, and Soni Sangwan. 2005, December "Paying for Terror." *U.S. News and World Report* 139 (21). Available at http://www.usnews.com/usnews/news/articles/051205/5terror_10.htm. Accessed January 23, 2007.

Kenney, Michael. 2007. *From Pablo to Osama: Trafficking and Terrorist Networks, Government Bureaucracies, and Competitive Adaptation.* University Park: The Pennsylvania State University Press.

Kouri, Jim. 2008, August 26. "Enforcement Strategy to Combat Threat of Organized Crime." Available at www.canadafreepress.com/index.php/article/2774.

Kushner, Harvey. 2003. *Encyclopedia of Terrorism.* Thousand Oaks, CA: Sage.

Lacey, Robert. 1992. *Little Man: Meyer Lansky and the Gangster Life.* New York: Little, Brown.

Lal, Rollie. 2005, Spring. "South Asian Organized Crime and Terrorist Networks." *Orbis:* 293–304.

Landler, Mark. 2009, March 26. "Clinton Says U.S. Feeds Mexico Drug Trade." *New York Times:* http://www.nytimes.com/2009/03/26/world/americas/26mexico.html. Accessed December 10, 2009.

Langewiesche, William. 2006, December. "How to Get a Nuclear Bomb." *Atlantic Monthly:* 80–98.

Lilley, Peter. 2006. *Dirty Dealing: The Untold Truth about Global Money Laundering, International Crime and Terrorism.* London: Kogan Page.

Lintner, Bertil. 2003. *Blood Brothers: The Criminal Underworld of Asia.* New York: Palgrave Macmillan.

Longrigg, Clare. 2009. *Boss of Bosses: How One man Saved the Sicilian Mafia.* London: John Murray.

Lunde, Paul. 2004. *Organized Crime: An Inside Guide to the World's Most Successful Industry.* New York: DK Publishing.

Lupsha, Peter A., and Sung-Kwon Cho. 1999. "The Future of Narco-terrorism: Colombia—A Case Study." In *Organized Crime: Uncertainties and Dilemmas,* ed. S. Einstein and M. Amir, 423–437. Chicago: Office of International Criminal Justice.

Mabrey, Daniel. 2003, March. "Human Smuggling in China." *Crime and Justice International:* 5–11.

Madinger, John. 2006. *Money Laundering: A Guide for Criminal Investigators.* Boca Raton, FL: Taylor and Francis.

Makarenko, Tamara. 2005. "The Crime-Terror Continuum: Tracing the Interplay between Transnational Organized Crime and Terrorism." In *Global Organized Today and the Changing Face of Organized Crime,* ed. Mark Galeotti, 129–145. London: Routledge.

Marsden, William, and Julian Sher. (2006). *Angels of Death: Inside the Bikers' Global Crime Empire*, London: Houghton and Stodder.

Mathers, Chris. 2004. *Crime School: Money Laundering—True Crime Meets the World of Business and Finance*. Buffalo: Firefly Books.

McAfee. 2005, July. "McAfee Virtual Criminology Report." Available at http://www.mcafee.com. Accessed March 13, 2008.

McCusker, Rob. 2006. "Transnational Organized Crime Cyber Crime: Distinguishing Threat from Reality." *Criminal Law and Social Change* 46: 257–273.

McGrath, Ben. 2006, May 1. "Kiss City: The Unmaking of the Mafia Cops." *The New Yorker*: 54–65.

McShane, Larry. 2006, April 7. "2 Ex-NYPD Detectives Convicted of Being Mafia Hitmen." *Houston Chronicle*: A12.

Meiners, Stephen. 2009, March 26. "Central America: An Emerging Role in the Drug Trade." Available at http://www.stratfor.com/weekly/20090326_central_america_emerging_role_drig_trade. Accessed March 27, 2009.

Messick, Hank. 1969. *Syndicate In the Sun*. New York: Macmillan.

Michaletos, Ionnis. 2007, April 25. "The Balkans: the Soft Underbelly of the European Narcotics Market." Available at http://www.savekosovo.org/default.asp?p=5&leader=0&sp=271. Accessed October 9, 2009.

Milton, Pat. 2006, October 3. "U.S. Worrying about Collaboration." *The China Post*, http://www.chinapost.com.tw/editorial/detail.asp?onNews=&GRP=1. Accessed November 9, 2006.

Mutschke, Ralf. 2000, December 13. "Links Between Organized Crime and 'Traditional' Terrorist Groups." Testimony to U.S. House Judiciary Committee, Subcommittee on Crime. Available at http://www.russianlaw.org/Mutschke.htm.

Nackan, Alan, and Jonathan Cooperman. 2006. "New Directions in Fraud Investigation." *The Secured Lender*, 43–46, 68.

Naim, Moises. 2003. "The Five Wars of Globalization." *Foreign Policy* 134: 28–37.

Naim, Moises. 2005. *Illicit: How Smugglers, Traffickers, and Copycats are Hijacking the Global Economy*. New York: Anchor Books.

Nakamura, Rodolfo Mendoza. 1999. "The Use of the Shining Path Myth in the Context of the All-Out War against the Narco-Guerrilla." In *Global Organized Crime and International Security*, ed. Emilio C. Viano, 99–116. Aldershot, UK: Ashgate.

Nance, M. W. 2003. *The Terrorist Recognition Handbook*. Guilford, CT: Lyons Press.

Napoleoni, Loretta. 2003. *Modern Jihad: Tracing the Dollars behind the Terror Networks.* London: Pluto.

Nardini, William J. 2006. "The Prosecutor's Toolbox: Investigating and Prosecuting Organized Crime in the United States." *Journal of International Criminal Justice* 4: 528–538.

NDIC (National Drug Intelligence Center). 2009. *National Drug Threat Assessment.* Washington, D.C.: U.S. Department of Justice.

Noble, Ronald K. 2003, July 16. "The Links between Intellectual Property Crime and Terrorist Financing." Text of speech from Interpol director. Available at http://www.interpol.int/Public?ICPO/Speeches/SG20030716.asp.

O'Connor, Anne-Marie. 2009, April 25. "More Guards, but Less Security, for Guatemalans." *Houston Chronicle:* A17.

O'Neil, Siobhan. 2007, May 24. "Terrorist Precursor Crimes: Issues and Options for Congress." Available at http://www.fas.org/sgp/crs/terror/RL34014.pdf.

Perl, Raphael. 2003, May 20. "Testimony of Raphael Perl before U.S. Senate Committee on the Judiciary." Available at http://judiciary.senate.gov/hearings/testimony.cfm?id=764&wit_id=2115.

Potter, Gary. 2008. "Drug Trafficking and Organized Crime: The Rise and Evolution of International Drug Cartels." In *Organized Crime: From Trafficking to Terrorism,* Vol. 1, ed. Frank G. Shanty and Patit Paban Mishra, 184–189. Santa Barbara: ABC-CLIO.

Powell, Stewart M. 2009, March 13. "Official Use of Guard Is a Last Resort." *Houston Chronicle,* http://articles.sfgate.com/2009-03-13/news/17214937_1_national-guard-border-security-homeland-security. Accessed January 4, 2010.

Powis, Robert E. 1992. *The Money Launderers.* Chicago: Probus Publishing.

Rashbaum, William K. 2004, February 11. "Officials Say Mob Stole $200 Million Using Phone Bills." *New York Times:* A1.

Reader, John. 1998. *Africa: A Biography of the Continent.* New York: Knopf.

Richards, Justin. 2006, July 11. "Growth of Cybercrime Is among Top Global Threats to Security, Says FBI." *Computer Weekly,* Available at http://www.accessmylibrary.com/coms2/summary_0286-15950350_ITM.

Roth, Mitchel. 2000, March. "Organized Crime in the Balkans." *Crime and Justice International:* 7–8.

Roth, Mitchel P., and Murat Sever. 2007. "Barriers to Police Cooperation in the Age of Terrorism." In *Understanding and Responding to Terrorism,* eds. Huseyin Durmaz, Bilal Sevinc, Ahmet S. Yayla, and Siddik Ekici, 1–16. Amsterdam: IOS Press.

Russo, Gus. 2001. *The Outfit: The Role of Chicago's Underworld in the Shaping of Modern America.* New York: Bloomsbury.

Schaan, Joan Neuhaus. 2009, April 12. "Beware Drug-Cartel Corruption." *Houston Chronicle:* B10, B11.

Schmid, Alex. 2005, January 27. "Links Between Terrorism and Drug Trafficking: A Case of Narco-Terrorism?" Available at http://english. safe-democracy.org/causes/links-between-terrorism-and-drug-trafficking-a -case of narcoterrorism.html.

Schmitt, Richard B. 2008, April 24. "Attorney General Targeting International Organized Crime." *Los Angeles Times,* http://latimes. com/news/nationworld/washingtonc/la-na-crime24apr24.

Serio, Joseph. 2006, November–December. "Has the Market Tamed the Mafia?" *Crime and Justice International:* 47.

Serio, Joseph D. 2008. *Investigating the Russian Mafia.* Durham, NC: Carolina Academic Press.

Shaw, Mark. 2002, September. "Typologies of Transnational Organized Crime Groups." Center for International Crime Prevention, United Nations Office of Drugs and Crime. Available at http://www.iss. co.za/pubs/PAPERS/28?Paper28.html.

Sheets, Lawrence Scott, and William J. Broad. 2007, January 26. "Smuggler's Plot in Georgia Boosts Fear over Uranium." *Houston Chronicle:* A19.

Shelley, Louise I. 2003. "Organized Crime, Terrorism and Cybercrime." Available at http://crime-research.org/library/terrorism_cybercrime. pdf. Accessed October 10, 2009.

Shelley, Louise I., and John T. Picarelli. 2005, Winter. "Methods and Motives: Exploring Links between Transnational Organized Crime and International Terrorism." *Trends in Organized Crime* 9 (2): 52–67.

Shelley, Louise I., and Robert Orttung. 2006, September/October. "Criminal Act: How Organized Crime Is a Nuclear Smuggler's New Best Friend." *Bulletin of the Atomic Scientists:* 22–23.

Skaperdas, Stergios, and Constantonos Syropoulos. 1995. "Gangs as Primitive States." In *The Economics of Organized Crime,* ed. G. Fiorentini and S. Peltzman, 61–84. New York: Cambridge University Press.

Sung, Hung-en. 2004, May. "State Failure, Economic Failure, and Predatory Organized Crime; A Comparative Analysis." *Journal of Research in Crime and Delinquency* 41 (2): 111–129.

Taylor, Robert W., Tory J. Caeti, D. Call Loper, Eric J. Fritsch, and John Liederbach. 2006. *Digital Crime and Digital Terrorism.* Upper Saddle River, NJ: Pearson.

Thomas, Dana. 2007, September 3. "Counterfeits Are Literally Terrorism's Purse Strings." *Houston Chronicle:* B7.

Thompson, Tony. 2003, June 15. "Ulster Terror Gangs Links Up with Mafia." Available at http://www.guardian.co.uk/2003/jun/15/northernireland.

Thoumi, Francisco E. 2003. *Illegal Drugs, Economy, and Society in the Andes.* Washington, D.C.: Woodrow Wilson Press.

USAID Bureau for Latin American and Caribbean Affairs Office of Regional Sustainable Development. 2006, April. *Central America and Mexico Gang Assessment.* Available at http://www.usaid.gov/locations/latin_america_caribbean/democracy/gangs_cam.pdf.

Varese, Federico. 2001. *The Russian Mafia: Private Protection in a New Market Economy.* Oxford, UK: Oxford University Press.

Volkov, Vadim. 2002. *Violent Entrepreneurs: The Use of Force in the Making of Russian Capitalism.* Ithaca, NY: Cornell University Press.

Walsh, Mary Williams, and Richard Boudreaux. 1994, August 17. "German Police Seize Weapons-Grade Plutonium." *Houston Chronicle:* A24.

Washington Office on Latin America (WOLA). 2007, October. *The Captive State: Organized Crime and Human Rights in Latin America.* Available at http://www.wola.org/index.php?option=com_content&task=sectionp&id=1&Itemid=2&topic_filter=Security+Policy. Accessed August 4, 2009.

Watson, Julie. 2007, April 13. "Campaign of Fear Hits Public Stage." *Houston Chronicle:* A19.

Weinberg, Neal. 2007, February 1. "Kasperskys on Cybercrime: Don't Blame the Russian Mafia and Why We Need Anti-Anti-Anti-Virus Software." Available athttp://www.,networld.com/cgi-bin/mailto/x.cgi?pagetosend=/export/home. Accessed March 13, 2008.

White, Jonathan R. 2009. *Terrorism and Homeland Security,* 6th ed. Belmont, CA: Wadsworth Cengage.

Wright, Alan. 2006. *Organised Crime.* Devon, UK: Willan Publishing.

Zaidi, S. Hussain. 2003. *Black Friday: The True Story of the Bombay Bomb Blasts.* New Delhi: Penguin Books.

3

Global Organized Crime Groups

Italian Organized Crime Groups

The Sicilian and Italian-American Mafias

Although both the Sicilian and American permutations of the Mafia share some tendencies and cooperate in the drug trade, they operate in different dimensions. More important, the American version has long stood on the periphery of society, but the Sicilian version has long been a dominant presence in the region's economic and political life. The American and Sicilian versions of the mafia remain distinct from one another, linked on occasion by personal contacts and business associations. For example, a Sicilian Mafioso could not appear in the United States and expect to become a made (official) member of a mafia family without the traditional long waiting period that used to be required. Conversely, when Lucky Luciano was deported from America to Naples, he had no formal status in Mafia-related matters in his native country (Stille 1995).

Few cases illustrate the international links between the Old and New World Italian syndicates better than the infamous "Pizza Connection" case of the 1980s when Sicilian and Italian American gangsters used pizzerias as a front to dispense almost $1.6 billion in profits from heroin sales (Kaplan 2006). The operation was later tied to New York's Bonanno family (which had the strongest ties to Sicily of an American Mafia family), but the actual operation was largely run by Sicilian immigrants who distributed heroin manufactured in Sicily. Both proved to be distinct groups; they were not subservient to one another, but simply separate, almost parallel, factions. The new Sicilians, sometimes pejoratively referred to as *zips* (origin of word is obscure), began appearing in the United States in the 1970s. Rather than joining domestic Italian America gangs, however, they reported to their Sicilian boss Gaetano Badalamenti, who introduced the scheme to use pizza parlors as fronts for heroin trafficking.

The evolution of Sicily's Mafia traditions can be traced back to an ancient feudal past often obscured by myth and legend. The island's history has been characterized by its conquest by a succession of rapacious oppressors that included Phoenicians, Carthaginians, Romans, Byzantines, Arabs, Normans, Spanish, Austrians, and the French. This has resulted in a deeply ingrained distrust of foreigners and central authority. In time a Mafia culture developed that emphasized traditional Sicilian values such as respect, honor, family ties, and *omerta* (code of silence). Although honor and respect were at the heart of the Mafia ethos, profit became the motivation for its existence in the 20th century. What began as bribery, corruption, and the extortion of businessmen and the merchant class, branched out to international and then global criminal enterprises. Nothing illustrates this more than the 20th-century illicit drug trade.

Most recent scholarship asserts that the Mafia as understood in the modern era harkens back to 19th-century western Sicily, a period of failed social rebellions and reform efforts. In fact the very word *mafia* cannot even be found in an Italian dictionary before the early 1860s. There is no simple agreed upon definition of the word *mafia*. Perhaps no other five-letter word conjures up more misconceptions and misguided ethnic stereotypes than this word that has been routinely applied to a wide range of criminal enterprises and behaviors. Historian Denis Mack Smith suggests that "Mafia is the only word from the Sicilian dialect to be incorporated into all the main world languages" (Smith 1995, 7).

Scholars and policymakers have long debated the persistence of the Sicilian Mafia. For many years it was convenient for Italian prosecutors to view the Sicilian Mafia as a single monolithic, hierarchical organization directed by a commission of top bosses, called the *cupola*. According to this model, members expressed their solidarity by abiding by unwritten rules based on strict internal discipline, job specialization, and a strong sense of duty and honor.

Recent revelations by a series of high-level informants (*pentiti*) have revealed that traditional Sicilian Mafia families do indeed operate according to a strict hierarchical structure and with clearly defined membership. The Sicilian Mafia is not a monolithic organization replete with a headquarters and a central leadership. Most observers compare it to a loose association of gangs, a relationship that most scholars compare to the bundled leaves of an artichoke, or *cosche*. Most towns have a family (*cosca*), with larger cities such as Palermo having more than one. Families range in size from 15 to several hundred. These gangs coexist in a state of mutual suspicion that occasionally breaks into bloody intermissive warfare. Each family claims a monopoly over the illicit activity on its turf (Follain 2008). Each family is headed by a Boss (*Capofamiglia*). In descending order follows a Counselor (*Consigliere*) and an Underboss (*Sotto capo*). Under them are Field Leaders, or *Capodecima* (head of 10) who oversee the *Uomini d'onore*, variously referred to as men of honor or soldiers. Three or more neighboring families are headed by a district boss or *capomandamento*, selected from among the three bosses.

Contrary to their penchant for secrecy, some Sicilian families have risen to prominence because of their involvement in global trafficking schemes and campaigns of violence against the state. None has earned more opprobrium than the faction out of Corleone in western Sicily, 20 miles from Palermo. The so-called Corleonese faction made its presence known soon after World War II when 153 people were murdered on the streets of Corleone between 1944 and 1948 (Follain 2008). From the 1950s to the present its leadership was under three men—Luciano Leggio, Toto Riina, and Bernardo Provenzano. Provenzano was finally captured in 2006 after 43 years on the run. He held sway over the Corleonese after the arrest of Leggio and then Riina. Although Provenzano was complicit in a number of high-profile murders, including those of special prosecutors Giovanni Falcone and Paolo Borsellino in 1992, he was credited with essentially reviving the Mafia at a time when it was losing its political connections. His strategy was to eschew murder and become almost invisible outside the parallel economy of Italy's underworld (Longrigg 2009). Testimony to his success were estimates the year that he was captured that suggested 80 percent of Sicily's businesses were paying protection money in order to survive. According to one expert, if one combined the profits of the major Italian organized crime groups (Sicilian Mafia, 'Ndrangheta, and Camorra), it would come to 42 billion pounds, or 10.5 percent of the country's GDP (Follain 2008, 317). Despite the well-publicized, anti-Mafia campaign of the 1990s, any successes that might have been claimed have been short-lived. Today the Italian government has shifted it priorities to fighting urban street crime, terrorism, and other forms of organized crime. If one thing is clear in the docile response of the Sicilian people, it is that they fear the Mafia more than they trust the Italian state.

An Italian investigation centered in Palermo in 2008 dubbed "Old Bridge" revealed attempts at restoring Old and New World Mafia contacts revolving around New York City's Gambino crime family (Hays 2008). A subsequent roundup of 87 suspects in New York City coincided with the arrest of 23 suspected organized crime figures in Palermo, although the cases were unrelated. Both American and Italian investigators, however, saw signs of efforts to reignite the close relationship between the Gambino family and the Sicilian Mafia (Rashbaum 2008). This raid was the biggest since the Pizza Connection arrests in the mid-1980s.

The Americanization of the Mafia

The word *mafia* first entered the American vocabulary (and imagination) soon after the arrival of Italian immigrants in the 19th century. Although there is still debate over when the Mafia first appeared in America, most accounts lean toward New Orleans sometime in the 1880s. Waves of Italian immigrants changed the demographics of New Orleans as newspapers and city rumor mills worked overtime conjuring sensational accounts of sinister Mafia and Camorra activity. The murder of New Orleans police chief David Hennessey in 1890, allegedly by Mafia assassins, led to an outpouring of rage against Italian immigrants. The purported suspects were acquitted after a trial in 1891. A mob estimated up to 20,000 strong stormed the jail and killed 11 Italian prisoners, including three who had been acquitted, three who had received a mistrial, and five awaiting trial (English 2005). It should not be surprising that many fellow immigrants fled to other urban centers, especially New York City.

Before 1931, the most prominent Italian crime bosses in New York City were Old World bosses from Sicily, often referred to as the "Mustache Petes." Giuseppe "Joe the Boss" Masseria, from Palermo, and Salvatore Maranzano from Castellemmare Del Golfo were the leaders of two factions competing for dominance of New York City's Italian American underworld. Masseria gunman Charles "Lucky" Luciano engineered the murder of his boss and then convincingly pledged his fealty to his new boss Maranzano.

A devotee of Julius Caesar, Maranzano had visions of becoming the New World "boss of bosses" (or *capo di tuti capi*). According to his vision "Cosa Nostra" or "Our Thing" would be arranged around five families led by bosses or "men of honor." Prospective members were expected to take part in an initiation ritual and promise to follow a code of silence, *omerta*. Thanks to the machinations of Luciano, Maranzano soon followed his nemesis to the grave, thereby ending the era of the Mustache Petes. This chain of events is considered a watershed event in the history of Italian American organized crime, a turning point that marked the emergence of the new and modern Mafia.

America's best-known Mafia families are the five in New York. The Gambino, Genovese, Lucchese, Colombo, and Bonanno families emerged out of the 1931 murders of the Mustache Petes. The Chicago version of the Mafia is known as the Outfit; in New England it is referred to as the Office. Each is structured differently, but the New York families come closest to mirroring the Sicilians. The organizational structure of Cosa Nostra has been well-chronicled with most accounts listing 24 separate gangs or families. Italian American Mafia families have a similar hierarchical structure to their Sicilian counterpart. This structure was laid out more than 100 years ago. At the top is the boss, who is assisted by a counselor or *consigliere*. Second to the boss is the underboss. In descending order are capos, soldiers, and associates. The numbers of each vary by organization. The underboss typically is called on to resolve disputes between members, although in more serious cases the boss might be called in. The boss appoints the underboss and capos. Soldiers, or "made men," are the lowest level of La Cosa Nostra membership. A soldier "makes his bones" and becomes a "made member" after proving himself by taking part in a murder (does not have to actually be the killer, but must be willing). Associates are not actual members of the family but engage in criminal activities with the blessing of made members. Virtually anyone who has criminal acumen and is an "earner" can become an associate without restriction of ethnicity. Membership is restricted to men of Italian American descent. It was not too long ago that both parents had to be Italian, but in the modern era one Italian American parent is sufficient. What differentiated the Americanized version of the Mafia from its Sicilian counterpart was the lack of support for a "Boss of Bosses," although over the years some overly ambitious Italian American bosses unsuccessfully tried to claim this honor.

Camorra [Naples, Italy]

The Camorra originated in the prisons of Naples during the 19th century. As members were released from jail, they extended their reach beyond the walls of prison. During the 1820s, Neapolitan police were able to document the organization's policies and rituals. In the second half of the 19th century, the Camorra were deeply entrenched in the city's gambling and theft rackets, as well as extorting cargo loaded at the city's docks. In response police launched a crackdown, arresting many *camorristi*, with other fleeing to the New World where they opened branches in New York City and elsewhere. Naples is currently Italy's most violent city, with perhaps 100 Camorra gangs with between 30 and 40 members, each battling for control of various rackets (Saviano 2008). Each gang has a hierarchical structure, with a boss at the top and in descending order capos (captains) in charge of crews of members and associates. Until the 1970s they favored gambling, loan sharking, extortion, tobacco smuggling, and political corruption. They soon became more involved in transnational crime through drug trafficking and money laundering. But by the end of the decade, the profits from the international drug trade and other global enterprises were too much to resist. Tobacco smuggling has been an especially lucrative enterprise. Consider that as far back as 1959 a case of cigarettes could be purchased in Morocco for $23 and sold in Europe for $170 (Lunde 2004, 75). By taking this trade from the Corsicans in the 1960s, the Camorra catapulted to the top ranks of European organized crime groups. The publication of Robert Saviano's best-selling book *Gomorrah* in 2006 convincingly revealed the ascendance of the Camorra over the past decade. In it the investigative journalist claims that the Camorra gang network is now the most formidable in terms of both power and violence in Italy. His revelations now require him to live under police protection in Naples.

'Ndrangheta [Calabria, Italy]

In 2008, Italy's anti-Mafia commission reported that the 'Ndrangheta, entrenched in Calabria and far southern Italy was not only "a worldwide threat" but had actually surpassed the power of the Sicilian Mafia, both in clout and international contacts reaching as far as Latin America, North Africa, Canada, the United States, and Africa. According to one spokesperson for the commission, the modern 'Ndrangheta "is the most modern organization" that has readily adapted to globalization, controlling much of the import of cocaine into Europe (*New York Times* 2008).

Some observers refer to the 'Ndrangheta as the "Honored Society" or brotherhood and have compared it to the Sicilian Mafia; however, both have distinct structures. The Sicilian Mafia typically has some type of understood hierarchy, but the 'Ndrangheta has no single leaders and depends on a number of cooperative strategies. Like Sicily, Calabria has a history of resistance against government oppression; today it is Italy's poorest and most crime-ridden region.

The origins of the name 'Ndrangheta are from the Greek word *'ndrina*, which refers to "a man who does not bend" (Varese 2006, 423). The *'ndrina* is the basic organizational unit, akin to a Sicilian Mafia family. It typically controls a small town and if by chance another *'ndrina* is operating in the area, they would band together into a *locale* (Paoli 2003). Each *'ndrina* is autonomous on its own turf, with no formal authority above the local boss. Each unit is composed of men from the same family unit, a factor that solidifies each *'ndrina* and makes it more difficult for outsiders or informants to infiltrate its ranks. Several studies in the mid-1990s found that *'ndrina* had 2.6 percent *pentiti* (witnesses for the government) compared to 6.9 for their Sicilian counterparts (Varese 2006, 423–424). One distinguishing feature of the 'Ndrangheta is that it does not try to limit the amount of blood members in the group. Most other organizations, however, consider this a weakness, as too many blood relatives can create cabals within the group or lead to dissension among members as a result of favoritism.

For more than 50 years 'Ndrangheta bosses have held annual summits called *crimini*, which gives them an opportunity to recount that year's activities in their territories, including murders, kidnappings, and other serious crimes (Paoli 2003). Bosses have reportedly attended these meetings from as far as Canada and Australia (Varese 2006). Despite these annual meetings, the gangs are often at war with each other as demonstrated by an outbreak of violence between members in Germany that left 20 dead, including six at one time. The 'Ndrangheta was thrust into the international spotlight in August 2007 after the machine gun drive-by killings of six men as they left a pizzeria in Duisburg, Germany. Italian authorities were aware of the migration of members into Germany and other parts of Europe; however, they were slow to warn their counterparts in other countries. In this particular incident, 'Ndrangheta members were believed to be attempting to launder money through legitimate business far from the prying eyes of Italian law enforcement. By 2007, Germany had more than a half-million Italian immigrants, second only to Turkey (Landler and Fisher, 2007). Although most Italian immigrants have assimilated into German society, their numbers indicate a strong recruitment pool for crime syndicates.

Authorities suggest that the 'Ndrangheta and other Italian gangs have taken advantage of crackdowns on the Sicilian Mafia since the 1990s and have flourished thanks to the drug trade and direct connections with the Colombian cocaine trade. Members have engaged in tobacco smuggling, gambling, kidnapping, and extortion and have been increasingly turning to legitimate business ventures such as construction, restaurants, and supermarkets. Beginning in the 1970s, they turned to the international heroin and cocaine trade. Members are well respected for their money-laundering acumen and have been identified in a number of countries. Today there are an estimated 100 'Ndrangheta families with more than 5,000 members in Italy and at least 10,000 counting the branches beyond Italy. These have been established through immigration to Germany, Belgium, Holland, France, Eastern Europe, the United States, Canada, and Australia (Varese 2006).

The Corsicans

In the years between the World Wars, the international heroin trade was mainly in the hands of Corsican gangs and independent operators located in Marseilles, France. Strategically located in the Western Mediterranean, this port city had long been at the center of many smuggling operations and by the mid-1930s was among the region's busiest ports. Marseilles provided an ideal transit point for ships bringing in morphine base from Turkey and French Indochina. During this era heroin labs operated around the clock. Their operations, however, came to prominence under the leadership of Corsican crime boss Paul Carbone, who directed the heroin trade including most of the heroin entering the United States. Over the years this source for heroin became known as the "French Connection." Observers have pointed out the similarities between the Corsicans and the Sicilians—both are clannish islanders sharing an Italian dialect. Using their connections in the American underworld, the Sicilians were the Corsicans' most reliable customers, helping transship heroin through Sicily to the United States, often packed clandestinely in shipments of typical Italian import items. The Corsicans continued to dominate the French underworld until the 1950s. After World War II, however, their power was threatened by the growing clout of the local Communist Party. Although the political party had little to do with criminal activity, its mere presence during the nascent Cold War proved alarming to American authorities (as it did in Italy). The emerging Central Intelligence Agency (CIA from the OSS) developed a strategy to support non-Communist Socialists in France. By some accounts, this might have included supplying the Corsican gangs with money and weapons as long as they harassed and attacked Communist officials and activists. Ultimately, the Corsicans were restored as leaders of the underworld thanks to American assistance. From the late 1940s to the 1960s, Hong Kong and Marseilles were the world's main heroin-refining sites. The largest postwar seizure of narcotics took place in New York in 1947 after a Corsican seaman was arrested while leaving a recently docked French vessel with seven pounds of heroin. The next month an even larger bust took place on another French ship. World War II had virtually stopped the international heroin trade, but these busts and others signaled investigators that the global trade was back in business thanks in no small part to the "Corsican connection." The inexorable expansion of the global heroin trade became much more dispersed in the 1960s as other heroin trafficking groups from Southeast Asia and Europe became major players, diminishing the role of the Corsicans (Inciardi 1992).

Russian Organized Crime (ROC)

During the Soviet era it was de rigueur to downplay the existence of organized crime within its borders. Recent research, however, reveals that the foundations of Russian organized crime dates back to the Soviet system itself more than 70 years ago. Between the 1920s and 1990s, Soviet labor camps, or gulags, gave birth to an elite criminal fraternity, or *vory-v-zakone*, which lived according to a thieves' law, an unwritten system of rules and behavior. By most accounts, modern ROC grew out of this phenomenon, as well as various characteristics of the Soviet system itself, exemplified by individual high-level officials developing beneficial relationships with these criminals. According to one expert, ROC groups emerged in the 1960s thanks to a state apparatus that "encouraged, facilitated and protected it" (Wright 2006, 148). During the Brezhnev regime in the 1970s and early 1980s, it became increasingly clear that the country was in the hands of corrupt Communist bureaucrats that some even had the temerity to brand a "kleptocracy." It even became fashionable to call this corruption "Mafiya." Rather than referring to a traditional structured hierarchy, however, it referred to the day-to-day inequalities of the Russian Communist system. According to one Russian journalist, "We apply 'mafiya' to practically anything—shops, creative unions, hospitals, diplomats, prostitutes, butchers, chess players, cities, regions and republics" (quoted in Serio 2008, 13). Nonetheless, the Soviet system did indeed institutionalize a culture of thievery as well as an underground economy.

In the late 1980s and through the 1990s, the release of price controls and the new free market economy drew thousands of entrepreneurs and merchants to open shop in Moscow and its environs. Many came from distant regions in Central Asia and elsewhere. Fledgling businessmen, migrants, and refugees were soon drawn into the orbit of developing crime syndicates that were trying to control most of the new markets. Savvy crime bosses used the newcomers to dispense narcotics, counterfeit liquor, and other illegal commodities. At the same time the merchants were allowed to engage in their own rackets, as long as they turned over a percentage to the crime bosses. It was during this period that the term *mafiya* was freely used by ethnic Russians in response to rising crime, high prices, and a decaying infrastructure as a pejorative label for these individuals. The unrestrained use of the term *mafiya*, however, obscured the fact that not all gangs were equal in structure, power, and influence, leading to the widespread illusion of one monolithic Russian mafiya.

In the aftermath of the collapse of the Soviet system in 1991, hundreds, if not thousands, of new criminal groups emerged in Russia to take advantage of the democratization process. The new gangster class included former KGB agents and military defectors, government specialists, and former prison inmates. Russian crime syndicates quickly grasped the opportunities of the confused state of affairs and the shortage of goods as they formalized a black market that would eventually spread into Eastern and Western Europe, as well as the United States. Many Russian émigrés landed in Israel and the United States where they flourished in coastal urban areas such as Boston, New York City, Miami, Los Angeles, and

San Francisco. The Russian Ministry of Interior estimated that as many as 110 Russian gangs were operating in 44 countries in the 1990s. One investigative journalist asserted that 30 Russian syndicates were operating in at least 17 American cities (Friedman 2000). Although several powerful criminal organizations emerged, there is no evidence that a single gang or group of gangs controls the Russian underworld.

Among the few syndicates with a recognizable hierarchy is Moscow's largest group, the *Solntsevo*, named after the suburb where it was created. In the mid-1990s, it had a reputed 9,000 members, although others place the figure much lower (Dunn 1997). According to one leading authority, it functions as an umbrella organization with different crews active in different countries (Varese 2001), but it does operate under a supreme council composed of 12 individuals who are considered the leaders of various factions. It meets on a regular basis. Although size estimates vary for this group, it runs against the typical ROC group profile that officials describe as small in numbers (Serio 2008).

More recently observers have argued that ROC is hardly quantifiable. What has never been made clear is what Russian gangs fell under the rubric of organized crime, whether the various numbers floated about refer to street gangs, mafiya clans, criminal societies or associations, or bandit groups. Some scholars have suggested that "the Russian underworld is maturing, as larger, more professional networks" subsume the hundreds of smaller organizations and gangs that emerged in post-Soviet Russia (Galeotti 2005, 55).

Mexican Drug Cartels

Strategically located on the American border, Mexican drug trafficking cartels are in position to quickly react to changing drug trends in the United States, where most users reside. Violent war between Mexican gangs over the lucrative drug trade is increasingly spilling over the border into the United States, leading to bombings with grenades, decapitations, and shoot-outs along the almost 2,000-mile border with Mexico. Officials have identified 230 cities where they operate including Boston, Anchorage, and Atlanta. More recently Mexican drug gangs have begun targeting the European drug market. Officials cite the weak American economy, a stronger euro, the ongoing Calderon military campaign, less aggressive law enforcement, and more open markets for shifting their strategies toward Europe (Schiller 2009). Soon after taking office in December 2006, President Felipe Calderon launched an all-out anticrime campaign. Calderon has deployed more than 40,000 troops and federal police throughout Mexico (more than U.S. troops in Afghanistan before the surge in 2009) (Hawley 2009). More than 10,000 people have died since then. According to the 2009 Justice Department's National Drug Threat Assessment, Mexican drug trafficking organizations have spread out across the United States, in the process forming alliances with urban street gangs and "now represent the greatest organized crime threat to the United States" (National Drug Intelligence Center 2009, iii). In March 2009, the Mexican government initiated a program that offered $2 million rewards for information leading to the capture of two dozen recognized drug kingpins. Officials have also offered $1 million rewards for the capture of less prominent bosses working for the country's six main syndicates.

Juarez Cartel

During its heyday, the Juarez cartel was thought to have been moving 70 percent of the illegal drugs into the United States from Mexico. Based in the border town of Ciudad Juarez (on the border across from El Paso, Texas), this organization came to prominence under the aegis of Amado Carrillo Fuentes (1956–1997), who was known as the "Lord of the Skies" for his strategy of converting Boeing 727 jets into cocaine transports. During the 1990s, the organization was Mexico's most powerful drug-trafficking syndicate. The Juarez cartel uses regional bases in Guadalajara, Hermosillo, and Torreon, Mexico to store drug shipments before transshipment to locations along the American border. After Carrillo Fuentes died during a botched plastic surgery operation in Mexico City in 1997, his brothers took over the gang. Unable to fill the shoes of their dead brother, they were replaced by a string of other traffickers, none of whom would attain the prominence and success of the "Lord of the Skies." Testimony to the cartel's reach into the highest level's of the Mexican government was the case of a former governor of the Yucatan state, who was convicted of accepting $30 million in bribes for police and political protection from the Juarez cartel between 1993 and 1999. Sometime in the first years of the new millennium the Juarez cartel transitioned into an alliance of three drug lords from the border states of Chihuahua, Durango, and

Sinaloa, sometimes referred to as the "Golden Triangle Alliance." In April 2009, Mexican police arrested major Juarez drug kingpin Vicente Carrillo Leyva (son of Carrillo Fuentes) while he was exercising in a Mexico City park, in no small part due to the Mexican government strategy of placing $2 million rewards for the country's top dug traffickers. At the time of his arrest, he was one of the two Juarez members on the list (*Reuters* 2009).

Sinaloa Cartel

Based in the Pacific Coast state of Sinaloa, this organization is led by Joaquin "El Chapo" Guzman and Ismael "El Mayo" Zambada, the two most wanted men in Mexico. The cartel is considered Mexico's "most important drug trafficking organization" (Althaus 2008, A12). This region has long been a key location for the cultivation of opium poppies for the making of heroin, controlled by the Sinaloa cartel. Since 2001, the cartel has been at war with the Gulf cartel over control of the strategic border town of Nuevo Laredo. By most accounts the Gulf cartel has had an upper hand, with an almost two-to-one advantage in gunmen. Nuevo Laredo is key to the Mexican-American drug trade, with the city offering extensive trade facilities and processing more legitimate cargo than any other crossing point along the almost 2,000-mile border between the two countries. In the United States the cartel is most active in Arizona. Since 2007, more than 750 individuals have been arrested for links with the group. The United States has placed a $5 million reward for the capture of its leader Guzman (Bogan 2009).

Tijuana Cartel [Arrellano-Felix Organization]

Also known as the Arrellano-Felix organization, this cartel has been based in Tijuana since the mid-1980s. After the arrest of its founder, Miguel Angel Felix Gallardo, in 1989 for his role in the slaying of U.S. Drug Enforcement Administration (DEA) agent Enrique "Kiki" Camarena, the organization was divided up among family members and subordinates. Unable to control the organization from prison, Gallardo by most accounts met with his lieutenants and divided the Mexican border crossings among them. According to one 2008 report, Sinaloa/Arizona, Laredo/Nuevo/

Laredo, and El/Paso/Juarez were turned over to Amado Carrillo Fuentes (Wallace-Wells 2007). During the 1990s, the Tijuana cartel dominated the flow of cocaine, marijuana, and heroin into California and the West Coast. In 2006, Mexico extradited Francisco Rafael Arrellano Felix to the United States, the first time the country had ever extradited a major drug kingpin across the border. The Tijuana cartel was considered Mexico's most ruthless and feared drug syndicate at one time. After the death and arrest of two leading Arrellano-Felix brothers in 2002, however, its influence briefly diminished. Since then the Tijuana cartel has been linked to hundreds of murders in that city alone, including 840 in 2008. Much of the deaths are attributable to the ongoing war between several factions within the cartel. In 2009, the U.S. State Department made waves when it issued an official travel warning for Americans contemplating visiting Mexico, including Tijuana, on spring break.

Gulf Cartel and Los Zetas

Considered Mexico's bloodiest gang, the Gulf cartel operates out of the Mexican cities bordering South Texas and controls narcotrafficking and sales throughout the Gulf Coast region. Based in the Mexican border towns of Matamoras, Reynosa, and Nuevo Laredo, the cartel's best known and most feared members work for its paramilitary arm known as *Los Zetas*. Many were veterans of Mexican Special Forces before deserting to the Gulf Cartel for better pay as killers. Dallas, Texas is the Gulf's most prominent U.S. drug-distribution destination. The organization is the brainchild of Juan Garcia Abrego and now operates in 17 Mexico states. The award-winning motion picture *Traffic* was reportedly based on his rise and fall from power. Arrested in 1996, Abrego is now serving 11 life sentences following his extradition to the United States. At his zenith he guaranteed Colombian cartels that their cocaine would reach destinations for 50 percent of each load. After Abrego's arrest, Osiel Cardenas Guillen took charge and was credited with luring the original Zetas to his syndicate. They adopted the name Zetas in homage to their original leader who was killed in 2002 and was identifiable by his radio name *Zeta* (Lloyd and George 2007). Cardenas was arrested in 2003 and has since been extradited to the United States.

Formerly members of Mexico's Army elite, a number of Zetas joined the drug cartels as hit men in the late 1990s. They were among the roughly 120,000 Mexican soldiers who deserted in that era. Mexican cartels now have a pool of military trained killers to draw from (Lloyd 2007). Among the more prominent Zetas was Heriberto Lazcano, a former member of the elite Special Forces. He was credited as among the first to work for the Gulf cartel as enforcers. Since 2006, Los Zetas have become so influential even their former handlers are incapable of controlling them. In recent years they have expanded their operations as they attempt to control drug routes and oust traditional cartel leaders (Corchado 2007). By most accounts, Los Zetas are now a managing partner for the Gulf cartel. In May 2009, the FBI warned law enforcement that the Zetas had formed a Texas cell on a secluded ranch where it trains hit men how to "neutralize" competitors in the United States. This has become increasingly necessary to collect debts and spy on competitors. Zetas are also used to protect cocaine and heroin shipments bound for Houston where drugs are repackaged and shipped to other states (Schiller 2009). They are also active in parts of Guatemala, where they are involved in aerial and overland drug trafficking (Meiners 2009).

Guadalajara Cartel [Amezcua-Contreras Organization]

Founded by the four Amezcua-Contreras brothers in the 1990s, the Guadalajara organization specializes in the illegal methamphetamine traffic. During the halcyon days of the 1990s, the brothers were dubbed "the kings of methamphetamine." At its zenith the cartel was probably the world's leading producer of that drug. It was able to accomplish this feat by securing huge quantities of precursor chemicals from India and Thailand. It was then distilled in laboratories on both sides of the Mexican-American border. Despite the arrests of the brothers in 1997, the networks continue to flourish. The meth business proved especially attractive to Mexican organizations. For years they had moved Colombian cocaine for only a percentage of the profits; with methamphetamine there was no sharing. So in effect they made the transition from middlemen to vertically controlling every aspect of the business, from production and distribution to sales (Owen 2007). Although the Tijuana and Juarez cartels tried to break into the market, the brothers became the most important because they were the first to grasp the commercial potential of the trade and were able to quickly adapt to the changing conditions of the marketplace, such as making the switch from ephedrine powder to pseudoephedrine pills (precursor chemicals). In 1995, Congress was finally convinced by the DEA to control ephedrine in order to disrupt the product of methamphetamine. The Amezcuas responded by switching to pills; and when this source was unavailable, they found new ones in Canada. What distinguished this group was its ability to get along with competing drug syndicates, as witnessed by its alliance with the Tijuana and Juarez cartels. Most observers trace the success and longevity of this organization to an insulated structure that recruited relatives, extended family members, and longtime friends (DEA 1998).

Mara Salvatrucha (MS-13) [Central America, Mexico, United States]

Gangs such as Mara Salvatrucha engage in transnational organized crime involving kidnapping, extortion, trafficking of people and contraband, and even assassinations. The success of these groups is in part blamed on the American policy of deporting gang members back to their countries of origin without notifying the receiving authorities. A number of transnational gangs originated in Los Angeles, organized by immigrants who fled Central America during the civil wars of the 1980s. Once exposed to gang life in urban America, they brought their knowledge of gang culture back to Central America. These international links have only helped foster gang culture throughout the region (USAID, April 2006). Today MS-13 has an estimated 30,000 to 50,000 members worldwide, with about 25 percent of them in the United States. It is unique among American gangs, as it is involved in drug trafficking through Central America and Mexico as well as the United States (Burton and West, 2009). Members have been known to work with Mexican Mafia members on both sides of the border.

Mara Salvatrucha, better known as MS-13, was named after *La Mara,* a street in El Salvador, as well as for the Salvatrucha guerrillas who fought in the country's bloody civil war in the early 1980s. It has been estimated that up to 100,000 people died in the conflict and that perhaps up to 1 million others fled to the United States (Vaquera and Bailey 2004). Many landed in southern California. Some were veterans who had served in the paramilitary Farabundo Marti National Liberation Front and were adept at using weaponry and explosives. Not long after moving into southern Los Angeles with its myriad gangs, the new immigrants organized their own gang for self-protection. Gang members are identifiable by the blue and white colors of their native flag, and many are heavily tattooed on their bodies and faces. MS-13 is no longer a purely southern California phenomenon. Investigators have traced members from coast to coast. Just as alarming, members have exported their criminal activities (and recruiting) back to Central America. For example, in 2004 Honduras was home to a reported 36,000 members (Domash 2005).

American law enforcement was in part complicit in the expansion of MS-13. During the 1990s a number of members were deported back to El Salvador, but their connections were not revealed. Once home they reconstituted the gang, with many returning to America. In 2005, the National Drug Intelligence Center of the U.S. Justice Department estimated there were between 8,000 and 10,000 members in the United States and more than 50,000 internationally (Harman 2005).

MS-13 made the transition from gang culture to transnational organized crime group in a rather short time as a result of its flexibility and mobility. Members are involved in a variety of criminal enterprises including car thefts, which are sometimes traded to Latin American drug cartels for drugs. Members have been connected to home invasion robberies, extortion, rapes, witness intimidation, and carjackings. Drug trafficking tends to include cocaine, marijuana, heroin, and methamphetamine. They have also moved into other rackets including the taxing of other gangs and even prostitutes.

The gang has flourished thanks to its mobility and ability to adapt to new law enforcement strategies. For example, when it feels the pressure in El Salvador or Honduras, it moves its operations into Mexico. To avoid detection, when gang members notice they are under surveillance, they respond by changing colors and other subterfuge.

Asian Organized Crime Groups

Triads [China]

Triads have been compared to decentralized cartels made up of independent gangs that assume similar organizational structures and rituals to unite their groups together (Chu 2005). What often confounds investigators is that not all Triad societies are Chinese criminal syndicates and not all Chinese organized crime members necessarily belong to a Triad. The term *Triad* is actually an English designation derived from the sacred emblem of the Society, consisting of a triangle, with each side representing the three basic powers of Heaven, Earth, and Man (Morgan 1960). Before the return of Hong Kong to China in 1997, Triads were often referred to as the *Sam Hop Wui* (Three United Association), *Tin Tei Wui* (Heaven and Earth Association), *Hung Mun* (Hung Sect), or more recently the *Hak Sh'e Wui* (Black Society Association).

The first Triad Society was founded in 1761. Better known as the "Heaven and Earth Society," it functioned more as a type of mutual aid group providing help in an unpredictable frontier region of China. The name Triad was not coined until 1821, alluding to the magic number 3, which, according to Chinese numerology, denoted the balance between Heaven, Earth, and Man (Gaylord and Fu 1999).

As mentioned previously, Triads are decentralized, lacking a central body capable of uniting all the groups or giving universally accepted commands. Triad structure has become increasingly flexible and decentralized over the years, and their initiation ceremonies have been simplified. Modern Triads have been able to operate quite freely by joining in alliances with high-ranking Chinese army members and Communist Party functionaries, allowing them to continue to operate gambling, protection, and prostitution rackets. The Chinese government has even used Triad member to silence critics and exiles. What's more they play an important role in suppressing the unpredictable activities of petty common criminals such as thieves and purse snatchers—both bad for business (Lintner 2005).

Between 1914 and 1939, almost 300 Triad societies were created in Hong Kong (Chu 2005). By 2005, about 50 still existed, 14 of whom were constantly on police radar including the Sun Yoo On, 14K Hau Group, 14K Tak Group, 14N Ngai Group, Wo Shing Wo, Wo Hop To, Wo On Lok (Shui Fong), and Luen Ying Sh'e (Chu 2005).

Chinese Triads became involved in global organized crime around 1917, when the British stopped importing opium into China, leaving an estimated 150 million Chinese craving a fix (McCoy 1992). Triads stepped in to fill the void, effectively passing on the opium trade from the British to the Chinese underworld. By the next decade Shanghai's drug syndicates were bringing in 10 tons of heroin from Japan and Europe each year. In the 1930s, the Japanese had established labs in northern China to produce large amounts of heroin. By most accounts, Mao-Tse-Tung was so outraged by the Triad drug trade when he came to power in 1949 that it was his main raison d'être for driving out the Triads in the 1950s. After the Communist victory, Chiang Kai-Shek and his followers and many Triad members fled to Hong Kong (under the British), Taiwan, and elsewhere. Mao consolidated his victory by executing or imprisoning many Triad members, but tens of thousands escaped.

Before the Communist victory over Chiang Kai-shek's nationalist forces in 1949, the Nationalist government secret police and Kuomintang (Nationalist Party) officers played a role in creating new Triads to be used against the rising tide of communism. This should not be surprising as Chiang Kai-shek was a longtime member of the Green Gang and a Triad member, with a background that included extortion, armed robbery, and art theft.

Most academics and law enforcement officials suspected that after Hong Kong was returned to mainland Chinese control in 1997, there would be a mass exodus of Triad members to Western countries. Recent scholarship has found otherwise, however; most surprisingly some members have had the temerity to enter Chinese markets (Chu 2005). Officials had expected 90,000 Chinese gangsters to flee Hong Kong. Instead "the reverse turned out to be true" (Lintner 2005, 85). Rather than hightail it for Australia, Canada, and the United States, all popular destinations for Chinese immigrants, Hong Kong Triads have entered into negotiations with new Chinese officials in the former British colony who allowed them to continue many of their rackets, albeit unofficially. At the same time Triads have made inroads on the mainland, lured by the country's transition from old socialist traditions to the fledgling market economy.

Triads are currently involved in a variety of activities in Hong Kong, including heavily investing in legitimate businesses such as bars, nightclubs, restaurants, dance clubs, and even the movie industry. At the beginning of the 1990s, the Hong Kong film industry was ranked third behind Hollywood and India's Bollywood. During this era Triads moved in for a piece of the action, coercing leading stars to act in their pictures. When peaceful overtures could not cajole the stars to participate, threats of violence followed. No less a star than martial arts actor Jackie Chan was ordered to participate in a film backed by the Wah Ching Triad, which is considered an American-Chinese organized crime group. When he demurred, citing his current obligation to the film *Cannonball Run II*, the film's main office in San Francisco was raked with gunfire. The Triad next tried to extort $4 million from Chan for the embarrassment he had caused the gang's leader. Upon Chan's return to Hong Kong, a 14K member came to collect the "debt." It is unknown whether this was ever paid (Dubro 1992; Booth 1999). Nonetheless the film industry has been a lucrative industry for the Triads. Related rackets include protection schemes targeting film props, exposing film, and forcing stars to buy security. They have even targeted foreign productions, demanding rent for filming on location and intimidating film crews and staff. Triads continue to try to monopolize emerging markets as well, including interior decoration and real estate sales.

Like other tradition-bound organized crime groups, the Triads have been going through a transition period. In times past a lengthy ceremony and initiation were required to join; new members are bound by oral agreements with their Big Brother (higher ranking member). Discipline has also become an issue, with Triads finding it increasingly difficult to enforce strict discipline over new members. In addition it is now easier for members to transfer from one Triad to another group. This breakdown in esprit de corps has had the unanticipated consequence of making the Big Brothers feel less obligated to look after their followers when they encounter problems (Chu 2005).

Big Circle Boys [China]

The Big Circle Boys is one of the newest examples of Chinese organized crime. Also recognized as the "Big Circle Gang" and "Dai Heun Jai," it is considered a "mainland (China) based Triad." It is distinct from other Triads because of its membership of mostly former Red Army guards who had served stints in Chinese prison camps. On maps these government camps are identified with a red circle, hence the name. Members are known for their brutality and knowledge of weaponry and favor activities such as heroin trafficking and jewelry store robberies. Although the Big Circle Boys is not technically a Triad, most of its members belong to various Triads. In recent years members have expanded their activities into Canada, the United States, and South America, where they have expanded into credit card fraud, counterfeiting, and trafficking in drugs and humans. In the new millennium membership was estimated to be close to 5,000, making it one of the more prominent examples of Chinese organized crime. One former member claimed to have molded a highly organized gang out of the group known as the Flaming Eagles, which was involved in international heroin trafficking and other crimes (Huston 1995).

The Green Gang [China]

Once an organization composed mostly of peasants and unskilled laborers, the Green Gang made the transition to a criminal organization at the end of the 19th century, specializing in drug trafficking, extortion rackets, and bribery. Unlike most of the other Triads historically linked to Hong Kong and Taiwan, the Green Gang developed in Shanghai, home to the Great Circle Triad, one of China's oldest and most powerful Triads. Shanghai's tremendous growth since the 1970s has facilitated the rise of the Great Circle Triad and other criminal organizations. Green Gang members are expected to take secret oaths and promise unwavering loyalty to the gang. Members recognize each other through a sequence of signals that also broadcast their position with the gang. Signals might include the way someone takes a cigarette out of a wrapper or how one uses an eating utensil. Any violation of the rules results in severe sanctions ranging from kneecapping and bone breaking to severing an ear or execution. According to one leading expert, the Green Gang is China's "first modern secret society" and should be considered the first Triad to become embroiled in the production and distribution of such modern narcotics as heroin and morphine (Lintner 2002, 54).

Tongs and Chinese Street Gangs [United States and Canada]

Tongs are considered the American incarnation of the Triads; however, one should not equate all tongs with criminal activity. Tong members are typically self-employed; there are tens of thousands of dues-paying members. The most common form of hierarchy includes in descending order a president, vice president, treasurer, auditor, several elders, and a public relations administrator (Chin, Kelly, and Fagan 1994). Only Tong officers and employees are allowed into the decision-making process. Elections for these positions are held annually or biannually. In any case the vast majority of Tong members are law abiding and legally employed as workers and merchants.

Historically, each Tong had an identifying name and membership exclusively composed of Chinese immigrants. Some were based on the region of China where they immigrated from; others were created around a particular job or trade, such as laundry Tongs, railway Tongs, and so forth. Not all Tongs operated in a single community; for example, the mineworkers Tong had members throughout the country.

Over time some Tongs expanded their activities to include criminal enterprises such as selling opium, prostitution, and making usurious loans to Chinese immigrants (a practice that was legal in China). Others paid protection to local police to protect gambling and opium dens. Tongs toed the line between the underworld and the upperworld (or legitimate world) as they observed their civic and legitimate duties in public while conducting rackets out of sight.

Similar to other criminal societies, over time various Tongs became involved in a variety of criminal enterprises including prostitution, loan sharking, drug dealing, and extortion. Tongs originated sometime in the mid-19th century, at a time when the first Chinese immigrants found work building railroads and mining gold in the American West. Chinese immigrants usually cloistered themselves in Chinatowns because of racism, discrimination, and the vagaries of immigration policy. Immigrants who were Triad members were quick to seize power in the nascent Chinatowns, forming what became known as Tongs, which literally translated to "lodges," "halls," or "meeting places." Early Tongs served as self-help organizations for Chinese newcomers, although law enforcement noticed early on their involvement in such criminal enterprises as illegal gambling, prostitution, extortion, and other crimes. In any case, Tong leaders would become local powerbrokers and mediators to the Chinese communities. New York City and San Francisco have the richest Tong traditions, dating back to the 19th century.

New York's Chinatown is the country's largest, and its most prominent Tong is the On Leong Tong (the country's first). The West Coast has a larger number of high-profile Tongs including the Hip Sing in San Francisco and the Ying On in Los Angeles. Both the Hop Sing and Suey Sing Tongs have Pacific Coast and East Coast offices.

A new wave of Chinese immigration reached American shores after the passage of the Immigration and Naturalization Act in 1965.

Among them were progenitors of the modern Chinese street gang phenomenon who would become inextricably linked to Tongs in the late 20th century. Despite their inherent legitimacy, Tong leaders have been linked to Chinese-American street gangs from at least the late 1960s. Tongs would have a difficult task controlling criminal activities without the assistance of Chinese street gangs. Many are hierarchically organized. With so many new immigrants, Tongs recruit from a ready supply of street criminals. Tong bosses usually select an individual tasked with coordinating the activities of the Tongs with the street gangs. The *Dai Dai Lo,* or "Big Brother," serves as a buffer between the Tong bosses and the street criminals, effectively insulating them from direct involvement in criminal activity. Among the more prominent street gangs are Ghost Shadows, the Flying Dragons, and others, each with its own codes of behavior and loyalty oaths. More often than not these gangs are ephemeral in nature, each disappearing or being subsumed by other gangs once they have fulfilled their usefulness. Once the street gangs were decimated by informants, killings, and arrests, they were deemed superfluous.

Once just a coastal big city phenomenon, Tongs and Chinese street gangs expanded throughout mostly urban America as cities such as Houston, Boston, and Chicago and others became more diversified with flourishing Asian communities.

In 1966, the Wah Ching street gang emerged and soon dominated the rackets in the Chinatowns of New York City, Los Angeles, and San Francisco. In 1989, they were severely tested by the arrival of Wo Hop To Triad members from Hong Kong. Subsequently both groups made concessions, consolidated their power, and emerged as a powerful criminal enterprise. Tongs and Chinese gangs have combined forces in the United States to control various Chinatown rackets including gambling parlors, promoting prostitution, human and drug smuggling, and protection rackets, with human smuggling still among their most lucrative activities.

Yakuza [Japan]

Recent scholarship traces the origins of the Japanese Yakuza to the late 1700s (Hill 2005). The Yakuza of the 21st century is a product of two distinct traditions, embracing both gamblers (*bakuto*) and traveling peddlers and stall keepers (*tekiya*). Both groups were suppressed during the Tokugawa era (1600–1867). Both of these terms are still occasionally used to describe Yakuza members. After

World War II a third group was added to the mix called gangsters, or *gurentai*. All three of these groups emerged from similar backgrounds, typically coming from the poor dispossessed classes, delinquents, and misfits. The etymology of the word *Yakuza* refers to a losing hand of cards, hence its traditional association with gambling rackets. The term was borrowed to also indicate a worthless person, a loser, or an outcast. Members seem to relish their image as societal rejects much in the way outlaw motorcycle gangs such as Hells Angels bask in a similar reputation.

After Japan's defeat in World War II, Yakuza members earned a degree of acceptance and respect in Japanese culture. Most carried business cards and even rented office space and did little to hide their affiliation. As the economy recovered in the 1950s, crime syndicates focused on the new opportunities offered by the increasing number of new clubs, bars, restaurants, and sexually oriented businesses. The Yakuza flourished thanks to alliances with politicians at all levels of government, inadequate policing, and fear of extreme left-wing activity by students and labor groups. The government knew it could count on the vehemently anticommunist gangsters to suppress radical activities when called on. Yakuza membership peaked at 180,000 in 1963 before declining to 120,000 by the end of the decade (Hill 2005). During the 1970s, larger Yakuza groups expanded their operations after a crackdown on gambling rackets, moving into the methamphetamine trade. Since the 1970s, Yakuza activities have run the gamut from corporate extortion, gambling, and loan sharking to prostitution, international sex tours, money laundering, stock manipulation, and pornography. Although they operate throughout Japan, the most powerful are located in Tokyo, Kyoto, and Kobe.

In the early 1990s, the Yakuza was targeted by the government with the passage of the Act for Prevention of Unlawful Activities by Boryokudan Members (1992). Since then they have lost much of their prestige and respect as a Japanese institution.

Today there are roughly 22 Yakuza crime syndicates, with 85,000 members (Onishi 2008). The Yakuza has traditionally managed protection, gambling, and sexually oriented rackets. Authorities have typically left them alone because they viewed these businesses as a necessary part of society. By allowing the Yakuza to operate openly, they believed they could keep them under surveillance. The Yakuza's position in Japanese society has taken a number of hits in recent years. Just several years ago it would have seemed unthinkable to take the Yakuza to court. But in 2008, one neighborhood had wearied of the local Donjinkai Yakuza, who were situated in a six-story office building in a central commercial area of Kurume, Japan. Concerned over factional warfare in the area that began in 2006 and had left several dead, 600 residents brought a court action against the syndicate. Although residents and the Donjinkai had coexisted there since 1986, recent events led a group of residents to demand the removal of their headquarters from their neighborhood (Onishi 2008).

The Yakuza has a fairly complex hierarchy, with most groups organized into paternalistic "families" based on the *oyabun-kobun*, or parent-child relationship. The *oyabun* or father figure is the supreme boss who offers advice and mentors and protects gang members in a paternalistic relationship that treats his minions like his children. Every new member is expected to accept this relationship. Until the mid-1980s, it was common for 5,000 youths to join each year, about the same number that drop out each year (Jameson 1985). In recent years standards for membership have been lowered to fill the ranks. Where in times past they could depend on a ready supply of prime recruits, today's members are drawn from motorcycle riding hoodlums or street tribes known as *bosozoku*. In fact in the modern era, it has become routine for the Japanese Police Agency to make less of a distinction between Yakuza and other crime syndicates, preferring to regard them all generically as the violent ones, or *Boryokudan* (Hill 2003).

Yakuza members first appeared in America in the early 1900s when a major Japanese drug distribution network began selling opium-based products and amphetamines to California crime syndicates. In recent years they are most likely to be found in Hawaii where they have established links with local crime syndicates, partnering activities including weapons and drug trafficking and pornography (usually smuggled from America to Japan). Hawaii serves as the main American destination in no small part because of the large number of Asian tourists and immigrants they can blend in with.

Yamaguchi-gumi [Yakuza gang]

Kobe is home to the Yamaguchi-gumi, the country's largest Yakuza gang. Formed in the early 1900s out of syndicates that organized labor on the city's docks, members are recognizable by diamond-shaped badges that in gangland circles were regarded as signs of prestige. The badge is emblazoned with the Japanese characters *yama* (mountain) and *guchi* (mouth). By the early 1980s, the

Yamaguchi-gumi controlled close to 2,500 businesses, earning $500 million each year (Lunde 2004). It flourished in no small part because of its political connections and willingness to innovate and diversify. The gang received its best publicity after the 1995 Kobe earthquake by offering relief to city residents before the government stepped in. In the 1990s, the organization expanded into Tokyo despite an agreement by its most powerful adversary, the Inagawa-Kai, not to do so. To get around the proviso of not opening offices there, Yamaguchi-gumi members opened up legitimate businesses as fronts and operated without an official gang headquarters. By 2002, the number of members in formerly sacrosanct Tokyo had doubled. Favored activities included loan sharking and real estate and construction rackets.

Membership estimates range as high as 40,000 today, but numbers are probably much lower (Neill 2009).

Organized Crime Groups in Other Regions

Jamaican Posses [Caribbean, United Kingdom, United States]

Jamaican gangs adopted the name "posse" as a result of the influence of the American Western genre popular in the 1950s and 1960s. They would eventually thrive in the rampant poverty of the capital city of Kingston. Most were based on neighborhood boundaries and political affiliations. In the 1960s and 1970s, politicians recruited armed gangs to get out the vote and enforce party loyalty, and over time they made the transition from simply street gangs to crime syndicates. By the 1980s, posses emerged in the United States (and as Yardies in Great Britain). When the ruling parties could not afford to fund the gangs in the 1980s, they turned to the drug trade and other organized crime activities. According to one estimate, there were 10,000 posse members in the United States in the 1990s, representing 40 different gangs (Valentine 1995). The majority were located in urban centers. In most cases they adopted the names of their hometowns. The Jungle Posse and the Jungle Lites Posse, for example, originated in a Jamaican township known as the Jungle, where they were known as *Junglelites*. In 1989, some non-Jamaican gangs began adopting the *posse* moniker. In response some of the real posses began referring to themselves as *massives* instead.

The first inkling of the Jamaican posses in America began in the early 1970s when a group was identified dealing marijuana in Kansas City. By the next decade posses were fighting indigenous American gangs over the drug trade in South Florida. Before long they were well established in the United States, and they began migrating from bases in Brooklyn and Miami to smaller cities, where they played an important role in the spreading crack cocaine trade. The two largest groups were the Shower and Spangler Posses. Few organized crime groups had such a well-earned reputation for violence as the posses in their heyday.

The posses' connection with the crack epidemic of the 1980s has been well documented. During his 1986 trial, former Gambino family boss John Gotti claimed that one posse leader was "one of the first drug dealers to introduce crack to the streets of New York" (Gunst 1995, 160). The posses operated out of a vertical structure that allowed them to control the sale of crack from its manufacture to its distribution, allowing for a higher profit margin. One gang specialist suggested that one posse managing 50 crack houses could expect a profit of $9 million per month (Valentine 1995). Some of the gangs were vertically structured, which allowed for more flexibility in controlling costs, some were "multilayered," and still others were structured based on family and kinship ties.

Jamaican posses are known for their reverence for high-powered weapons. Some observers have gone as far as suggesting the roots of their gang activity in the United States coincided with earning money to buy weapons to control their neighborhoods back in Jamaica. Weapons are rarely acquired legally. Posses acquired guns by home invasion robberies, raiding gun shops, breaking into armories, and hijacking vehicles carrying weapons. Attempts to acquire them through subterfuge include having a member set up a residence and acquiring required documentation in states where residence requirements are less than 90 days. This short-term residency allows the member to purchase weapons that can be transported to others states and sold for a substantial profit. There is still considerable debate as to whether posses should be considered organized crime groups or glorified street gangs. Although some would argue that posses are locally organized syndicates with affiliations that allow them to expand their trafficking networks, others suggest that unlike organized crime groups, posses typically operate independently of each other and are less cooperative with their counterparts than traditional organized crime families.

Nigerian Gangs [Africa]

Nigerian gangs have been reported in 80 different countries (Liddick 2004). These gangs are distinct for their ability to adapt to the conditions they find in any country. Congressional Hearings on Intelligence and Security reported they launder money in Asia, purchase cocaine in South America, and direct prostitution and gambling rings in Spain and Italy. As the so-called African Connection, Nigeria emerged as a leading transshipment point for Southeast heroin going to the United States and Europe in the 1990s. In the late 1990s, the New Jersey State Commission of Investigation announced Nigerian complicity in the international heroin trade. The investigation revealed a structure that included a "God Father" who directs six smugglers (mules), who transport money and drugs into Nigeria from abroad. Usually the operation begins with a juvenile or woman being sent to a "Black Magic House" for instructions on swallowing heroin sealed in condoms. Authorities learned that the Nigerians received most of their heroin from Southeast Asia; indeed three of every five couriers arrested in Thailand for heroin smuggling were Nigerian nationals. In the opening years of the 21st century, the DEA regarded Nigeria as Africa's most important transshipment point (Naim 2005). Demonstrating the global magnitude of Nigeria's involvement, the country's heroin processing labs were handling opium brought in from Afghanistan and Myanmar (which also transited through Pakistan, Uzbekistan, Thailand, or China).

Nigerian crime syndicates appear in a variety of incarnations, with most preferring a modicum of organization that might include a leader at the top with lieutenants acting under him; in most cases the actors are affiliated with government agencies or officials. But unlike the traditional monolithic structure of organized crime, some authorities claim Nigerian gangs more closely resemble "cell-like syndicates," of three to five core individuals (Nicaso and Lamothe 2005). Others, however, have identified well-organized structures resembling an "old fashioned pyramid of hierarchy" connected with criminal operations around the world (United Nations 2005). In any case, as a result of weak money laundering laws and crime bosses who often operate with the tacit approval of high-ranking officials, Nigeria remains among the major players in global organized crime networks.

Since the 1990s, Nigerian criminals have become identified with "419" frauds, or advance fee fraud. The "419" refers to a particular Nigerian criminal statute—Nigerian Decree 419, which made the fraud illegal in 1980 (Robinson 2000). According to the U.S. Secret Service and the State Department, this scam nets hundreds of millions of dollars each year. Nigerian fraudsters conduct extensive research before selecting targets to scam, and almost anyone with a fax or e-mail can be victimized. The scam is usually introduced through a communication purported to be from some high-ranking official or luminary who wants to share a fortune with the victim, but characteristically requires that he turn over a bank address/fax/telex number, bank account number, and other information. To show good faith, the mark is expected to send an advance payment to guarantee what is really a fictitious money transfer. In cases where the response is positive, once the victim sends money, communication is typically cut off. Individuals in more than 60 countries have been victimized in this way. Until 2006, the United States was considered the most lucrative market, with losses approaching $800 million (Chaudhuri 2007). Most of the frauds originate in Nigeria, the Netherlands, the United Kingdom, or South Africa. More recently, India has become the third fastest-growing market for the fraud. In 2006, victims lost $32 million (Chaudhuri 2007). The United Kingdom comes in second at $530 million in losses.

Hells Angels [United States, Western Europe, Canada, Australia]

In 1983, the U.S. Congress held hearings on organized crime. Most of the focus was on organized drug trafficking. What made these hearings such a landmark was that the focus had shifted from traditional Italian American organized crime groups such as La Cosa Nostra to the growing clout of outlaw motorcycle gangs (OMGs), prison gangs, and street gangs. When it came to international organized crime, none of these was as prominent as Hells Angels. This gang is among a handful of other gangs that have developed international connections that give them access to wholesale quantities of narcotics. One 2004 case exemplified the international nature of the Hells Angels. In this incident four members of the Dutch Hells Angels were killed after the theft of $11 million in cocaine. The subsequent investigation revealed international ties to Colombian drug dealers. In this case the drugs had been shipped from the Revolutionary Armed Forces of Colombia to Amsterdam via a new chapter on the Caribbean island of Curacao (Marsden and Sher 2006).

The two decades after the return of servicemen from World War II are considered the formative years of what would later become outlaw motorcycle gangs. Between 1947 and 1967, major motorcycle clubs absorbed smaller ones or pushed them aside, and formal structures were put into place. In the 1960s and 1970s, the OMGs, especially Hells Angels, began unprecedented expansion, much of it stimulated by the growing drug trade. It was this era that saw its members make the transition from mostly drug abusers to major traffickers. What makes these gangs so unique in the world of organized crime is their penchant for flaunting their colors and other links to their criminality. They share with more established syndicates most of the traditional characteristics including operating legitimate businesses as fronts for money laundering, a structured hierarchy, drugs and weapons trafficking, sophistication, secret rules and restricted membership, and others.

In 2006, Canada's Criminal Intelligence Service described the Hells Angels as the "foremost organized crime group in the country, topping traditional Mafia and ethnic gangs" (CBC 2006, 2). With 32 active chapters and 500 full members, the Angels are more prominent in Canada than in the United States (CBC 2006; Marsden and Sher 2006). The largest and most prominent chapter was established in Montreal in 1977. In recent years the Angels' influence in Canada has been growing in British Columbia and Ontario through its ties with Italian organized crime groups; likewise it shows signs of diminishing in Quebec and Atlantic Canada.

Many organized crime observers have commented on the organizational similarities between traditional organized crime and the Angels. Hierarchically, the Angels have a Chapter President equivalent to a mafia boss and in descending order the equivalent positions of both respectively include Secretary/Consigliere, Vice President/Underboss, Sergeant of Arms/Caporegima, and members/soldiers.

If any event demonstrated the transnational reach of the Hells Angels and other OMGs it was the so-called Great Nordic OMG War between 1994 and 1997, when the Angels fought the rival

Bandidos over supremacy of Denmark. During this conflict the gangs were involved in hundreds of violent incidents leaving 11 dead and at least 100 wounded. Experts on OMGs have been unable to explain why this country has the highest concentration of them in Europe (Marsden and Sher 2006). Nonetheless, between 1998 and 2005, both organizations doubled in size.

References

Althaus, Dudley. 2008, January 22. "Alleged Leader of Powerful Mexican Drug Cartel Nabbed." *Houston Chronicle:* A12.

Althaus, Dudley. 2009, May 1. "Mexican Drug War Not Slowed by Flu Fight." *Houston Chronicle:* A16.

Arlacchi, Pino. 1993. *Men of Dishonor: Inside the Sicilian Mafia.* New York: William Morrow.

Bogan, Jesse. 2009, March 30. "Cocaine King." *Forbes*, http://www.forbes.com/forbes/2009/0330/102-cocaine-king.html.

Booth, Martin. 1999. *The Dragon Syndicates: The Global Phenomenon of the Triads.* New York: Carroll and Graff.

Burton, Fred, and Ben West. 2009, April 15. "When the Mexican Drug Trade Hits the Border." *STRAFOR*, www.stratfor.com.

CBC News Online. 2006, April 10. "Biker Gangs in Canada." Available at http://www.cbc.ca/news/background/bikergangs.

Chaudhuri, Pramit Pal. 2007, March 9. "U.S. to Find Means to Stop Spread of 419 Fraud." *Hindustan Times*, http://home.rica.net/alphae/419coal/news2007.htm.

Chin, Ko-lin, Robert J. Kelly, and Jeffrey Fagan. 1994. "Chinese Organized Crime in America." In *Handbook of Organized Crime in the United States*, ed. Robert J. Kelly, Ko-lin Chin, and Rufus Schatzberg, 213–244. Westport, CT: Greenwood Press.

Chu, Yiu Kong. 2005, Spring. "Hong Kong Triads after 1997." *Trends in Organized Crime* 8 (3): 5–12.

Corchado, Alfredo. 2007, June 11. "Cartel's Enforcers Outpower Their Boss." *Dallas Morning News*, http://www.dallasnews.com/sharedcontent/dws/news/world/stories/o61107dnintzetas.3a36.

Dash, Mike. 2009. *The First Family: Terror, Extortion and the Birth of the American Mafia.* London: Simon and Schuster.

Domash, Shelly Feuer. 2005. "America's Most Dangerous Gang." *Police Magazine*, http://policemag.com/Articles/2005/02/America-s-Most-Dangerous-Gang.aspx.

Drug Enforcement Administration (DEA). 1998, June 2. "DEA Confirms Arrest by Mexican Authorities of Amezcua-Contreras Brothers." Press Release. Available at http://www.fas.org/irp/agency/doa/dea/product/pr980602.

Dubro, James. 1992. *Dragons of Crime: Inside the Asian Underworld.* Ottawa, Ontario: Octopus Publishing.

Dunn, Guy. 1997. "Major Mafia Gangs in Russia." In *Russian Organized Crime: The New Threat?*, ed. Phil Williams, 63–87. London: Frank Cass.

English, T. J. 2005. *Paddy Whacked: The Untold Story of the Irish American Gangster.* New York: Regan Books.

Follain, John. 2008. *The Last Godfathers: The Rise and Fall of the Mafia's Most Powerful Family.* London: Hodder and Stoughton.

Friedman, Robert I. 2000. *Red Mafiya: How the Russian Mob Has Invaded America.* New York: Little, Brown.

Galeotti, Mark, ed. 2005. *Global Crime Today: The Changing Face of Organized Crime.* London: Routledge.

Gaylord, Mark S., and Hualing Fu. 1999. "Economic Reform and 'Black Society': The Re-Emergence of Organized Crime in Post-Mao China." In *Organized Crime: Uncertainties and Dilemmas,* ed. S. Einstein and M. Amir, 119–134. Chicago: Office of International Criminal Justice.

Gunst, Laurie. 1995. *Born Fi' Dead: A Journey Through the Jamaican Posse Underworld.* New York: Henry Holt.

Harman, Danna. 2005, February 24. "U.S. Steps up Battle against Salvadoran Gang MS-13." *USA TODAY:* 4A.

Hawley, Chris. 2009, February 23. "On the Border, a Crisis Escalates." *USA Today:* 1A, 2A.

Hays, Tom. 2008, February 8. "N.Y. Raids New Dozens of Accused Mobsters." *Houston Chronicle:* A3.

Hill, Peter B. E. 2003. *The Japanese Mafia: Yakuza, Law, and the State.* New York: Oxford University Press.

Hill, Peter B. E. 2005. "The Changing Face of the Yakuza." In *Global Crime Today,* ed. Mark Galeotti, 97–116. London: Routledge.

Huston, Peter. 1995. *Tongs, Gangs, and Triads: Chinese Groups in North America.* Boulder, CO: Paladin Press.

Inciardi, James A. 1992. *The War on Drugs II.* Mountain View, CA: Mayfield.

Jameson, Sam. 1985, May 20. "Japan Gangs Not Really Underworld." *Los Angeles Times:* A1, A10.

Jonnes, Jill. 1999. *Hep-Cats, Narcs, and Pipe Dreams: A History of America's Romance with Illegal Drugs.* Baltimore: Johns Hopkins Press.

Kaplan, David E. 2006, September 8. "Ba-Da-Bing: Return of the Mafia's Pizza Connection." Available at http://www.usnews.com/usnews/news/badguys/060908/badabing_return_of_the_mafias.htm?s_cid=rss:site1.

Landler, Mark, and Ian Fisher. 2007, August 16. "German Police Link 6 Dead Men to an Italian Mob Feud." *New York Times,* http://www.nytimes.com/2007/08/16/world/europe/16italians.html.

Liddick, Donald Jr. 2004. *The Global Underworld: Transnational Crime and the United States.* Westport, CT: Praeger.

Lintner, Bertil. 2002. *Blood Brothers: The Criminal Underworld of Asia.* New York: Palgrave Macmillan.

Lintner, Bertil. 2005. "Chinese Organized Crime." In *Global Crime Today,* ed. Mark Galeotti, 84–96. London: Routledge.

Lloyd, Marion. 2007, June 18. "New Fear in Mexico: Soldiers Fleeing for Cartels." *Houston Chronicle:* A1, A9.

Lloyd, Marion, and Cindy George. 2007, January 23. "Alleged Mexican Kingpins in Court." *Houston Chronicle:* A1, A8.

Longrigg, Clare. 2009. *Boss of Bosses: How One Man Saved the Sicilian Mafia.* London: John Murray.

Lunde, Paul. 2004. *Organized Crime: An Inside Guide to the World's Most Successful Industry.* New York: DK Publishing.

Maran, A.G.D. 2009. *Mafia, Inside the Dark Heart.* Edinburgh: Mainstream Publishing.

Marsden, William, and Julian Sher. 2006. *Angels of Death: Inside the Bikers' Global Crime Empire.* London: Houghton and Stodder.

McCoy, Alfred W. 1992. *The Politics of Heroin in Southeast Asia.* New York: Harper and Row.

Meiners, Stephen. 2009, March 28. "Central America: An Emerging Role in the Drug Trade." *STRATFOR,* http://www.stratfor.com/weekly/200090326_central_america_emerging_role_drug_trade.

Morgan, W. P. 1960. *Triad Societies in Hong Kong.* Hong Kong: Government Press.

Naim, Moises. 2005. *Illicit: How Smugglers, Traffickers, and Copycats are Hijacking the Global Economy.* New York: Anchor Books.

National Drug Intelligence Center. 2009. *National Drug Threat Assessment.* Washington, D.C.: U.S. Department of Justice.

Neill, David. 2009, April 10. "Gangster Boss Who Turned to God." *The Independent World,* http://www.independent.co.uk/news/world/asia/gangster-boss-who-turned-to-god-1666851.html.

New York Times. "Italy: Calabria Mob on the Rise." 2008, February 22.

Nicaso, Antonio, and Lee Lamothe. 2005. *Angels, Mobsters & Narco-Terrorists: The Rising Menace of Global Criminal Empires.* Toronto, Ontario: John Wiley and Sons Canada.

Onishi, Norimitsu. 2008, November 16. "Neighborhood in Japan Files Lawsuit in Bid to Oust Mafia." *International New York Times:* 14.

Owen, Frank. 2007. *No Speed Limit: The Highs and Lows of Meth.* New York: St. Martin's Press.

Paoli, Letizia. 2003. *Mafia Brotherhoods: Organized Crime, Italian Style.* New York: Oxford University Press.

Phillipp, Joshua. 2008, October 22. "Chinese Associations and Chinese Gangs." *Epoch Times,* http://www.theepochtimes.com/n2/content/view/6053.

Rashbaum, William K. 2008, February 8. "Dozens Held as Mob Case Links Gambinos to 3 Decades of Crime." *New York Times:* A1, A15.

Reuters. 2009, April 2. "Mexico Catches Senior Drug Baron from Juarez Cartel." Available at http://www.reuters.com/articlePrint?articleID=USTRE53154G20090402.

Robinson, Jeffrey. 2000. *The Merger: The Conglomeration of International Organized Crime.* New York: Overlook Press.

Saviano, Roberto. 2007. *Gomorrah: A Personal Journey Into the Violent International Empire of Naples' Organized Crime.* New York: Farrar, Straus and Giroux.

Schiller, Dane. 2009, May 20. "Cartel's Texas Cell Has Its Own Ranch," FBI Says." *Houston Chronicle:* A1, A15.

Serio, Joseph D. 2008. *Investigating the Russian Mafia.* Durham NC: Carolina Academic Press.

Smith, Denis Mack. 1995, November 30. "The Ruling Class." *New York Times Book Review,* 7.

Stille, Alexander. 1995. *Excellent Cadavers: The Mafia and the Death of the First Italian Republic.* New York: Random House.

United Nations Office on Drugs and Crime, Vienna. 2005. *Transnational Organized Crime in the West African Region.* New York: United Nations.

USAID Bureau for Latin American and Caribbean Affairs Office of Regional Sustainable Development. 2006, April. *Central America and Mexico Gang Assessment.* Available at http://www.usaid.gov/locations/latin_america_caribbean/democracy/gangs_cam.pdf.

Valentine, Bill. 1995. *Gang Intelligence Manual: Identifying and Understanding Modern-Day Violent Gangs in the United States.* Boulder, CO: Paladin Press.

Vaquera, Tony, and David W. Bailey. 2004, November–December. "Latin Gang in the Americas: Los Maras Salvatrucha." *Crime and Justice International:* 4–10.

Varese, Federico. 2001. *The Russian Mafia: Private Protection in a New Market Economy.* Oxford, UK: Oxford University Press.

Varese, Federico. 2006. "How Mafias Migrate: The Case of the 'Ndrangheta in Northern Italy." *Law and Society Review* 40 (2): 411–444.

Wallace-Wells, Ben. 2007, December 13. "How America Lost the War on Drugs." *Rolling Stone,* 91–119.

Wright, Alan. 2006. *Organised Crime.* Devon: UK: Willan Publishing.

4

Chronology

Second millennium BC	Earliest documented pirates are the Phoenicians.
1500 BC	Early Assyrian tablet inscriptions suggest that chariot racing was already an established sport.
1304	England creates Trailbaston commissions to suppress escalating organized crime activities in the rural localities.
1611	Poulterers' Case lays the foundation for modern conspiracy laws that have been so effective at targeting organized crime activity.
1644	Modern Triad societies trace their lineage to 1644 after the Chinese Ming Dynasty loses its battle to keep Manchurian invaders from taking over the Ming Dynasty. The Manchus (Ch'ing Dynasty) rule China for the next 268 years.
1650– 1725	This period is the "Golden Age" of piracy on the high seas.
1661	English Navigation Acts create opportunities for pirates in colonial America.
1682– 1725	During the reign of Peter the Great a vast network of Russian prison camps is created. Hardened criminals band together here.

English gangster Jonathan Wild rises to crime boss prominence as the London underworld's "thief taker general." As the city's leading thief taker, or bounty hunter, thief takers ply the thin line between crime and criminality. Thief takers are often powerful criminals who are protected from prosecution through bribes and graft. In a time before professional police officers, they act as the middlemen between thieves and victims. While Wild helps breakup competing gangs for rewards, he runs his own stable of thieves on the side. He is convicted of thief taking and hanged in 1725.

1735 The term *Camorra* first appears in print in reference to gambling dens in Naples where a game called *morra* is supervised by *capos*.

1773 The British East India Company gains control of India's Bengal opium fields.

1803 German pharmacist isolates the opium alkaloid, which he calls morphine.

1807 Great Britain criminalizes trade in slaves.

1812 End of feudalism in Sicily by order of King Ferdinand leads to emergence of absentee landlords called *gabelloti*.

1821 The term *triad* is first coined, referring to the magic number 3, which in Chinese numerology denotes the balance between Heaven-Earth-Man.

1834 Great Britain abolishes slavery in all of its colonies.

1839 Chinese Emperor's high commissioner confiscates and destroys a large cache of opium, setting off what becomes known as the Opium War the next year.

1855 Cocaine is first extracted from coca leaves.

1860s The word *mafia* is first found in Italian dictionaries.

1868 The first recorded instance of drug smuggling in the United States is reported after a Chinese merchant is arrested for smuggling opium for his opium den in Manhattan's Chinatown.

1870   More than 70,000 Chinese live in the United States, mostly on the West Coast. San Francisco becomes home to America's largest Chinatown and to early Chinese organized crime activity.

1874   Heroin is refined from opium.

1875   San Francisco passes the first antinarcotics legislation in the United States.

1878   Italian government crack down on Sicilian Mafia marks the beginning of the exodus of Sicilian mafiosi to the United States.

1880   New York's Chinatown has 700 residents.

1880s   Cuban immigrants introduce *bolita*, Spanish for "little ball," to the Tampa area of Florida.

A Select Committee in South Africa is appointed to investigate the illegal diamond trade, resulting in the Diamond Trade Act in 1882, which is geared toward suppressing this illicit trade.

1882   Chinese Exclusion Act is passed in the United States. This is the first federal legislation targeting a specific nationality or ethnic group. It is supported in part because of the association of the Chinese with the growing opium problem.

1890   According to some sources, this year is the first time the word *mafia* is printed in a foreign newspaper in the *Times of London* in connection with the murder of New Orleans police chief David Hennessey.

According to national census, Italians make up more than one-tenth of the population of New Orleans. By most accounts, during this period the first major mafia family in the New World is established in New Orleans.

1898   China leases Hong Kong and the New Territories to Great Britain for 99 years.

1899   New York City's first Tong War breaks out over the control of gambling rackets in Chinatown.

1905   New York City detective Giuseppe "Joe" Petrosino forms nation's first bomb squad and the elite "Italian branch" investigating Sicilian-America criminals.

1909   Passage of the Opium Exclusion Act opens up new opportunities for syndicated crime in the United States.

Joe Petrosino is murdered in the garden of Palermo's Piazza Marina, the only NYPD officer killed in the line of duty in another country.

1910   In 30 years, New York's Chinese population rises from 700 to more than 10,000. The rise in population is accompanied by the growing influence of Tongs and Chinese organized crime in New York's Chinatown.

1911–
1912   International Opium Conference is held at The Hague.

1914   America's Harrison Narcotic Act criminalizes the nonmedical use of opium, morphine, and coca leaf derivatives.

1919   Methamphetamine is first synthesized by a Japanese chemist.

On January 16, the 18th Amendment to the U.S. Constitution is ratified, prohibiting the manufacture, sale, import, or export of intoxicating beverages in the United States. On October 27, Congress passes the Volstead Act to enforce the amendment, beginning 13 years of alcohol prohibition.

1920   On January 16, 1920, Prohibition officially begins.

Great Britain passes the Dangerous Drugs Act, prohibiting the use of cocaine, morphine, opium, codeine, hashish, and barbiturates for nonmedical purposes.

1920s   West African immigrants introduce the *numbers* game to Harlem, New York.

1922   Mussolini comes to power, chasing many mafiosi overseas until 1943.

1923   The International Criminal Police Organization, or Interpol, is founded in Vienna.

1924   On a visit to Sicily, Mussolini is humiliated by the local Mafia establishment. While visiting the small town of Piana degli Albanesi (formerly Piana dei Greci), the dictator is chided by the town's Mafioso mayor, who teases Mussolini, who is traveling with a coterie of motorized guards. "There is no need for so many police. Your Excellency has nothing to fear in the district when you are with me." Mussolini is no doubt infuriated by the inference that he is not in total control of the island. Later that year he installs Cesare Mori, formerly police prefect of Bologna, as prefect of Palermo. Tasked with purging the government of all Mafia-connected bureaucrats, Mori suspends most legal protections on the island to purge the island of the Mafia. Hundreds of young Mafiosi leave the island for America. Among them are the young Carlo Gambino and Joseph Bonanno, who will make their marks in the future development of the American Mafia.

1928   Great Britain criminalizes the use of cannabis.

1929   Chicago's St. Valentine's Day Massacre makes Al Capone a household name, marking the beginning of the end for the mob boss. It also advances the movement to repeal Prohibition.

1929–
1931   The National Commission on Law Observance and Enforcement under the direction of George Wickersham conducts the first federal attempt to study organized crime in the United States.

1930   Congress establishes Federal Bureau of Narcotics, the forerunner of the modern Drug Enforcement Administration (1973).

1931   Murders of New York's Sicilian crime bosses Salvatore Maranzano and Joe Masseria set the stage for the "Americanization" of the Mafia in the United States.

Nevada becomes first state to legalize most forms of licensed gambling.

1931 *(cont.)*	Capone pleads guilty to tax evasion and is sentenced to 11 years in prison, effectively removing him from the free world of organized crime after a rather brief period as Chicago mob boss.
1933	Looking for the next big opportunity, Meyer Lansky reports that Havana, Cuba, is becoming a tourist hotspot and that the Cuban dictator Fulgencio Batista would be a compliant partner.
	Prohibition is repealed by the 21st Amendment on December 5.
1937	The United States criminalizes marijuana with the Marijuana Tax Act.
1938	Interpol is disbanded.
1943	The Allies invade Sicily. Role of the Mafia in these events is still debated but unclear.
	The Christian Democratic Party emerges in Italy. By 1948, it is in clear control of the government, thanks in no small part to the votes from Mafia-dominated areas. In the aftermath of this vote, Communist Party members are prohibited from holding office. Thanks to its support of the Christian Democrats, a new urban Mafia emerges. No faction is more powerful than the Corleone Mafia, which takes over many of Palermo's rackets.
1944	On March 2, Louis "Lepke" Buchalter becomes the first major gang boss to be executed in the United States.
1945–1953	The "Vor Wars" or "Bitches War" in Russia pits various prison criminal factions against each other. By its end, only the most hardcore have survived.
1946	Interpol is resuscitated after World War II.
	Benjamin "Bugsy" Siegel opens the Flamingo Hotel and casino in Las Vegas. Although he is not the first to

open such an establishment here, he is credited with bringing organized crime into the Las Vegas gambling rackets.

Charles "Lucky" Luciano is deported to Italy from the United States.

1948   Hells Angels are established in San Bernardino, California.

1949   Communists take over China from the Nationalists, forcing the Triad-connected Chiang Kai-shek to move his operations from the mainland.

1950–   The Kefauver Hearings, held in more than 14 U.S. cit-
1951   ies, "establishes" organized crime as an Italian phenomenon synonymous with the Mafia rather than a product of the American system.

1956   Interpol adopts its formal name and is now located in Lyons, France.

1957   The Grand Hotel des Palmes meeting in Palermo on October 12 lays the groundwork for the international drug trade, especially heroin. More important, the Sicilian Mafia sets up a 12-member commission known as the Cupola, containing the leaders of the Mafia families most interested in the new international drug trade.

On November 14, New York State police officer Edgar Croswell discovers the meeting of organized crime kingpins in rural upstate New York at a home in Apalachin, New York. This is a turning point in the American war on organized crime. FBI Director J. Edgar Hoover had previously denied the existence of organized crime in the United States. The sensational reports about the meeting force him to finally enter the fray, beginning a campaign of wiretapping and electronic surveillance that sees few victories until the 1980s.

Mexican Mafia is organized by Hispanic inmates in Tracy, California.

1959   On January 1, Castro's revolutionary army topples dictator Fulgencio Batista. Among the groups hit hardest by the change in administration are the American syndicates that controlled a gambling empire in Cuba, thanks to the collusion of the Cuban government. With the ascendance of Castro and the Cuban revolution, most of those connected to organized crime rackets leave the island.

Outlaw motorcycle gang, The Outlaws, is founded in Joliet, Illinois.

1960s   Establishment of military dictatorships in Latin America stimulates development of organized crime in this region by creating institutional conditions criminals need to operate freely. While the government pursues political repression and hunts subversives, traditional criminality receives little attention and operates under the government's radar.

1963   Murder of President John F. Kennedy is followed by an avalanche of books on various conspiracies. Of all the theories, the notion that organized crime is involved has remained among the most widely believed, but still unsubstantiated, scenarios.

Genovese family soldier Joe Valachi testifies before the U.S. Senate, the first American Mafia member to reveal mafia secrets in court.

Seven policemen are killed on June 30 in what has became known as the Ciaculli massacre. In response the Italian government launches a major crackdown on organized crime, passing new anti-Mafia legislation.

1965   Passage of Immigration and Naturalization Act leads to new wave of Chinese immigration to America, including future progenitors of the modern Chinese street-gang phenomenon.

1966   The Bandidos OMG is formed in Texas.

The Revolutionary Armed Forces of Colombia (FARC) is founded by Manuel "Sureshot" Marulanda. Most of its funding comes from the drug trade, including manufacturing and distribution, as well as by taxing cultivators of coca plants and laboratories.

1967   United States launches first federal Organized Crime Strike Task Force in Buffalo, New York.

President's Commission on Law Enforcement and the Administration Justice Task Force announces gambling is the greatest source of revenue for organized crime.

1969   Mario Puzo's *Godfather* and Donald Cressey's *Theft of the Nation* are published.

1970   President Richard M. Nixon signs the Organized Crime Control Act, which introduces the Witness Security Program (WITSEC) and the Racketeer Influenced and Corrupt Organizations Act (RICO) to the organized crime fighting arsenal.

U.S. Bank Secrecy Act requires currency transaction reporting for cash transactions over $10,000.

1971–   The Sicilian War of the Godfathers leaves at least 500
1978   mobsters and family members, as well as a number of public figures, dead as the Corleonese faction emerges as the island's prominent mafia syndicate.

1972   Turkey agrees to completely ban the opium crop.

Death of FBI Chief J. Edgar Hoover energizes the Bureau and frees up the required sources to fight organized crime.

1973   Calabrian gangs win international prominence after kidnapping for ransom J. Paul Getty III, heir to the oil billionaire's fortune. Two million dollars is paid after kidnappers send one of Getty's ears to his grandfather.

1975   First wave of Vietnamese refugees arrive in the United States, Canada, Australia, England, France, and Germany. One of the more unforeseeable results is the

1975 (*cont.*)	transferring of conflicts between the Chinese and the Vietnamese to America.
1976	Cocaine kingpin Carlos Lehder purchases part of Norman's Cay in the Bahamas for use as an airstrip for refueling airplanes delivering cocaine to the United States from Colombia.
1977	New Jersey becomes the second state to legalize gambling after public referendum passes the Casino Control Act allowing gambling casinos in Atlantic City.
1979	Facing 99 counts of fraud, perjury, and misappropriation of funds, and probably 25 years in prison, Sicilian banker Michele Sindona, financial advisor to the Vatican, goes on the run.
1980	Cuba's Marielito boatlift between April 15 and October 31 brings an estimated 125,000 Cubans to America. Among them are some of Cuba's most dangerous felons who would have been otherwise rejected.
	Yugoslavian leader Marshal Tito dies. With his death new party leaders, such as Secretary Slobodan Milosevic, take a more antagonistic stand toward ethnic minorities, promoting a brutal brand of Serbian nationalism that will result in the explosion of the Balkans in the 1990s after the fall the Soviet Union.
	Nigerian Decree 419 makes advance fee fraud illegal.
1980s	Yardie gangs from Jamaica begin to appear in England. Within a short time they make dramatic inroads into the cocaine and crack trade. They are linked to their first murder in 1987.
1982	The assassination of general Carlo Alberto Dalla Chiesa, a well-respected military commander who had been recently appointed prefect of Palermo to head the campaign against organized crime, leads to a fledgling anti-Mafia movement on the island led by a consortium of lawyers, church officials, and reform-oriented politicians. The burgeoning movement will attain ephemeral success with the Palermo Maxi Trials beginning in 1986.

1983   Peruvian president Belaunde Terry coins the term *narcoterrorism*.

The white supremacist group known as The Order and The Silent Brotherhood begins one of the most profitable crime sprees in U.S. history. Following the script provided by *The Turner Diaries*, during its one-year spree it knocks off armored cars and produces counterfeit currency. After the arrest of almost two dozen members for racketeering, robbery, counterfeiting, and murder, the defendants are tried under the RICO statute, the first time it is used in a political case.

1984   President's Commission on Organized Crime Hearings on Organized Crime of Asia Origin is formed.

Mafia pentito Tommaso Buscetta reveals the inner workings of the Sicilian and American mafias. This is the first testimony by a major figure in the Sicilian Mafia and is considered one of the biggest challenges to this phenomenon since Mussolini in the 1920s.

End of the military dictatorship in Brazil leads to growth of domestic cocaine market and development of new organized crime groups and the expansion of the Brazilian numbers racket, *jogo do bichos*, and its concomitant involvement in the drug trade.

Medillin drug cartel is responsible for assassination of Colombia's Minister of Justice Rodrigo Lara Bonilla, as well as a subsequent attack on the Colombian Supreme Court.

1984–   Jamaican Posse gangs in the United States are linked to
1987   at least 800 drug-related killings.

1985   Mikhail Gorbachev is elected president of the U.S.S.R., inaugurating a new era of free-market economy. This sets the stage for the emergence of numerous crime syndicates.

Sonora cartel kidnaps and murders DEA agent Enrique "Kiki" Camarena Salazar in Guadalajara, Mexico.

1985
(*cont.*)

U.S. government promulgates the notion of "narcoguerrillas" as the alliance between drug smugglers and arms dealers in support of terrorists and guerrillas.

1986

Financial advisor to the Vatican Michele Sindona commits suicide in his cell with strychnine.

On March 11, four of the top leaders of the Chicago-based El Rukns street gang fly from Chicago to Casablanca, Morocco, and then to Libya, violating travel prohibitions at the time. The Libyan government pays their expenses after El Rukns convinces Gadhafi that they have the ability to carry out a terrorist campaign in the United States. The FBI learns of the arrangement before it is finalized. In 1986, a 50-count indictment is handed down, naming six members of El Rukns as defendants. Four of the defendants are found guilty and receive sentences ranging from 80 years in prison and a $225,000 fine to suspended sentences. This is the first time in U.S. history that citizens have been found guilty of planning a terrorist act for a foreign government for money.

Between 1986 and 1988, President Ronald Reagan's Commission on Organized Crime publishes seven volumes of hearings and reports. Its findings are significant for broadening the government's interpretation of the organized crime problem by moving beyond the parochial view that organized crime is synonymous with Italian gangsters. In marked contrast to previous investigations, this commission expands the emphasis to include nontraditional forms of organized crime such as outlaw motorcycle gangs, prison gangs, and Chinese, Vietnamese, Japanese, Cuban, Colombian, Irish, Russian, and Canadian criminal organizations.

Money Laundering Control Act makes money laundering a federal offense in the United States.

In the Commission Case, or *U.S. v. Salerno*, the heads of four of New York's five major crime families and other key figures are prosecuted for operating a "Commission," similar to a board of directors for organized crime. On November 19, a jury finds the defendants guilty of racketeering acts, leading to long prison terms and effectively dismantling the upper echelon of New York's Mafia families.

1986– 1987   Palermo Maxi Trials begin after testimony by Mafia boss.

Tommaso Buscetta links hundreds of mobsters to mafia activities in Sicily.

1987   Colombian government extradites Carlos Lehder, one of the founders of the Medillin cartel, to the United States. Lehder had introduced the then novel idea of transporting cocaine to the United States on small private planes from transshipment points in the mid-1970s.

(Late) 1980s Mara Salvatrucha (MS-13) organizes in Los Angeles.

1988   The investigation of the Bank of Credit and Commerce International, better known as BCCI Scandal, is launched after its branch in Tampa, Florida is implicated in the laundering of drug money.

U.S. Congress passes the Indian Gaming Regulatory Act, allowing the nation's sovereign Indian nations to open gambling casinos on their reservations.

The UN Convention against Illicit Trafficking in Narcotic Drugs and Psychotropic Substances, the so-called Vienna Convention, is adopted. It requires signatory countries to criminalize the laundering of drug money and to confiscate it wherever it is found.

1989   Collapse of socialism across Eastern Europe and the fall of the Berlin Wall open borders between Western and Eastern Europe, facilitating the increase in illegal smuggling operations.

In December, a military expedition dubbed "Operation Just Cause" invades Panama to capture President Manuel Antonio Noriega Moreno.

1989 Pablo Escobar is ranked the world's seventh richest
(*cont.*) man by *Forbes* magazine.

Medillin cartel is responsible for bombing of Avianca
passenger jet, killing 111 people on board, and level-
ing the 12-story headquarters of the National Security Forces in Bogotá, leaving 70 dead and hundreds
wounded.

The G-7 group of industrialized countries sets up a task
force to share money-laundering expertise, forming
the Financial Action Task Force (FATF) in an attempt to
"spread 'clean' financial practices."

1990 On January 3, Noriega is flown to the United States for
trial on eight counts of drug trafficking.

1991 After laundering millions of dollars in illicit cash, the
Bank of Credit and Commerce International (BCCI) is
declared worthless and shut down for good.

The breakup of the Soviet Union has tremendous implications for global organized crime. When Yeltsin bans
the Communist Party, 15 new republics emerge, facilitating the expansion of Russian organized crime syndicates.

End of communist rule in Albania leads to social and
political chaos and collapse of the rule of law.

Collapse of Soviet Union leads to creation of the Central Asian Republics of Kazakhstan, Kyrgyzstan, Tajikistan, Turkmenistan, and Uzbekistan. Organized crime
in these countries is shaped by common issues of political instability, endemic corruption, and trafficking of
illegal commodities. Organized crime here is patterned
more on political cliques and kinship groups.

BCCI officials are indicted.

1992 Noriega is convicted by a federal court and sentenced
to 40 years in prison.

Croatia, Slovenia, Macedonia, and Bosnia-Herzegovina declare independence, launching bloody conflict that will alter the balance of organized crime groups in Eastern Europe and create new opportunities for them in the process.

Italian magistrates Giovanni Falcone and Paolo Borsellino are murdered.

Russian mobster Vyacheslav Ivankov enters the United States for the first time, claiming on his visa that he is involved in the motion picture business.

The Piracy Reporting Center is established to collect and distribute information on marine piracy.

Japanese government passes the Act for Prevention of Unlawful Activities by Boryokudan Members, beginning a major offensive against organized crime and forcing hundreds of Yakuza to attempt to rejoin law-abiding society. With almost 40 percent of them missing at least a portion of one finger, however, any chance at regular employment is thwarted. Subsequently at least one doctor develops a specialty of amputating a toe and grafting it on to the missing finger part.

On March 12, Salvatore Lima is assassinated. He is considered the leading Christian Democratic politician in Palermo and is regarded as the "Mafia ambassador" to the Italian government. His murder is apparently the result of his inability to fix the Maxi Trials that revealed the relationships between his political party and Cosa Nostra.

1993   A single European Market is created with the Treaty on European Union. Designed to further European integration by making it easier for goods and people to cross European borders, in a parallel way it has been used by organized crime groups to create cross-border syndicates and expand their operations into new markets and territories.

On March 12, a terrorist attack in Mumbai, India, kills more than 250 and injures 700. It is now believed that

1993 (*cont.*)	several prominent South Asia crime syndicates were involved, offering a graphic lesson on the modern convergence of organized crime and terrorist groups.

On May 27, Cosa Nostra detonates a huge bomb in front of the Uffizi Gallery in Florence, killing five civilians and destroying a number of art works. That same day two more bombs are exploded in Rome, damaging several churches.

On June 6, a ship named the *Golden Venture* carrying human cargo runs aground on a sandbar 150 yards from a New York beach, not far from midtown Manhattan and Wall Street. Crew members encourage the 300 passengers to jump into the 53-degree water and swim to shore. Of the 200 who actually jump, at least 8 drown. This incident leaves an indelible imprint on the American consciousness and puts a face on human smuggling.

While on the run from authorities and the Los PEPES vigilante group, Pablo Escobar is cornered and killed in a shootout on December 2 by members of the Colombian National Police in a middle class Medillin neighborhood.

Brazil's most powerful criminal organization, the First Capital Command (PCC), is organized at Sao Paulo's Taubate Penitentiary.

More than 250,000 European cars disappear without a trace.

According to one survey in 1993, 45 percent of the Yakuza members are missing at least one finger joint after performing *yubitsume*, a form of apology that requires the Yakuza to sever a finger joint and present it to his superior as a plea for forgiveness.

1994   The passage of the North American Free Trade Agreement (NAFTA) opening free trade between the United States, Canada, and Mexico leads to unprecedented growth for Mexican criminal syndicates as they quickly adapt their businesses to advantages wrought by globalization. Mexican cartels can now deal with Colombians and other traffickers from positions of strength, as they control border crossings into the United States. In this way they are able to sell routes to smaller syndicates for exorbitant prices ranging up to 60 percent of each shipment's value.

Apartheid in South Africa is ended in favor of a constitutional democracy. As the country makes the transition from police state to democracy, criminal organizations take advantage of the discontinuity in government by creating new alliances with both local and international criminal groups as the evolving police force plays catch-up.

The FBI opens an office in Moscow.

Canadian biker war between the Hells Angels and the Rock Machine begins.

Interpol states that "Nigerians are the third largest ethnic smuggling groups in the world."

1995   After the devastating Kobe earthquake, Yakuza are lauded for assisting citizens.

Russian criminologist Alexander Gurov coins term *Red Mafiya*, in reference to Russian-organized crime in Germany.

Europol is created by the European Union convention Council Act on July 26. Its intent is to improve police cooperation among the member states to combat terrorism, drug trafficking, and other forms of illegal trafficking.

Bosnian War ends in December with signing of the General Framework Agreement, better known as the Dayton Agreement.

1996   The U.S. Congress passes the Comprehensive Methamphetamine Control Act (MCA), which forces all U.S. dealers of ephedrine to register with the DEA. It extends its restrictions to the transmission of ephedrine

1996 (*cont.*)	and similar chemicals by mail or courier to nonpharmaceutical individuals; this covers the sale of powdered pseudoephedrine, but not the sale of cold tablets.
1996– 2001	Terrorist group Hezbollah reaps almost $1.5 million from cigarette smuggling in the United States.
1997	On June 30, Hong Kong is returned to China by the British. Many think this will lead to an exodus of Triad members from Honk Kong to other Asian countries.
1998	UN Security Council passes Resolution 1173, a sanction against diamonds from Angola, and Resolution 1176, a sanction against diamonds from the Sierra Leone rebel group Revolutionary United Front (RUF).
	Interpol reports that the Kosovo Liberation Army (KLA) is a major player in the trade of drugs for weapons.
	The leader of the Egyptian terrorist group al Gamaat al Islamiyah is arrested for trading guns for drugs with Colombian rebels, demonstrating the nexus between global organized criminal and terrorist groups.
	Protestant and Catholic paramilitary groups sign permanent ceasefire in Northern Ireland. Both groups had long participated in organized crime activities to fund their operations.
	A Russian Organized Crime Task Force (ROCTF) recognizes that Russia's definition of organized crime is substantially different from that of the American FBI.
1999	Noriega's 40-year prison sentence is reduced to 30 on appeal.
	Jaime Gonzalez, nicknamed "The Hummer," deserts the Mexican Army and forms the Zetas, which act as enforcers for the Gulf cartel. Until his capture in 2008, he directs Zeta operations in Mexico City and seven Mexican states out of Reynoso, Mexico.

Colombian President announces that "The terrorist group FARC has financed its activities with $600 million from the Colombian drug dealers."

2000   The Budapest Project is an innovative strategy of cooperative law enforcement. A joint FBI-Hungarian National Police Organized Crime Task Force is created in Budapest in April and is tasked with focusing on organized crime groups that had become active in Central Europe after the fall of communism. In one of its main successes, Ukrainian-born crime kingpin Semion Mogilevich flees Budapest for Moscow, one step ahead of Philadelphia organized crime strike force indictments charging him and three others with a panoply of money laundering, securities fraud, and RICO conspiracy charges.

Mexican presidential election ends decades of one-party rule. The transition to democracy is followed by increased violence between the various drug cartels that continue into 2009.

In June a container carrying 58 Chinese asylum seekers who were illegally smuggled is found on the Dover docks. All 58 are dead.

UN Convention on Transnational Organized Crime is signed in Palermo, Sicily on December 14. It adopts a broad definition of organized crime groups.

UN Security Council passes Resolution 1306, prohibiting all countries from importing rough diamonds from Sierra Leone until a certification process is designed.

The FATF declares 29 offshore jurisdictions to be deficient and labels the 15 worst "non-cooperative countries and territories." The G-7 asserts it will blacklist the worst offenders from doing business with member country banks. Within months the Bahamas, Cayman Islands, Cook Islands, Israel, Liechtenstein, the Marshall Islands, and Panama make progress toward increased compliance by passing new laws and increasing oversight of banks.

2000–   Officials estimate that almost $12 billion in drug money
2001   was laundered in South America's Tri-border region
linking Puerto Iguazu, Argentina; Foz de Iguaçu, Brazil;
and Ciudad del Este, Paraguay.

2001   In April Italian authorities arrest members of a Russian
and Ukrainian criminal syndicate suspected of supplying more than 13,500 tons of weapons to groups fighting in the Balkans.

The September 11 terrorist attacks put organized crime
on the back burner as most federal funding is directed
toward fighting terrorism.

U.S. Patriot Act becomes law, establishing new tools that
could be used against terrorists and organized crime
groups, including new money laundering laws and
granting extensive powers to the U.S. attorney general.

A study of organized crime in Northern Ireland links
more than half of its 78 criminal gangs to either Republican or Loyalist paramilitary groups.

2002   The United Nations endorses the Kimberley Certification Process for diamonds of uncertain origin.

According to the Piracy Reporting Center, the Indone-
sian, Bangladeshi, and Indian coastlines are the top
three sites of reported pirate attacks.

After long negotiations, China joins the World Trade
Organization.

2003   In April two tunnels are discovered running under the
border between Tijuana, Mexico and Otay Mesa, California.

U.S. State Department's *International Narcotics Control
Strategy Report* asserts that Bosnia has become a regional
transshipment point and storage center for the illegal
drug trade and has become increasingly involved in
the production of synthetic drugs.

U.S. Treasury Department designates Dawood Ibrahim, formerly India's most prominent gang boss, a "global terrorist" for allowing al Qaeda to use his smuggling routes and supporting jihadists in Pakistan.

The World Health Organization proclaims methamphetamine "the most widely used illicit drug after marijuana." The meth trade heats up in Mexico.

United Nations High Level Panel on Threats, Challenges, and Change releases a report linking terrorist and organized crime groups, noting that they "were more interrelated today than ever before."

The United Nations Convention against Transnational Organized Crime becomes law and finally offers a definition of organized crime acceptable to most countries.

2004 Spain's 9/11 on March 11, 2004, is in part funded by the drug trade. Investigations reveal 70 pounds of hashish were bartered for high-velocity dynamite from a Spanish crime group.

The U.S. Secret Service announces it has cracked a "global organized cybercrime ring" in *Operation Firewall*. More than 28 individuals are arrested, including residents of eight different states and six foreign countries. The suspects are charged with identity theft, computer and credit card fraud, and conspiracy. *Operation Firewall* began the previous year as a national operation but soon expands into a global investigation targeting international credit card fraud and identity theft.

The European Union increases from 15 to 25 member states.

2005 Internet use triples to almost 900 million users since 1999.

2006 Robert Saviano's best-selling book *Gomorrah*, revealing the Camorra's deadly secrets and forcing the young investigative journalist to go into hiding, is published.

2006
(cont.) Taking advantage of China's booming economy, Macau's gambling operations takes in over $500 million more than Las Vegas between January and November.

On March 29, former Liberian warlord-turned-president Charles Taylor becomes the first African head of state to be indicted for war crimes. American investigators in 1996 estimated that between 1990 and 1994, Taylor brokered close to $75 million a year in financial transactions stemming from his control of Liberia's natural resources, including diamonds, timber, iron ore, and rubber. By most accounts, until he stepped down from power in 2003, organized crime groups from China, Israel, Russia, South Africa, and the Ukraine operate simultaneously with his full blessing in Liberia.

Toward the end of the year, Mexican president Felipe Calderon initiates an aggressive war on drug trafficking by sending in more than 25,000 soldiers and federal police to combat the drug cartels.

After 40 years on the run, Sicily's top Mafia boss Bernardo Provenzano is captured in April on a farm near Corleone.

2007 'Ndrangheta Gang War announces its presence outside Italy after six men are killed in drive-by shooting as they left a pizzeria in Duisburg, Germany.

Having lost the 1846–1848 war with America, Mexico was forced to cede half of its territory to its northern neighbor. Partially as a result, the Mexican military has traditionally refused most American aid. This did not begin to change until the administration of Vicente Fox in 2000–2006. During the summit meeting on a mutual drug-control strategy between Mexican President Felipe Calderon and President George W. Bush, their cooperation leads to the Merida Initiative, marking a change in the historically tense relationship between the two governments.

2008 Arms dealer Viktor Bout is arrested on March 6 in Bangkok, Thailand.

In February, the Italian Parliament's anti-Mafia commission warns that the 'Ndrangheta crime organization rooted in Calabria and far southern Italy "was on the rise worldwide and had eclipsed the Sicilian Mafia in power and international reach."

Parallel raids in New York City and Palermo, Sicily, target mob groups in both countries that are trying to strengthen their criminal ties. The Italian operation is dubbed "Old Bridge."

FARC founder Manuel "Sureshot" Marulanda dies of a heart attack, the third senior member of the rebel group to die in 2008.

On January 23, 2008, Semion Mogilevich is arrested by Russian police in connection with an investigation into an alleged $2 million tax evasion scheme. Others suggest the real motive for his arrest is his involvement in the clandestine multibillion-dollar natural gas trade between Russia and Ukraine. Others have linked him to the trafficking in nuclear materials, drugs, prostitutes, precious gems, and stolen art.

Residential neighborhood in Japan files lawsuit in bid to oust the Dojinkai Yakuza syndicate from its six-story headquarters in Kurume, Japan.

In August, U.S. prosecutors bust what they call "the largest hacking and identity-theft ring ever." Eleven people from five different countries (United States, Estonia, Belarus, China, and Ukraine) are charged with stealing more than 41 million credit and debit card numbers. This case like many others illustrates the changing nature of organized crime, which has become increasingly multinational and more technologically sophisticated.

More than 5,300 murders in Mexico are connected to the country's ongoing war between the drug gangs. Almost 90 percent of the 28,000 weapons seized over the past two years originate in the United States.

The November pirate hijacking of a super-tanker 450 miles off the coast of East Africa is unprecedented.

2008 Somali pirates capture the 1,000-foot long Sirius Star,
(*cont.*) owned by a Saudi Arabian company and carrying almost 2 million barrels of oil valued at more than $100
million.

2009 In late July Mexican marines seize a cocaine-filled sub-
marine 120 miles off Pacific Coast containing almost
six tons of cocaine valued at between $50 and $100 million.

The U.S. Bureau of Alcohol, Tobacco, Firearms and Explosives announces that Houston, Texas, is the number
one origin for weapons later recovered from gangsters
in Mexico, where they are illegal. By most accounts the
transactions are arranged through U.S. citizens with no
felony convictions and are able to pass federal background checks.

In March a top Homeland Security official tells Congress that National Guard troops will be dispatched to
the U.S.–Mexico border to counter drug cartel violence
only as a "last resort."

Russia becomes the world's largest heroin consumer.
According to that nation's head of the Federal Drug
Control Service, it has become "the world's absolute
leader in the opiate trade and the number one heroin
consumer," posing a threat to national security.

Forbes magazine lists alleged Sinaloa cartel drug kingpin Joaquin "El Chapo" Guzman as one of the world's
richest men. Arrested in 1993, he escaped prison eight
years later. According to the recent report he is listed as
tied for 701st place, with a fortune of $1 billion.

5

Biographical Sketches

Global Organized Crime Figures

Juan Carlos Ramirez Abadia [Chupeta; Lollypop] (1963–)

This Colombian cocaine kingpin has been overshadowed by the likes of Pablo Escobar and others, but in recent years few Colombians moved more cocaine than his organization. Abadia, or "Chupeta" meaning lollypop in Colombian Spanish, rose to prominence in the 1990s, moving large amounts of cocaine and ordering hits on informants and police in several countries. By some accounts his Norte del Valle cartel was considered Colombia's most powerful drug cartel in the mid-1990s. Despite recent plastic surgery to obscure his identity, Abadia was arrested in August 2007 in Sao Paulo, Brazil and charged with transporting tons of cocaine into Europe and the United States. Authorities attributed his arrest to the $5 million reward for information leading to his capture. Much of Abadia's operations had been moved to Brazil, which was becoming an important transit point for Colombian cocaine. Brazilian investigators seized weapons and drugs related to his operations in six different Brazilian states; in addition they found that the organization laundered profits from Europe and Mexico by purchasing property, cars, and hotels in Brazil.

Jose Miguel Battle (1929–1997)

The emergence of Cuban organized crime activity on American soil dates back to the 1959 exodus of gangsters from Castro's Cuba.

149

The most prominent organization was the "Corporation," which originated in 1964, although its roots date back to the Cuban Bay of Pigs fiasco of 1961. By the 1990s, it was among the largest Hispanic crime syndicates in the United States. By 1986, the syndicate was led by Jose Miguel Battle, who was then one of Dade County Florida's richest men, with a net worth approaching $180 million. Over the years Battle eluded law enforcement by organizing his syndicate like a "crime family" and relying on individuals known as "corrupters" to bribe politicians and other officials to stay out of his affairs. In the 1990s, Battle diversified his organization and expanded into territories once ruled by Italian American families. The so-called El Padrino or the Godfather had begun his career as a police officer in Havana in the 1950s where he made friends with Meyer Lansky and Santos Trafficante Sr., connections that he would later use to open gambling operations in Florida. He was arrested, however, for a string of murders and in 1997 he was sentenced to prison for a parole violations, where he died of kidney disease later that same year.

Viktor Bout (1967–)

Born in Tajikistan to Russian parents, Bout became the most prominent weapons dealer of the late 20th century, inspiring books and the 2005 movie *Lord of War* and earning such sobriquets as "Merchant of Death" and "Embargo Buster." He began his military career as a young man and rapidly rose through the ranks before earning a degree in economics from Moscow's Soviet Military Institute of Foreign Languages.

Bout was a gifted linguist and was fluent in at least six languages. A number of sources suggest he was associated with the KGB at one time or another. He was on assignment in Angola when the Soviet state collapsed, but apparently he did not miss a beat with the opening of free trade opportunities. He made his first arms deal in 1992 and is estimated to have earned more than $50 million between 1992 and 1995 in various weapons transactions. Much of his early activities were centered in Sub-Saharan African nations, where conflict was the norm in the 1990s. He supplied civil wars, coups, and rebellions in Sierra Leone, Congo, Liberia, and the Ivory Coast among others. During the 1990s, he counted the Taliban and even the United States among his many customers. He finally appeared on police radar screens in 1997 while working out of Belgium but was able to slip out and into the United Arab Emirates, where he found the accommodations much more to his liking. After the September 11, 2001, terrorist attacks, revelations about his association with the Taliban led to arrest warrants from various international authorities and the freezing of his bank accounts by the United Nations. Bout was arrested in Bangkok, Thailand in a sting operation on March 6, 2008, and remains in custody awaiting trial. Investigative reporters Douglas Farah and Stephen Braun claimed Bout was worth $6 billion at the time of his arrest, most of it held in a complicated maze of fronts and ever-changing companies. Although he went out of his way to avoid notoriety, his omnipresence in the weapons trade ultimately led to his demise.

Klaas Bruinsma [De Dominee] (1953–1991)

The leading authorities on Dutch organized crime consider Bruinsma the "first Dutch godfather." The scion of a wealthy Dutch businessman, he entered the drug trade full-time in 1974, selling hashish. After a stint in jail he changed his name to Frans van Arkel and immersed himself further in the shadowy Dutch underworld, where he formed the "Organization" with several others, and by the 1980s, his activities reached beyond Holland as he began looking for legitimate ventures for laundering his profits. At his zenith he commanded 200 men and was regarded as the most prominent drug supplier in Europe. He became increasingly erratic after several large seizures of his products, however, and soon upped the ante by setting his sights on taking over the entire Amsterdam underworld. His schemes included forcing coffee shops to buy his slot machines and reaching into the red-light district prostitution rackets. His increasingly violent behavior soon caused the organization to unravel and led his associates and competitors to come gunning for him. The Dutch tax authorities were on to him as well, but before he could be arrested, an ex-cop hit man working for a Yugoslavian syndicate killed him at the age of 37.

Tommaso Buscetta (1928–2000)

The youngest of 17 children, Buscetta was born into a middle-class Palermo family. He found his calling in the post-World War II Mafia. After a first arrest for bootlegging cigarettes in 1959, he began traveling extensively to Brazil and the United States. He opened a chain of pizzerias in New York City's Little Italy as a front for drug trafficking operations. In 1970, he was arrested as an illegal alien and escaped to Brazil. At the end of the 1970s, he was arrested and extradited to Italy to serve a sentence for conspiracy and kidnapping. In 1980, he returned to Brazil under an alias and once more became involved in heroin and cocaine trafficking with the Sicilian and American mafias. Buscetta made history as the first executive-level Mafioso to turn informant, or *pentito*.

During his subsequent interrogation and trial, Buscetta described in rich detail the inner workings of Sicilian Mafia families. From an international perspective, Buscetta's revelations led authorities in America and Italy to reevaluate their understanding of organized crime, as well as their methods for suppressing it.

Ibrahim Dawood (1955–)

One of eight sons born to a struggling policeman, Dawood rose from petty crime to head of the Mumbai underworld. What most distinguishes him is his reputation as both a crime kingpin and terrorist leader. By the early 2000s, he was directing criminal syndicates from Bangkok to Dubai from the relative safety of his Pakistani sanctuary. In 2003, the U.S. Treasury Department designated him a "global terrorist" for permitting al Qaeda to use his smuggling routes and supporting jihadists in Pakistan. He first came to the attention of terrorist hunters in 1993 when, along with his brother Anis, Dawood masterminded serial bombings in Mumbai that left 257 dead and more than 700 wounded; however, he had been supporting Islamic extremists with his criminal activities since the early 1990s. He is considered by many officials "South Asia's Al Capone," directing a network of contract killers, smugglers, drug traffickers, and extortionists across at least 14 countries. As the leader of his "D Company" syndicate, he is considered the most wanted man in India. He reputedly built his syndicate by smuggling black market gold and other commodities into India's closed economy and forced his way into the nation's Bollywood film industry. After leaving India he fled to Dubai. He has flourished in Pakistan where he maintains a number of legitimate and illegitimate businesses, leading to his emergence as the "don of Karachi," where his organization made huge investments in real estate and plays an important role in the country's parallel credit system business, the *hundi*. Some have even credited him with having rescued Pakistan's Central bank by floating loans during a financial downturn at one point.

His syndicate has been linked to large-scale drug shipments to the United Kingdom and Western Europe.

Pablo Emilio Escobar-Gaviria (1949–1993)

By the 1980s, Escobar had become the face of the international cocaine trade. An admirer of Al Capone, he poured millions of dollars from the drug trade into Medillin, Colombia, building houses, new schools, sewers, sports plazas, and health clinics. But he saved the best for himself. At his zenith he owned 16 homes in Medillin and a country house capable of sleeping 100. To top it off, he had a 7,000-acre spread that boasted Colombia's best zoo. Formerly a stealer of tombstones and cars, his talent for subterfuge included hiding a landing strip under mobile houses on wheels; residents pushed them aside for planes to land and unload drugs before moving them back on departure. Escobar cultivated his own stable of hired killers and pioneered new methods of killing such as putting assassins on the back of motorcycles, which residents observed worked well in Bogotá's perpetual traffic jams. Escobar's prominence was important to the 1980's Bush Administration "War on Drugs" by putting a human face on a formerly anonymous enemy. During the 1980s and early 1990s, he was among the world's leading drug traffickers; and, in 1989, *Forbes* magazine reported he was the seventh richest man in the world. Escobar was elected to Congress in 1983, but the following year the United States demanded his extradition. The Colombian government had been extraditing low-level dealers, but Escobar, capable of waging war on the state, was another matter. In the end his decision to wage war on Colombia led to his death and the demise of the Medillin drug organization. Some estimates suggest his war against the state left 1,000 judges and officials dead. He also engineered the murders of several presidential candidates who favored extradition. Escobar took his campaign of violence to new levels in 1989 when he masterminded the bombing of an Avianca passenger jet, killing all 110 passengers. Around this time, the United States began sending financial aid to the Colombians to cover the ensuing manhunt, making Escobar the world's most wanted man. In 1991, he surrendered after an agreement was met in which he would be jailed in a facility of his own making—more fashionable resort than prison. From there he continued to run his operations and engineer the murder of opponents. When he found out he was to be placed in a military prison, he walked away from his "jail," leading to a massive manhunt by Colombian and American agents. They were soon joined by a vigilante group known as LOS PEPES, an acronym for "People Persecuted by Pablo Escobar." With a large reward on his head and a constant manhunt following his every move, he could stay in one place only for several hours; and on December 1, 1993, authorities traced him from a phone call and he was located and killed in a shootout the next day.

Don Vito Cascio Ferro (1862–1943)

Born in Palermo, Sicily, Ferro became an early international crime figure in 1901 when he purportedly visited New York City and advised Black Hand extortionists on various criminal rackets. He was arrested by the Italian American detective Joe Petrosino in 1903, but escaped to Sicily. In 1909, Petrosino went to Palermo to investigate ties between that city's Black Handers and those in New York, but was almost immediately assassinated. Most researchers suggest that Ferro was complicit in his death. Despite almost 70 arrests, Ferro stayed out of jail and even became a regular on the Palermo society circuit. His career ended during the fascist Mafia purges in the 1920s, and he died in prison during an Allied bombing raid in 1943.

Gregorio Sauceda Gamboa (1965–)

A former Mexico state police detective, Sauceda was a top member of the Gulf Cartel when he was arrested by Mexican police in April 2009. He was just one of more than 20 high-level mobsters targeted by the Mexican government with million-dollar rewards. He is considered a founding member of the bloody Gulf Cartel almost a decade ago, when he was given control of trafficking through Reynosa, near McAllen, Texas, by the cartel's boss Osiel Cardenas. He is also often credited as one of the founders of the Gulf cartel's hit squad, Los Zetas. By most accounts Sauceda was selected as boss because of his "violent character." Authorities estimate that the Gulf cartel trafficked 10 tons of cocaine and 30 tons of marijuana across the American border each month. After Sauceda's arrest, a police spokesman admitted that he had headed the gang only for a short time and at his arrest his own involvement had been drastically reduced in recent years.

Osiel Cardenas Guillen [Fanstasma; Ghost; El Patron (Boss)] (1968–)

Born in Matamoras, the former federal policeman made the transition to the drug business, and by the 1990s his network was bringing four to six tons of cocaine across the south Texas border each month. Cardenas took over the Gulf cartel in 1996 after the arrest and extradition of its founder, Juan Garcia Abrego. Among his greatest accomplishments was luring dozens of army deserters known as the Zetas. Their function as hit men was critical to establishing his organization as one of the region's most powerful crime syndicates. Cardenas had his first brush with organized crime while still in his teens, when he took care of a car for a famous hit man known as "the Nice One" for his penchant of letting his victims know their deaths were not personal, "just business." Cardenas was convicted of organized crime activities in Mexico in 2003 before being extradited to the United States, where he was indicted for leading the Gulf cartel and threatening the lives of federal agents. His extradition in 2007 ended the career of one of Mexico's most violent drug lords and was considered the most prominent drug trafficker extradited from Mexico. What distinguished Cardenas from his fellow kingpins was his unwillingness to build alliances with other cartels or to keep a low profile.

Joaquin Guzman [El Chapo, Shorty] (1957–)

Born in La Tuna, Sinaloa, Mexico, Joaquin "Shorty" Guzman is among the preeminent drug traffickers in Mexico today. By most accounts he was mentored by Miguel Angel Felix Gallardo, often referred to as "The Godfather" and among the country's most legendary kingpins. Guzman, at 5' 6" is tough to keep behind bars. Arrested in Guatemala and extradited to Mexico in 1993, he managed to escape from a maximum security prison in 2001, driving out in a laundry truck. His trafficking strategies have included building complex tunnels under the border between Mexico and Arizona and, in one instance, reportedly smuggling seven tons of cocaine inside cans of chili peppers. In 2009, *Forbes* magazine featured him on a list of billionaires, something that did not sit well with the Mexican government.

Vyacheslav Ivankov [Yaponchik; Little Japanese] (1938–)

Born in Vladivostok in the Far Eastern Soviet Union, Ivankov was given the moniker "Yaponchik" or "Little Japanese" by police for his faintly Asian appearance. Ivankov first rose to prominence as the leader of the *Solontsevskaya* gang in Moscow in 1980, leading a crew of gangsters who, under the guise of police officers, conducted home invasion robberies at the houses of wealthy Muscovites. He was subsequently arrested and sentenced to 14 years in a Siberian prison. He bribed his way out in 1991 and two years later landed in New York City. Ivankov joined the clutch of crime lords attempting to take advantage of the growing Eurasian drug trade. Controversy has always swirled around Ivankov, with some reports suggesting he was sent to the United States by peers to explore business opportunities, and others suggesting he was trying to stay one step ahead of Chechen and Turkish mobsters. His gang was considered the most powerful Russian syndicate in New York City, but his career here was short-lived, and in 1995 he was among a group of gangsters convicted with wiretap information revealing the attempted extortion of a Manhattan investment firm owned by Russian-born businessmen. His legacy was mixed, with some regarding him as a formidable gang boss, but in reality he was never a monolithic crime boss in the tradition of a mafia don; his gang was never more than a dozen or so loosely affiliated gangsters who engaged in organized crime activities.

Daut Kadriovski (1955–)

Born in Macedonia, Kadriovski came to prominence as a heroin smuggler in the 1970s, when he operated a network reaching from Turkey to Yugoslavia. He used a variety of legitimate businesses as a cover to launder proceeds in Germany, Hungary, Italy, and the United States. He towed the traditional Albanian line by trying to work with only blood kin in other countries. At his arrest in Albania in 2001, he was considered the boss of one of Albania's "15 families." Other countries filed charges against him as well. Because Italy claimed him first, he was extradited there in 2002, where he was tried, convicted, and sent to prison for 12 years.

Yoshio Kodama (1911–1984)

Throughout his long career, Kodama had a penchant for subterfuge. During World War II he reportedly directed an Asian espionage and spy ring. At the same time he used his contacts to line his own coffers, providing Japan's war machine with raw materials such as radium, copper, and nickel. Despite projecting an upstanding profile with his connections to the government, he was deeply involved in heroin trafficking. By the end of the war, he was worth a reported $175 million and had been awarded the honorary rank of rear admiral. After World War II, Kodama was sentenced to two years in prison by the Allies for war crimes. After a general amnesty in 1948, Kodama was released and the U.S. government relied on his diplomatic skills as an intermediary between the allied forces intelligence corps (G-2) and the Yakuza. During the next 20 years, he was able to rally Yakuza thugs for political bosses and the Allies whenever they were needed. His power reached from Japan into much of Asia, leading one observer to refer to him as "the most powerful man" in Japan and another as a "visionary godfather." During his early years Kodama was involved in ultranationalistic activities and was a rabid anticommunist (not unlike most Yakuza members). By most accounts his peacemaking among the gangster syndicates was due in part to a perception that warring Yakuza groups could be a national threat to Japan's anticommunist unity. During the 1970s, Kodama earned millions of dollars representing the Lockheed aircraft corporation in Japan and establishing links between politicians and the Yakuza. His implication in the subsequent Lockheed scandal in 1976 led to his descent from power. Before he could be imprisoned, he was felled by a stroke and died eight years later.

Luciano Leggio (1925–1993)

Born in rural poverty in Sicily, Leggio is considered a transitional figure in the history of the Sicilian Mafia. Straddling two distinct eras, he came up as a cattle rustler in the feudal countryside and participated in the transformation of the Mafia into an international player in the developing global drug trade. He originally was used as a hired killer for the Corleone family under Michele Navarra in the late 1940s and early 1950s. Leggio even kept a private ravine on his land to get rid of bodies; however, his boss tired of his bloodthirsty protégé. Leggio escaped, and with the help of two killers who would create their own legacies in Mafia lore, Salvatore Riina and Bernardo Provenzano, proceeded to hunt down Navarra and his supporters. Leggio's ascendance marked a new era in the Sicilian Mafia as it moved away from its agrarian roots. By the mid-1950s, Leggio was moving into the urban Palermo rackets, extorting the booming construction industry and collecting protection money from virtually every business in his territory. His ability to avoid capture over the years earned him the sobriquet, the "Scarlet Pimpernel of Corleone." His reputation lost its luster, however, when he was arrested in 1974. He would die in prison, but he left a legacy of moving the Mafia into global organized crime circles.

Heriberto Lazcano [The Executioner; El Lazca; Z-3] (c. 1976–)

Lazcano was born in Veracruz, Mexico, but not much is known about this shadowy drug trafficker except that he commands Los Zetas of the Gulf Cartel. His recruiting fliers for recruits have been posted widely along the border towns, advertising "The Zetas want you, soldier or former soldier. We offer good salary, food and family care. Don't go hungry any longer." Lazcano joined the military and matriculated through the elite Airborne Special Force Group. After his unit was sent north to battle the drug gangs, however, he defected along with 30 others to the Gulf Cartel. He took control after the two officers ahead of him were killed, and he has molded the Zetas into a formidable paramilitary force.

Arturo Beltran Leyva (1961–2009)

Born in Sinaloa, Mexico, Beltran rose to prominence in 2007 for his role in several assassinations and commanding a group of paramilitary hit men. During his early years he was reportedly mentored by "Chapo" Guzman. By 2005, he was running a formidable group of hired guns that included members of the MS-13 street gang, as he battled to control border routes in northeastern Mexico. After his brother was captured in early 2008, Beltran ordered hits on prominent federal officials in the state capital at Culiacan. Subsequent police action led to the capture of some of his killers in Mexico City. What troubled investigators was their possession of high-powered weapons and grenades, as well as bullet-proof jackets emblazoned with the Spanish acronym FEDA, which stood for

Special Forces of Arturo (Beltran Leyva). Leyva was killed along with three of his gang members on December 16, 2009 after he was tracked down at an upscale apartment house and gunned down during a 90-minute shootout with elite members of the Mexican military. One of the Special Forces marines was killed and later buried with full military honors. The next day, gunmen killed members of the hero's family, including his mother.

Charles "Lucky" Luciano (1897–1962)

Born Salvatore Lucania in Sicily, Luciano became one of the most significant organized crime figures of the 20th century. He moved to the United States with his family in 1906, earning his first arrest before the age of 18 for heroin possession. After serving a six-month sentence, he was released and rose as one of the leaders of the multiethnic Five Points Gang, becoming fast friends with future Jewish mob luminaries Meyer Lansky and Benjamin "Bugsy" Siegel. During Prohibition he entered into alliances with a variety of ethnic gangsters, transcending the traditions of the Sicilian Mafia that required all members to have Italian-born parents. In 1931, he figured prominently in the deaths of the Old World Sicilian bosses Joe "the Boss" Masseria and Salvatore Maranzano (the so-called Mustache Petes) and is credited with playing an important role in the Americanization of Italian American organized crime, which saw increased cooperation between different ethnic groups. Under Luciano's guidance, organized crime became more businesslike and professional, moving into developing lucrative rackets such as construction and narcotics trafficking. In the early 1930s, he was targeted by mob-buster Thomas Dewey, who in 1936 engineered Luciano's arrest and conviction for running organized prostitution. His conviction was probably the first time a major American organized crime figure was sent to prison for promoting this crime. Luciano was sentenced to from 30–50 years, but later had his sentence commuted and was released and deported to Italy in 1946. Although he was able to run the mob from behind bars, once deported to Italy his influence diminished. He died of a heart attack at the Naples airport.

Semion Mogilevich (1946–)

Born in Kiev, Ukraine, Mogilevich first came under Russian police scrutiny in the 1970s. The so-called Brainy Don has an economics degree and at his zenith was worth more than $100 million. He did not hit the upper echelons of international crime until the 1980s, when he began purchasing the possessions of Jews immigrating to Israel and promising to send them their profits in Israel (which never arrived). During the 1990s, he was considered among the world's most feared crime kingpins and was wanted for weapons and drug trafficking, as well as several murders. On January 23, 2008, he was arrested by Russian police while operating under one of his six pseudonyms. His apprehension was connected to an alleged $2 million tax evasion scheme run in connection with a chain of cosmetics stores called Arbat Prestige, whose owner was arrested along with Mogilevich. Other observers, however, have suggested that his arrest was probably connected to his involvement in a clandestine multibillion-dollar natural gas deal between Russia and Ukraine. He has also been linked to the illegal trafficking of a host of other commodities ranging from precious gems and stolen art to drugs, prostitutes, and nuclear materials.

Manuel Antonio Noriega Moreno (1938–)

Born into a poor rural family in Panama City, Noriega rose to the presidency of Panama but then fell to becoming the first head of state to be convicted of felony charges by the United States. Two years after the death of then-President General Omar Torrijos in a mysterious plane crash in 1981, Noriega assumed the leadership of the nation, a position he would use until his arrest to become wealthy through the international drug trade and other related activities. As America's drug problems got worse in the 1980s, President George H. W. Bush was forced to act, starting by freezing Panamanian assets in U.S. banks and then cutting off all military and economic assistance to the Central American country. In 1988, a U.S. Senate report revealed what many suspected—Noriega was in cahoots with the Colombian cocaine syndicates. His doom was sealed, however, when the Panamanian strongman proclaimed a state of war existed between the two countries the next year. Following the death of an American soldier by Panamanian Defense Force troops, American forces invaded the country in "Operation Just Cause." Although its main goal was the arrest and extradition of its leader to the United States to stand trial, thousands of Panamanian civilians were killed in the process. On January 3, 1990, Noriega was captured and taken to Miami and held there for the next two years while investigators put their case together. During a trial that lasted more than eight months, 100 witnesses testified in what some called the "drug trial of the century." In 1992, Noriega was found guilty on 8 of 10 charges and sentenced to 40 years (reduced on appeal to 30) in federal prison for his role in money laundering and protecting Colombian drug traffickers who were using Panama as a transshipment point for bringing drugs into the United States.

Cheng Chui Peng [Sister Ping] (1949–)

Cheng Chui Peng was reportedly born in the small farming village of Shengmei. Her father was by most accounts involved in human trafficking long before "Sister Peng" rose to prominence as a "snake-head." She was arrested in connection with the *Golden Venture* smuggling case, in which 10 passengers drowned after the ship ended up stranded off the coast of Queens, New York, a 17,000-mile voyage from China. She was an important cog in a huge smuggling network that included contacts in China, Thailand, Belize, Kenya, South Africa, Guatemala, Mexico, and Canada and was credited with setting up the route from China to New York's Chinatown in the 1980s. Her efforts at smuggling undocumented workers into the United States reportedly earned her $40 million during a two-decade career. Although Ping had little in the way of a formal education and knew little English, she was able to become a prominent business-woman in Manhattan's Chinatown after immigrating in 1981. She was the 23rd person convicted in the Golden Venture case and in 2005 was sentenced to 35 years in prison.

Ze'ev Rosenstein [Fat Man] (1954–2008)

Israel's foremost crime boss was born in Jaffa, adjacent to Tel Aviv. The son of Romanian Jewish immigrants, "Fat Man" controlled one of the world's largest international trafficking rings and survived at least seven assassination attempts before being killed in 2008. Rising from petty jewel thief to international drug smuggler to international drug kingpin, Rosenstein had a criminal career that parallels the rise of global international crime in the 1990s. During this period Israel emerged as a transit point of criminal routes reaching from Moldova to Dubai to Southern Florida.

Khun Sa (1934–)

Khun Sa was born in Myanmar's (formerly Burma) Shan State. The offspring of a prince, he was well accustomed to opulence by the time he became known as the "Opium King" and the "Prince of Death." In 1960, he formed his militia, the *kakweye*, which would become the nucleus of his Shan United Army (SUA). Over the next 10 years, his 1,000-strong army was often embroiled in conflict with competitors over the opium trade. Since the transition from democracy to military dictatorship (as Myanmar), Khun Sa has been at war with the military. He has claimed that his only involvement in the drug trade has been to finance his fight for the independence of the Shan people. In 1993, he proclaimed himself the leader of an independent Shan state, but this has only brought him into conflict with neighboring countries. The next year Thailand and DEA agents took part in "Operation Tiger Trap," which led to the arrest of some of his important contacts and successfully sealed the border against his drug-trafficking network. In 1995, he stepped down as leader, vowing to lay down his weapons and leave the drug trade. Subsequent negotiations led to his surrender and release without trial. He purportedly now lives in Yangon, Myanmar.

Charles Ghankay Taylor (1948–)

Born near Monrovia, Liberia, Taylor received a degree in economics from Bentley College in Massachusetts in 1977 before landing a job at the Liberian Consulate in New York City. After several scrapes with law enforcement, Taylor fled the United States for Libya, where he reportedly studied guerrilla tactics before moving on to Cote d'Ivoire and establishing the National Patriotic Front of Liberia in 1989 with the intention overthrowing the Liberian government. Taylor came to prominence during a protracted civil war using "child soldiers," better known as "small boy units." He made the transition from warlord to Liberian president in 1997. As warlord he controlled Liberia's diamond-rich regions, as well as timber concessions, iron ore deposits, and rubber plantations. Between 1990 and 1994, he reportedly made close to $75 million a year through his tightfisted control of these natural resources. As president his control brought in millions more. Before being unseated in 2003, he spent heavily on weapons and created a mercenary army to protect his interests. International officials traced his banking accounts to institutions throughout West Africa, Europe, Panama, and the Caribbean Islands. Authorities suspect he used at least 30 front companies to hide his assets, using couriers to transfer large shipments of cash. During his years as warlord and president, he helped destroy two of West Africa's most prosperous countries (Liberia and Sierra Leone), as he established links with various organized crime groups and terrorist organizations. Officials claimed that in 2000 organized crime groups from China, Israel, Russia, Ukraine, and South Africa operated simultaneously in Liberia with the consent of Taylor. In March 2006, he was arrested by Nigerian security officials ands sent to The Hague to stand trial for war crimes.

Tu Yueh-sheng [Big Eared Tu] (ca. 1888–1951)

Tu was born into one of Shanghai's worst slums and was lured into the criminal life while still in his teens, earning a reputation as a drug runner and contract killer. He took over a number of gangs and became second in command of the preeminent Green Gang by the 1910s. His wealth was counted in the tens of millions of dollars as he held sway over most organized crime activities along the Yangtze River in Shanghai, as well as the opium-growing regions. What brought his downfall was his opposition to the increasingly powerful Communists. Despite using gang members to beat up or kill thousands of students and Communist supporters, the Maoist victory in 1949 forced him to flee for Hong Kong where he died two years later.

Crime Fighters

Harry Anslinger (1892–1975)

Born in Altoona, Pennsylvania, Anslinger entered public service with the War Department shortly after graduating law school. In 1926, he joined the Treasury Department. During the early years of Prohibition, he attended seminars on international drug and alcohol smuggling. By 1929, he was appointed commissioner of the Prohibition Bureau. During the 1920s, the association of the Narcotics Division with the Prohibition Bureau led to public disenchantment with it, in no small part as a result of the bureau's ineptitude and the unpopularity of the Prohibition laws. In 1930, Congress removed drug enforcement from the Prohibition Bureau and created a separate agency, the Federal Bureau of Narcotics (precursor to the DEA), within the Treasury Department. Appointed to lead the new bureau (until 1962), Anslinger took a get-tough nonpragmatic stance against drug abusers, leading the crusade against marijuana that culminated in the Marijuana Tax Act of 1937. During World War II, Anslinger claimed (without substantiation) that the Japanese were using an "opium offensive" as part of their strategy to enslave conquered countries. The U.S. government was sufficiently alarmed to grant him use of the Coast Guard, the U.S. Customs Service, and the Internal Revenue Service in the battle against narcotics traffickers.

Thomas Dewey (1902–1971)

Born in Michigan, Dewey earned a law degree from Columbia Law School before entering the legal profession. He rose to prominence in the 1930s when the New York governor appointed him to investigate organized crime. Between 1935 and 1937, he successfully targeted police corruption and organized crime figures and was credited with restoring the integrity of the New York Police Department. He caught the public's attention by engineering the demise of criminals Lucky Luciano and Dutch Schultz. He became a national hero and revered racket buster and went on to serve as the state governor three times. As New York's crusading district attorney, Dewey is remembered as America's quintessential crime-buster.

Giovanni Falcone (1939–1992)

The Palermo-born anti-Mafia judge rose from urban poverty to iconic status during a career that ended on May 23, 1992, when he, along with his wife and three bodyguards, was blown up by a bomb hidden on the highway between Palermo and the city airport. Most evidence suggests that Corleone boss Toto Riina gave the orders for his death. One of the highlights of his career was convincing Tommaso Buscetta to return to Sicily from Brazil to testify at the Palermo Maxi Trial (and later at the Pizza Connection Trial in the United States). Buscetta's testimony led to the convictions of 340 mafiosi and associates. Falcone recognized that the success of the trial had sealed his demise, publicly stating he knew he would now have a price on his head for his victory. Despite the success of the trials, over the ensuing years political chicanery at the highest levels of government resulted in most of the convictions being overturned. Falcone's murder, and that of his fellow magistrate Paolo Borsellino two months later, led to the creation of the *Direzione Investigativa Anti-Mafia* (DIA) and the passage of a witness protection law, which was an overwhelming success as hundreds of *pentiti* (informers) came forth to testify against the Mafia.

Rudolph Giuliani (1944–)

Giuliani's controversial career as a public figure—New York City mayor, 9/11 presence, and presidential candidate—has been well chronicled. What is less well known was his role as U.S. attorney for the Southern District of New York in leading the so-called Commission case, *U.S. v. Salerno*, against the heads of New York's five crime families in the mid-1980s. After the former Bonanno family boss had the temerity to publish his autobiography, *A Man of Honor*, Giuliani famously opined that since Bonanno could profit from writing a book on the Commission, he could now indict it. He used the 1970 RICO statute to indict more Cosa Nostra members than in any previous case. The linchpin to the government case was proving the existence of the organization. On November 19, 1986, the jury found the defendants guilty of all 17 racketeering acts and 20 related charges involving extortion, labor payoffs, and loan sharking. All of the defendants except one (sentenced to 40 years) were sentenced to 100 years in prison.

Walter Maierovitch (Unknown)

Maierovitch is considered among Brazil's leading experts on that country's organized crime problems. He made his mark on the war against the Latin American drug trade during his one-year term as Brazil's first anti-drug secretary between 1998 and 1999. He had first come to prominence when he assisted Italian magistrate Giovanni Falcone in the early 1980s in persuading Mafia turncoat Tommaso Buscetta to return to Italy and give testimony during the 1986 Maxi Trial. Before taking the position of chief of the National Drug Office in 1998, he spent almost 30 years as a judge focused mostly on prosecuting dirty cops and drug traffickers. Appointed to the position by then President Fernando Henrique Cardoso, he introduced several measures that were stymied by other government officials. According to Maierovitch's strategy, suspicious plane purchases would be tracked. Following the planes, most of which were bought in the United States, once they landed in Brazil with ιoαus of drugs, the aircraft would be seized and the pilots interrogated. The Brazilian government, however, decided on a different tact, more in line with the American strategy, by allowing Brazilian fighter jets to shoot down planes suspected of narcotrafficking. Maierovitch did his best to convince the government his strategy offered the better chance of results, and on top of that the government could then sell the plane and put the profits into drug rehabilitation programs for addicts. Despite the intentions of Maierovitch and others, Brazil has become an important center for transnational criminal gangs, linking markets in Latin America with Europe, Africa, and North America.

Cesare Mori (1880–1942)

In 1969, the authors of the *Crime Confederation* remarked that any list of top Italian American organized crime's heroes would have to rank "Benito Mussolini at the top" since he unintentionally put into motion the exodus of Sicilian Mafiosi to the New World, where they would play a role in the creation of the Italian-American version of the Mafia. This could not have been accomplished without the work of his protégé, Cesare Mori, who has been accorded much of the credit for driving the Mafiosi from Sicily to the United States (and elsewhere) during the reign of Italian dictator Benito Mussolini. He chronicled his war against the pre-World War II Mafia in *The Last Struggle with the Mafia*, a book that demonstrated prescience about Sicilian organized crime unmatched to that time. Mussolini selected Mori as prefect of Palermo and in 1924 ordered him to make quick work of the Mafia outside the control of the fascist state. During a four-year campaign of torture and other extra-legal methods, he obtained hundreds of confessions and elicited false testimony from residents. Hundreds were jailed, and probably just as many fled to the United States, where many joined Italian American syndicates. Mori's campaign wound up in 1929 with the arrest of the island's most prominent Mafia leader, Don Vito Cascio Ferro. Those Mafiosi who had not been arrested or had fled pledged their support to the new regime, and for a time the Mafia seemed have been a figment of the past—that is until the Allied invasion of Sicily in 1943.

Giuseppe Petrosino (1860–1909)

Giuseppe "Joe" Petrosino was born in Padua, Italy and immigrated with his family to New York while barely in his teens. Ten years later he joined the New York Police Department, and in 1905 he was tabbed to lead the newly formed Italian Squad, tasked with suppressing crime in the Italian community. His background and familiarity with his homeland culture and language made him an ideal choice. Early on he earned a reputation for his investigative skills, sometimes masquerading as a day laborer, blind beggar, and even a gangster. During the first five years of the unit's operations, members made thousands of arrests with hundreds of convictions, a number leading to deportations. Much of his efforts were directed at cracking Black Hand extortion gangs that preyed on fellow countrymen. In 1909, he received permission to travel to Palermo, Sicily to gather information on Sicilian criminals active in the United States. His enemies were waiting for him, however, and he was murdered on March 12, 1909, soon after arriving. He is considered the first member of the NYPD to be killed outside the United States. His funeral in New York attracted more than 200,000 mourners.

Joseph D. Pistone [Donnie Brasco] (1939–)

The grandson of Italian immigrants, Pistone was born in Pennsylvania. He worked as a civilian special agent for the Office of Naval Intelligence before joining the Federal Bureau of Investigation in 1969, first with the Jacksonville, Florida office and then the Alexandria, Virginia office. While at the FBI Academy, he studied gambling investigation and took undercover and Special Weapons and Tactics (SWAT) training. In 1974, he was reassigned to the New York City office and used for undercover work. Using the alias "Donnie Brasco," Pistone infiltrated the American Mafia as a deep-cover agent for six years (1976–1981), the most successful infiltration of a mob family (the Bonanno family) by a government agent. Posing as a jewel thief he frequented mob hangouts before coming to the attention of Bonanno family member. His ruse was so successful that he was put up for Mafia membership, but first was expected to complete a murder contract. Fearing for his safety, the FBI pulled him out in 1981. Over the next few years, Pistone testified at mob trials across the United States. Despite the introduction of the 1970 RICO statute, government officials did not figure out how to use it until the Pistone investigations of the Bonanno family. Pistone's subsequent testimony sent more than 100 gangsters to prison. With a half-million dollar mob contract on his head, Pistone resigned from the FBI in 1986 and two years later published *Donnie Brasco: My Undercover Life in the Mafia.* Surprisingly, rather than enter the Witness Security Program, he changed his family name and moved far away from New York City.

Enrique Camarena Salazar [Kiki] (1948–1985)

The DEA agent "Kiki" Camarena was probably the best known American casualty of the "War on Drugs." He was kidnapped and tortured to death in Guadalajara, Mexico by cocaine cowboys from the Sonora cartel. Born in Mexicali, Mexico and raised in California, he was posted to Guadalajara after joining the DEA, where he started a program to monitor marijuana fields on the outskirts of the city. His "Operation Miracle" strategy led to a 1984 bust that retrieved 20 tons of marijuana. The next year Camarena testified before a congressional investigation that drug-related corruption reached into the highest branches of the Mexican government. Just before the publication of his revelations, however, he was kidnapped outside a Guadalajara bar. It was three months before his body was found not far from the home of the prominent legislator Manuel Bravo Cervantes. As law enforcement arrived to question Cervantes, a gunfight broke out resulting in the death of the legislator, his wife, and two children. Pressure from the American authorities led to the arrest of a former Mexican policeman who confessed to his role in the abduction and murder of Camarena. His testimony sent Sonora kingpin Caro-Quintero to prison for 40 years (the torture murder took place in his home), while the policeman received three life terms.

Researchers

Howard Abadinsky (1941–)

Howard Abadinsky is professor of criminal justice at St. John's University. He earned his doctorate in sociology from New York University. He worked as an inspector for the Cook County, Illinois sheriff for eight years and as a New York State parole officer for 15 years. He is the founder of the International Association for the Study of Organized Crime and served as a consultant to the President's Commission on Organized Crime. The author of several books, including *The Criminal Elite: Professional and Organized Crime* (1983) and *The Mafia in America: An Oral History* (1981), he is the author of *Organized Crime*, a textbook now in its ninth edition.

Jay S. Albanese (1953–)

Jay S. Albanese is professor in the Wilder School of Government & Public Policy at Virginia Commonwealth University. He received the PhD from Rutgers University School of Criminal Justice. He served as chief of the International Center at the National Institute of Justice (NIJ), the research arm of the U.S. Department of Justice, from 2002–2006. Dr. Albanese is author of numerous articles, and 10 books that include *Organized Crime in Our Times* (2007), *Criminal Justice* (2008), *Professional Ethics in Criminal Justice: Being Ethical When No One is Looking* (2008), *Comparative Criminal Justice Systems* (with H. Dammer and E. Fairchild) (2006), and a *NIJ Special Report: Commercial Sexual Exploitation of Children: What Do We Know and What Do We Do About It* (National Institute of Justice, 2007). He is editor of the books *Transnational Crime* (2005) and *Combating Piracy: Intellectual Property Theft and Fraud* (2009). Dr. Albanese has served as executive director of the International Association for the Study of Organized Crime, and is a past president of the Academy of Criminal Justice Sciences (ACJS).

Pino Arlacchi (1951–)

Arlacchi was born in Gioia Tauro in Calabria, Italy. In 1997, he was appointed director general of the United Nations Office at Vienna and executive director of the Office for Drug Control and Crime Prevention (ODCCP). During the early 1990s, Arlacchi rose to prominence as the senior adviser to Italy's Ministry of Interior and helped create the Direzione Investigativa Anti-Mafia (DIA), which spearheaded the fight against organized crime in Italy. He played an important role in the promotion of the United Nations Convention against Transnational Organized Crime (2000) that was adopted in 2003. In 1992, he was nominated as honorary president of the "Giovanni Falcone" Foundation. Falcone, a close friend of Arlacchi, was assassinated by the Mafia in 1992. Arlacchi served a variety of positions in Italy's national government and as a trained sociologist has taught at several leading universities. Currently he is professor of sociology at Sassari. He has written a number of articles and several books about transnational organized crime and is a well-respected expert on Italian organized crime. His best known work includes the books *Mafia, Peasants and Great Estates: Society in Traditional Calabria* (1983), *Mafia Business: The Mafia Ethic and the Spirit of Capitalism* (1986), and *Men of Dishonor: Inside the Sicilian Mafia* (1993).

Ko-lin Chin (1951–)

Ko-lin Chin received his PhD in sociology from the University of Pennsylvania and is now a professor in Rutgers University School of Criminal Justice. He specializes in street gangs, human smuggling and trafficking, and drug trafficking. Among his many publications are the books *Chinese Subculture and Criminality: Non-Traditional Crime Groups in America* (1990), *Chinatown Gangs: Extortion, Enterprise, & Ethnicity* (1996), *Smuggled Chinese: Clandestine Immigration to the United States* (1999), and *Heijin: Organized Crime, Business, and Politics in Taiwan* (2003). His most recent book, *The Golden Triangle: from Opium and Heroin to Methamphetamine* (2009), chronicles the drug trade in the Wa area of the Golden Triangle where Chin investigated cross-border drug trafficking along the China-Burma border.

T. J. English (1957–)

For more than a decade English has investigated the changing face of organized crime in America. As a journalist and investigative reporter, he has written a string of well-researched and bestselling books on various aspects of international organized crime including *The Westies: The Irish Mob* (1991), *Born to Kill: America's Most Notorious Vietnamese Gang and the Changing Face of Organized Crime* (1995), *Paddy Whacked: The Untold Story of the Irish American Gangster* (2005), and most recently *Havana Nocturne* (2008), an investigative account of American mob infiltration of Havana, Cuba, in the years leading up to the Cuban Revolution.

Cyrille Fijnaut (1946–)

Professor Fijnaut teaches international and comparative criminal law at the Law School of Tilburg University. His many research interests include organized crime and terrorism, international police and judicial cooperation, comparative criminal procedure and police law, the history of European criminology and of policing in Europe, and police and judicial cooperation in the Benelux. He has authored, co-authored, and edited 75 books and published hundreds of articles in learned and professional journals and edited books including (with L. Paoli) *Organised Crime in Europe: Concepts, Patterns and Control Policies in the European Union and Beyond* (2004). He has also served as an expert for a number of governmental and parliamentary committees of inquiry in Belgium and the Netherlands related to organized and professional crime problems over the past 15 years. Since 2005, he has a special chair, sponsored by the Dutch State Lottery, on the regulatory aspects of gambling.

James Finckenauer (1939–)

Professor Finckenauer has taught at Rutgers University School of Criminal Justice since 1974 and is currently distinguished professor. Most of his research and teaching interests have been devoted to international and comparative criminal justice issues, transnational crime, organized crime, crime policy, and evaluation research. He is the author or coauthor of nine books, as well as hundreds of articles, chapters, and reports. His most recent book is *Mafia and Organized Crime: A Beginner's Guide* (2007). He has received numerous awards and is in demand as a lecturer on organized crime issues around the world. Finckenauer has served as editor of *The Journal of Research in Crime and Delinquency* and *Trends in Organized Crime* and was past president of the New Jersey Association of Criminal Justice Educators, the International Association for the Study of Organized Crime, and the Academy of Criminal Justice Sciences. In 2008, he served as a U.S. expert for the State Department's U.S.–Russia Experts Forum on Transnational Organized Crime, and a consultant to the United Nations in developing an Organized Crime Threat Assessment Handbook. He is currently working on a project studying the trafficking of Chinese women for commercial sex work.

Robert J. Kelly (1938–)

Kelley is the Broeklundian Professor Emeritus at Brooklyn College and the Graduate School of the City University of New York. He served on the Manhattan Terrorism Task Force after 9/11 and consulted with the Department of Homeland Security (Northeast region) and the National Institute of Justice on Terrorism and Organized Crime. Kelly has published numerous articles and books on terrorism, organized crime, and social distress, including *Encyclopedia of Organized Crime in the United States*, published by Greenwood Press in 2000. Most recently he coauthored *Illicit Trafficking*, published in 2005 by ABC-CLIO.

Letizia Paoli (1966–)

Letizia Paoli received her PhD in social and political sciences from the European University Institute in Florence in 1997. Since the early 1990s, she has researched and published extensively on organized crime, drugs, and illegal markets. During the 1990s, Paoli served as consultant to the Italian Ministries of the Interior and Justice, the United Nations Office for Drug Control and Crime Prevention, and the United Nations Crime and Justice Interregional Research Institute. In 2001, she published *Illegal Drug Trade in Russia,* the first detailed study of illegal drug trafficking in Russia, which was based on her research on behalf of the UN Office for Drug Control and Crime Prevention. In 2003, she published *Mafia Brotherhoods.*

Kip Schlegel (1953–)

Professor Schlegel teaches at Indiana University. His research interests include organized crime and the social mechanisms used to control it, the jurisprudence of sentencing, and criminal justice planning and evaluation. Most of his recent research is related to various facets of organized crime including the organization and enterprise of illegal drug distribution. He is the author of *Just Deserts for Corporate Criminals* (1990) and co-editor of *White Collar Crime Reconsidered* (1992). More recently he examined the connections between technology and organized crime in an article with Charles Cohen, "The Impact of Technology on Criminality" (2007).

Joseph Serio (1958–)

During the months leading up to fall of the Soviet Union, Serio was the only American to work in the Organized Crime Control Department of the Ministry of Internal Affairs of the U.S.S.R. His internship there was sponsored by the Office of International Criminal Justice at the University of Illinois at Chicago. During his tenure at Soviet national police headquarters from September 1990 to June 1991, he conducted research on Soviet organized crime, assisted in the preparation of Soviet police documents for international conferences, and developed a network of law enforcement contacts. In the course of his research, he had access to police intelligence reports and the Ministry's National Police Academy archives. His research resulted in the document *Soviet Organized Crime,* which has been used as a reference by the FBI, the Italian Ministry of Interior, the Chinese Ministry of Public Security, and other foreign governments. Between 1993 and 1996, Serio returned to Moscow and served stints as a security and media consultant for three years and as a consultant in to Kroll Associates, a corporate investigation and business intelligence firm. He is the author of the publication *Guidelines for Safety and Security in Russia* and most recently *Investigating the Russian Mafia* (2008).

Louise Shelley (1952–)

Professor Shelley is the founder and director of the Terrorism, Transnational Crime and Corruption Center (TRaCC). A leading expert on transnational crime and terrorism, she currently teaches in the School of Public Policy at George Mason University. She is the recipient of numerous grants and awards including a MacArthur Grant to establish the Russian Organized Crime Study Centers. Shelley is the author of numerous articles and book chapters on all aspects of transnational crime and corruption and also an editor (with Sally Stoecker) of *Human Traffic and Transnational Crime: Eurasian and American Perspectives.* Her research interests include transnational crime and corruption, particularly money laundering and illicit financial flows, human smuggling and trafficking, national security issues, and the use of information technology by international crime groups.

Federico Varese (1965–)

Professor Varese is professor of criminology and fellow of Linacre College, Oxford. He is the author of a number of book chapters in edited volumes, and his articles have appeared in leading journals such as *Law and Society Review, Archives Européenes de Sociologie, Low Intensity Conflict and Law Enforcement, Political Studies, Cahiers du Monde Russe* and *Rationality & Society.* His book *The Russian Mafia* (Oxford University Press) won the Ed Hewitt prize of the American Association for the Advancement of Slavic Studies in 2002 and has been translated into Dutch and Polish. He is also the editor of the journal *Global Crime.* His main research interests are the study of organized crime, corruption, Soviet criminal history, and the dynamics of altruistic behavior. In 2009, he completed *Mob and Mobility: How Mafias Settle in New Territory,* forthcoming from Princeton University Press.

Klaus von Lampe (1961–)

Klaus von Lampe is assistant professor at John Jay College of Criminal Justice, Department of Law, Police Science and Criminal Justice Administration, in New York. He has previously practiced law as an attorney, and he has worked as a researcher at Freie Universität Berlin with a specialization in the study of organized crime. His research interests include the conceptual history and theory of organized crime; the empirical manifestations of organized crime in the form of cigarette smuggling, drug trafficking, and underworld power structures; and strategic analysis in the area of organized crime. Dr. von Lampe is the author, coauthor, and co-editor of numerous journal articles and books on crime, crime control, and crime analysis. He is editor-in-chief of the journal *Trends in Organized Crime* and associate editor of *Crime, Law and Social Change.*

Michael Woodiwiss (1950–)

Professor Woodiwiss is on the history faculty of the University of the West of England, Bristol. His research interests focus on organized, corporate, white supremacist, and transnational crime after the American Civil War. He has published widely on various aspects of organized crime in America. His books include *Crime, Crusades and Corruption: Prohibitions in the United States 1900–1987* (1988), *Organized Crime and American Power* (2001), and *Gangster Capitalism: The United States and the Global Rise of Organized Crime* (2005). He is also co-editor (with Frank Pearce) of *Global Crime Connections: Dynamics and Control* (1993).

6

Data and Documents

Facts and Statistics on Organized Crime

One of the darker and unforeseen consequences of globalization has been the widespread increase in all forms of illegal trafficking and smuggling. From the trafficking of weapons and drugs to the smuggling of humans and diamonds, no era has been impacted by these activities as much as the present one. Fortunately, the inauguration of the Internet and the information superhighway has been a boon to researchers and others tracking the development of global organized crime activities through documents and statistics. There are countless domestic and international sources for this information. The data and documents presented in this chapter reflect the sources available from U.S. government agencies, the United Nations, regional agreements, and other multilateral conventions. Especially helpful for anyone researching the convergence of organized crime and terrorism are periodic in-depth reports prepared under the auspices of the Library of Congress Federal Research Division Also useful are the reports issued by the Institute for Security Studies (ISS Monograph Series) that examine trends of African organized crime. The U.S. Department of Justice offers detailed reports on organized crime in the United States through its Office of Justice Programs Bureau of Justice Statistics Special Reports. For anyone studying drug trafficking organizations, annual drug threat assessment reports by the National Drug Intelligence Center are a must and are available through the U.S. Department of Justice (see http://usdoj.gov/ndic/pubs).

175

The United Nations Office on Drugs and Crime offers a number of indispensable sources on global organized crime and is especially useful for data gathering. One needs to cast a wide net with all of the resource materials available, and these aforementioned sources are just the tip of the iceberg.

Defining Organized Crime

Racketeer Influenced and Corrupt Organizations Act (1970)

The Racketeer Influenced and Corrupt Organizations Act (RICO, was passed in 1970 as Title 9 of the Organized Crime Control Act of 1970 (OCCA), revolutionizing the war on organized crime in the United States. It was originally intended to allow the government to allege and prove the entire history of a criminal organization beyond the normal statute of limitations. RICO introduced new racketeering laws that enabled prosecutors to link numerous members of criminal syndicates in a single overarching charging document, or a conspiracy. It also established that their combined association to commit multiple crimes constituted a pattern of racketeering activity worthy of its stiff sentencing guidelines. Although it did not create any new substantive offenses, it did combine 35 existing offenses under the rubric of racketeering activity. What most distinguishes this legislation is it finally offered a definition of organized crime that was useful in attacking entire criminal networks. It has been most notably used against New York City's Five Mafia families in 1986 in the so-called Commission Case, or U.S. v. Salerno. *The government's case was built on the notion that Cosa Nostra's commission of crime bosses constituted a criminal enterprise, meaning that each was either a member or functionary of the commission. The following excerpt is the description that is the linchpin of any RICO case. Most important is the definition of racketeering in which defendants (two or more) can be tied to a conspiracy if they committed two or more acts of racketeering in the support of the organization in a 10-year period. A federal RICO violation carries a maximum penalty of 20 years, which increases to potential life in prison if the underlying acts themselves include more serious crimes such as murder or large-scale drug trafficking. The following excerpts list the individual criminal (predicate) acts that lead to a charge of violating RICO. Over the years Congress has added more crimes since the original 35.*

Section 1961. Definitions

(1) "racketeering activity" means (A) any act or threat involving murder, kidnapping, gambling, arson, robbery, bribery, extortion, dealing in obscene matter, or dealing in a controlled substance or listed chemical (as defined in section 102 of the Controlled Substances Act), which is chargeable under State law and punishable by imprisonment for more than one year; (B) any act which is indictable under any of the following provisions of title 18, United States Code: Section 201 (relating to bribery), section 224 (relating to sports bribery), sections 471, 472, and 473 (relating to counterfeiting), section 659 (relating to theft from interstate shipment) if the act indictable under section 659 is felonious, section 664 (relating to embezzlement from pension and welfare funds), sections 891–894 (relating to extortionate credit transactions), section 1028 (relating to fraud and related activity in connection with identification documents), section 1029 (relating to fraud and related activity in connection with access devices), section 1084 (relating to the transmission of gambling information), section 1341 (relating to mail fraud), section 1343 (relating to wire fraud), section 1344 (relating to financial institution fraud), section 1425 (relating to the procurement of citizenship or nationalization unlawfully), section 1426 (relating to the reproduction of naturalization or citizenship papers), section 1427 (relating to the sale of naturalization or citizenship papers), sections 1461–1465 (relating to obscene matter), section 1503 (relating to obstruction of justice), section 1510 (relating to obstruction of criminal investigations), section 1511 (relating to the obstruction of State or local law enforcement), section 1512 (relating to tampering with a witness, victim, or an informant), section 1513 (relating to retaliating against a witness, victim, or an informant), section 1542 (relating to false statement in application and use of passport), section 1543 (relating to forgery or false use of passport), section 1544 (relating to misuse of passport), section 1546 (relating to fraud and misuse of visas, permits, and other documents), sections 1581–1591 (relating to peonage, slavery, and trafficking in persons), section 1951 (relating to interference with commerce, robbery, or extortion), section 1952 (relating to racketeering), section 1953 (relating to interstate transportation of wagering paraphernalia), section 1954 (relating to unlawful welfare fund payments), section 1955 (relating to the prohibition of illegal gambling businesses), section 1956 (relating to the laundering of monetary instruments), section 1957 (relating to engaging in monetary transactions in property derived from specified unlawful activity), section 1958 (relating to use of interstate commerce facilities in the commission of murder-for-hire), sections 2251, 2251A, 2252, and 2260 (relating to sexual exploitation of children), sections 2312 and 2313 (relating to interstate transportation of stolen motor vehicles), sections 2314 and 2315 (relating to interstate transportation of stolen property), section 2318 (relating to trafficking in counterfeit labels for

phonorecords, computer programs or computer program documentation or packaging and copies of motion pictures or other audiovisual works), section 2319 (relating to criminal infringement of a copyright), section 2319A (relating to unauthorized fixation of and trafficking in sound recordings and music videos of live musical performances), section 2320 (relating to trafficking in goods or services bearing counterfeit marks), section 2321 (relating to trafficking in certain motor vehicles or motor vehicle parts), sections 2341–2346 (relating to trafficking in contraband cigarettes), sections 2421–2424 (relating to white slave traffic), (C) any act which is indictable under title 29, United States Code, section 186 (dealing with restrictions on payments and loans to labor organizations) or section 501(c) (relating to embezzlement from union funds), (D) any offense involving fraud connected with a case under title 11 (except a case under section 157 of this title), fraud in the sale of securities, or the felonious manufacture, importation, receiving, concealment, buying, selling, or otherwise dealing in a controlled substance or listed chemical (as defined in section 102 of the Controlled Substances Act), punishable under any law of the United States, (E) any act which is indictable under the Currency and Foreign Transactions Reporting Act, (F) any act which is indictable under the Immigration and Nationality Act, section 274 (relating to bringing in and harboring certain aliens), section 277 (relating to aiding or assisting certain aliens to enter the United States), or section 278 (relating to importation of alien for immoral purpose) if the act indictable under such section of such Act was committed for the purpose of financial gain, or (G) any act that is indictable under any provision listed in section 332b(g)(5)(B);

Rico Definitions

The following excerpt from RICO lists the multitude of definitions enumerated by the law.

(2) "State" means any State of the United States, the District of Columbia, the Commonwealth of Puerto Rico, any territory or possession of the United States, any political subdivision, or any department, agency, or instrumentality thereof; (3) "person" includes any individual or entity capable of holding a legal or beneficial interest in property; (4) "enterprise" includes any individual, partnership, corporation, association, or other legal entity, and any union or group of individuals associated in fact although not a legal entity; (5) "pattern of racketeering activity" requires at least two acts of racketeering activity, one of which occurred after the effective date of this chapter and the last of which occurred within ten years (excluding any period of imprisonment) after the commission of a prior act of racketeering activity; (6) "unlawful debt" means a debt (A) incurred or contracted in gambling activity which was

in violation of the law of the United States, a State or political subdivision thereof, or which is unenforceable under State or Federal law in whole or in part as to principal or interest because of the laws relating to usury, and (B) which was incurred in connection with the business of gambling in violation of the law of the United States, a State or political subdivision thereof, or the business of lending money or a thing of value at a rate usurious under State or Federal law, where the usurious rate is at least twice the enforceable rate; (7) "racketeering investigator" means any attorney or investigator so designated by the Attorney General and charged with the duty of enforcing or carrying into effect this chapter; (8) "racketeering investigation" means any inquiry conducted by any racketeering investigator for the purpose of ascertaining whether any person has been involved in any violation of this chapter or of any final order, judgment, or decree of any court of the United States, duly entered in any case or proceeding arising under this chapter; (9) "documentary material" includes any book, paper, document, record, recording, or other material; and (10) "Attorney General" includes the Attorney General of the United States, the Deputy Attorney General of the United States, the Associate Attorney General of the United States, any Assistant Attorney General of the United States, or any employee of the Department of Justice or any employee of any department or agency of the United States so designated by the Attorney General to carry out the powers conferred on the Attorney General by this chapter. Any department or agency so designated may use in investigations authorized by this chapter either the investigative provisions of this chapter or the investigative power of such department or agency otherwise conferred by law.

Source: http://www.treas.gov/offices/enforcement/teoaf/publications/18usc1961-1968-rico.pdf.

United Nations Convention against Transnational Organized Crime (2000)

Although it took until 2003 for this Convention to be ratified, it finally offered a legal definition of organized crime acceptable to most countries and based on only a few criteria in regards to the number of members and group structure.

Article 1 Statement of Purpose

The purpose of this Convention is to promote cooperation to prevent and combat transnational organized crime more effectively.

Article 2 Use of Terms

For the purposes of this Convention:

(a) "Organized criminal group" shall mean a structured group of three or more persons, existing for a period of time and acting in concert with the aim of committing one or more serious crimes or offences established in accordance with this Convention, in order to obtain, directly or indirectly, a financial or other material benefit;

(b) "Serious crime" shall mean conduct constituting an offence punishable by a maximum deprivation of liberty of at least four years or a more serious penalty;

(c) "Structured group" shall mean a group that is not randomly formed for the immediate commission of an offence and that does not need to have formally defined roles for its members, continuity of its membership or a developed structure;

(d) "Property" shall mean assets of every kind, whether corporeal or incorporeal, movable or immovable, tangible or intangible, and legal documents or instruments evidencing title to, or interest in, such assets;

(e) "Proceeds of crime" shall mean any property derived from or obtained, directly or indirectly, through the commission of an offence;

(f) "Freezing" or "seizure" shall mean temporarily prohibiting the transfer, conversion, disposition or movement of property or temporarily assuming custody or control of property on the basis of an order issued by a court or other competent authority;

(g) "Confiscation", which includes forfeiture where applicable, shall mean the permanent deprivation of property by order of a court or other competent authority;

(h) "Predicate offence" shall mean any offence as a result of which proceeds have been generated that may become the subject of an offence as defined in article 6 of this Convention;

(i) "Controlled delivery" shall mean the technique of allowing illicit or suspect consignments to pass out of, through or into the territory of one or more States, with the knowledge and under the supervision of their competent authorities, with a view to the investigation of an offence and the identification of persons involved in the commission of the offence;

(j) "Regional economic integration organization" shall mean an organization constituted by sovereign States of a given region, to which its member States have transferred competence in respect of matters governed by this Convention and which has been duly authorized, in accordance with its internal procedures, to sign, ratify, accept, approve or accede to it; references to "States

Parties" under this Convention shall apply to such organizations within the limits of their competence.

Article 3 Scope of Application

1. This Convention shall apply, except as otherwise stated herein, to the prevention, investigation and prosecution of:
   (a) The offences established in accordance with articles 5, 6, 8 and 23 of this Convention; and
   (b) Serious crime as defined in article 2 of this Convention; where the offence is transnational in nature and involves an organized criminal group.

2. For the purpose of paragraph 1 of this article, an offence is transnational in nature if:
   (a) It is committed in more than one State;
   (b) It is committed in one State but a substantial part of its preparation, planning, direction or control takes place in another State;
   (c) It is committed in one State but involves an organized criminal group that engages in criminal activities in more than one State; or
   (d) It is committed in one State but has substantial effects in another State.

Source: United Nations Convention against Transnational Organized Crime, United Nations, 2000, pp. 1–2.

Categories of Transnational Criminal Offenses

The United Nations has identified 18 categories of transnational offenses whose inception, perpetration, and direct or indirect efforts involve more than one country. These include:

Money laundering	Computer crime
Terrorist activities	Environmental crime
Theft of art and cultural objects	Trafficking in persons
Theft of intellectual property	Trade in human body parts
Illicit arms trafficking	Illegal drug trafficking
Aircraft hijacking	Fraudulent bankruptcy
Sea piracy	Infiltration of legal business
Insurance fraud	Corruption and bribery of public or party officials

Source: Adapted from G. O. Mueller. 2001. "Transnational Crime: Definitions and Concepts." In *Combating Transnational Crime: Concepts, Activities and Responses,* ed. Phil Williams and D. Vlassis, 13–14. London: Frank Cass.

Drug Trafficking

People have used narcotics for medicinal, recreational, and religious purposes for millennia. It was not until the early 1800s, however, that the global trafficking of opium became an international concern. During the 19th century, China made a number of attempts to stop the opium trade with India, then a British colony, after legions of addicts were created. Before 1800, there were few reports of opium addiction in China. In 1773, the British gained control of India's Bengal opium fields and inundated China with the drug. Over the next century this created a serious addiction problem among Chinese users unfamiliar with the drug's propensities. In 1839, the Chinese confiscated and destroyed a large trove of British opium, setting off the Opium War. A subsequent treaty in 1842 forced China to accept the free trade of opium within its borders. It has been estimated that by 1900 at least one third of the Chinese had become users and perhaps 10 percent were addicted. Following the 1909 Shanghai Opium Commission and the 1911–1912 International Opium Conference held at The Hague, China began to suppress domestic cultivation that had led to a dramatic shift in the consumption of imported morphine and heroin from Europe and to the centralization of the Shanghai Triads over the illegal opiate trade, and by the early 20th century the opium trade had passed from the British to the Chinese underworld. By the 1920s, these syndicates were importing 10 tons of heroin from Japan and Europe per year and by the early 1930s, Japanese labs in north China were producing large amounts of heroin. The ascension of Communist China in 1949, together with punitive laws against drug use, ended much of the problem in China after 1949, and the trade shifted to Central and Southern Asia and later Mexico and Colombia.

Potential Worldwide Heroin Production, in Metric Tons, 2002–2006

Despite a number of initiatives targeting poppy growing and heroin trafficking around the world the production of heroin contin-

TABLE 6.1
Potential Worldwide Heroin Production, in Metric Tons, 2002–2006

	2002	2003	2004	2005	2006
Afghanistan	150	337	582	526.6	664
Burma	60	46	31.5	36	22
Mexico	6.8	11.9	8.6	8	12.7
Colombia	8.5	7.8	3.8	*	4.6
Pakistan	0.5	5.2	NA	3.8	4.2
Laos	17	19	5	2.7	1
Vietnam	1	NA	NA	NA	0.0
Thailand	0.9	NA	NA	NA	NA
Guatemala	NA	NA	1.4	0.4	NA
Total	244.7	426.9	632.3	577.5	708.5

Source: 2009 National Drug Threat Assessment, DOJ.
*Crime and Narcotics Center did not report for Colombia in 2005.
NA = Not available.

ues to increase in the 21st century, as street prices fall and purity increases. As the table demonstrates, Afghanistan continues as the major poppy source for the global heroin trade, with Burma (Myanmar) a distant second. According to the available sources interdiction efforts seem to be working best in Burma, Laos and Colombia, with all registering significant drops in production. However, the involvement and support of the Taliban in the opium growing regions of Afghanistan probably account for the recrudescence of the problem there.

International organized crime networks have persisted in parts of Latin America since the early 1960s. The Andean region is home to its cocaine trade, enveloping the nations of Colombia, Bolivia, and Peru. One recent estimate by the DEA and the Colombian National Police estimated that Colombia is home to more than 300 active drug trafficking groups. Peru and Bolivia have stepped up their participation in the refining and trafficking of cocaine as Colombia became the world's premier coca producer. Due in part to the stagnation of the American cocaine market in the late 1980s cocaine syndicates diversified their markets and products and began looking for new markets in Europe, the former Soviet Union and Latin America. At the same time Colombia became the leading importer of heroin into the United States.

Estimated Andean Region Coca Cultivation

This table shows how Andean coca production waxed and waned in the first years of the 21st century but since 2005 cultivation has increased in Colombia and Bolivia. Although the United States and Colombia launched a joint effort to diminish coca cultivation in the late 1990s production increased by 16% in 2007, its highest rise since 2001. Despite the reduction in coca in Bolivia in the late 1990s, since 2001 it has increased each year. Some blame recurring political challenges of having had five different presidents between 2000 and 2006. Peru has surpassed is coca eradication goals; however, coca cultivation continues to increase, especially with the reemergence in 2006 of the terrorist group the Shining Path who now protect the crops.

Estimated Amounts of Illicit Drugs Transiting or Produced in Mexico and Seized, 2000–2006

Despite recent attempts by the Calderon administration, Mexico remains mired in corruption as it continues its prominence as a major producer of heroin, methamphetamine, and marijuana. As a result Mexican gangs control much of the U.S. methamphetamine trade, while perhaps half the cocaine enters the U.S. across the Mexican border. Table 6.3 illustrates Mexico's stature at the epicenter of drug trafficking in the Americas. What is most striking

Table 6.2
Estimated Andean Region Coca Cultivation
(New cultivation hectares)

	2003	2004	2005	2006	2007
Bolivia	23,200	24,600	26,500	25,800	29,500
Colombia	113,850	114,100	144,000	157,200	167,000
Peru	29,250	27,500	34,000	42,000	36,000
Total	166,300	166,200	204,500	225,000	232,500

Source: Adapted from 2009 National Drug Threat Assessment, DOJ.

TABLE 6.3
Estimated Amounts of Illicit Drugs Transiting or Produced in Mexico and Seized,
2000–2006

Illicit drugs	2000	2001	2002	2003	2004	2005	2006
Cocaine (metric tons)							
Arriving in Mexico for							
Transshipment to U.S.	220	270	270	210	220–440	260–460	300–460
Seized in Mexico	20	10	8	12	19	21	10
U.S. border seizures	23	20	23	16	22	23	27
Heroin (metric tons)							
Produced	9	21	13	30	23	17	N/A
Seized in Mexico	.27	.27	.28	.31	.30	.46	.40
U.S. border seizures	.07	.35	.30	35	.29	.32	.47
Marijuana (metric tons)							
Produced	7000	7400	7900	13,500	10,400	10,100	N/A
Seized in Mexico	1619	1839	1633	2248	2208	1786	1849
U.S. border seizures	533	1083	1072	1221	1173	974	1015
Methamphetamine							
(kilograms)							
Seized in Mexico	560	400	460	750	950	980	600
U.S. border seizures	500	1150	1320	1750	2210	2870	2710

Source: U.S. Government Accountability Office, Appendix I, p. 25, Oct. 25, 2007.

is the amount of drugs transshipped through the U.S. compared to the minute quantities seized north and south of the Mexican border. References to seizures at the U.S. border include 88 border counties in Arizona, California, New Mexico and Texas and occur within 150 miles on either side of the U.S.–Mexico border.

Gangs Affiliated with the Sinaloa, Gulf, Juarez, or Tijuana Cartels

Mexican drug organizations flourish along the border competing with each other in bloody battles over the illicit drug trade. It has been estimated these gangs spend $3 billion each year in bribes for protection at all levels of government. As a result these so-called cartels are more transnational than ever, often involved in alliances with other Latin American syndicates. Table 6.4 notes the various American street and prison gangs that have entered into accommodations with the Mexican gangs.

TABLE 6.4
Gangs Affiliated with the Sinaloa, Gulf, Juarez, or Tijuana Cartels

18th Street	Latin Kings
Bandidos	Mara Salvatrucha (MS-13)
Barrio Azteca	Mexican Mafia
Black Guerilla Family	Mexikanemi
Bloods	Mongols
Crips	Nortenos
Florencia 13	Surenos
Gangster Disciples	Tango Blast
Hells Angels	Texas Syndicate
Hermanos de Pistoleros Latinos	Vagos

Source: Federal, state, and local reporting; 2009 National Drug Threat Assessment, DOJ.

The 20 Largest Cocaine Seizures Ever Reported

Table 6.5 lists the twenty largest cocaine seizures. What is most notable is the number that took place in the Eastern Pacific Ocean. Interdiction on the high seas has had a number of successes and as can be seen has largely been eliminated in the Caribbean. However this has been replaced by land-based operations controlled by Mexican gangs. It should not be surprising then that the largest cocaine seizure over the past twenty years took place in Mexico.

Drug Seizures in the Central Asian Region, 2005–2006

The so-called Golden Crescent of Central Asia, comprises the mountainous borderlands of Afghanistan, Iran, and Pakistan as well as the Central Asian countries of Kazakhstan, Kyrgyzstan, Tajikistan, Turkmenistan, and Uzbekistan. While drug trafficking has increased in Iran, Afghanistan, and Pakistan as this region retains its prominence in the heroin trade, new interdiction strategies and better cooperation between police forces have had more success in the other Central Asian countries for the most part between 2005 and 2006. In fact, at the end of 2007 new strategies had left the northern province of Balkh, adjacent to Uzbekistan and Tajikistan and 12 others virtually poppy free. However, farmers switched from growing opium poppies in favor of cannabis, which produces both the herb and the resin for hashish. Nonetheless, Afghanistan still supplies the majority of the world's opium.

TABLE 6.5
The 20 Largest Cocaine Seizures Ever Reported

Ranking	Kilograms	Year	Location
1	23,600	2007	Mexico
2	21,000	1989	U.S.-California
3	15,200	2007	Eastern Pacific Ocean
4	15,200	2007	Colombia
5	13,200	2007	Colombia
6	13,200	2004	Eastern Pacific Ocean
7	12,144	2004	Eastern Pacific Ocean
8	11,971	2001	Eastern Pacific Ocean
9	11,720	2007	Mexico
10	11,401	2002	Eastern Pacific Ocean
11	11,323	1995	Eastern Pacific Ocean
12	10,386	2007	Eastern Pacific Ocean
13	9,846	1997	Mexico
14	9,690	1999	Atlantic Ocean
15	9,650	1999	Eastern Pacific Ocean
16	9,267	2001	Eastern Pacific Ocean
17	9,017	2001	Eastern Pacific Ocean
18	9,000	2001	Eastern Pacific Ocean
19	8,895	2000	Chile
20	8,840	2006	Eastern Pacific Ocean

Source: 2009 National Drug Threat Assessment, DOJ.

TABLE 6.6
Drug Seizures in the Central Asian Region, 2005–2006

	Opium		Heroin		Cannabis herb		Cannabis resin	
	Kilograms							
	2005	2006	2005	2006	2005	2006	2005	2006
Kazakhstan	668	636	625	554	21,732	22,868	284	305
Kyrgyzstan	261	302	259	260	1,983	2,399	131	153
Tajikistan	1,104	1,386	2,344	2097	1,164	1,305	NA	NA
Turkmenistan	748	2,655	180	201	135	154	18	206
Uzbekistan	107	759	466	537	444	428	9	5

Source: An Assessment of Transnational Organized Crime in Central Asia, 2006–2007.

narcotics through their usual medical channels (physicians and pharmacists). Once someone was arrested in possession of narcotics, this was viewed as a violation unless the addict could produce a document testifying that the narcotics were obtained legally. Violations could incur a maximum five-year jail sentence, a $2,000 fine, or both. The following are excerpts from the Act:

Chap 1.—An Act To provide for the registration of, with collectors of internal revenue, and to impose a special tax on all persons who produce, import, manufacture, compound, deal in, dispense, sell, distribute, or give away opium or coca leaves, their salts, derivatives, or preparations, and for other purposes.

Be it enacted by the Senate and House of Representatives of the United States of America in Congress assembled, that on and after the first day of March, nineteen hundred and fifteen, every person who produces, imports, manufactures, compounds, deals in, dispenses, distributes, or gives away opium or coca leaves or any compound, manufacture, salt, derivative, or preparation thereof, shall register with the collector of internal revenue of the district, his name or style, place of business, and place or places where such business is to be carried on: Provided, that the office, or if none, then the residence of any person shall be considered for purposes of this Act to be his place of business. At the time of such registry and on or before the first of July annually thereafter, every person who produces, imports, manufactures, compounds, deals in, dispenses, distributes, or gives away any of the aforesaid drugs shall pay to the said collector a special tax at the rate of $1 per annum. . . .

It shall be unlawful for any person required to register under the terms of this Act to produce, import, manufacture, compound, deal in, dispense, sell, distribute, any of the aforesaid drugs without having registered and paid the special tax provided for in this section. . . .

Sec. 2 That it shall be unlawful for any person to sell, barter, exchange, or give away any of the aforesaid drugs except in pursuance of a written order of the person to whom such article is sold, bartered, exchanged, or given, on a form to be issued in blank for that purpose by the Commissioner of Internal Revenue. Every person who shall accept any such order, and in pursuance thereof shall sell, barter, exchange, or give away any of the aforesaid drugs shall preserve such order for a period of two years in such a way as to be readily accessible to inspection by any officer, agent, or employee of the Treasury Department duly authorized for that purpose. . . .

Sec. 4 That it shall be unlawful for any person who shall not have registered and paid the special tax as required by section one of this Act to send, ship, carry, or deliver any of the aforesaid drugs from any State or Territory or the District of Columbia, or any insular possession of the

United States, to any person in any other State or Territory or the District of Columbia or any insular possession of the United States. . . .

Sec. 6 That the provisions of this Act shall not be construed to apply to the sale, distribution, or giving away, dispensing, or possession of preparations and remedies which do not contain more than two grains of opium, or more than one-fourth of a grain of morphine, or more than one-eighth of grain of heroin, or more than one grain of codeine. . . . The provisions of this Act shall not apply to decocainized coca leaves or preparations made therefrom, or to other preparations of coca leaves which do not contain cocaine.

Sec. 9 That any person who violates or fails to comply with any of the requirements of this Act shall, on conviction, be fined not more than $2,000 or be imprisoned not more than five years, or both, in the discretion of the court.

Source: Harrison Tax Act of 1914, Pub. L., No. 223, Chap. 1, 38 Stat. 785, 63rd Congress (1914), pp. 785–790.

Marijuana Tax Act of 1937

At a meeting of the League of Nations in the mid-1930s, every country voted against an international ban on cannabis (marijuana). Most realized how impossible it would be to enforce the law. Federal Bureau of Narcotics director Harry Anslinger found that the only way to support it at home was through the adoption of a tax law that would place a prohibitive tax on the selling and buying of the drug, and in 1937 it went into effect, making the sale and possession of marijuana illegal through federal legislation. One of the more deceptive aspects of the law was the fact that penalties included five years' imprisonment, a $2,000 fine, or both—an excessive punishment for evading such a small tax. The Act has been criticized for its excessive length (more than 60 pages) and the confusing array of required affidavits, depositions, sworn statements, and constant Treasury Department police inspections in every instance that marijuana is involved in a transaction. The following are several excerpts from the Act:

Sec. 2 (a) Every person who imports, manufactures, produces, compounds, sells, deals in, dispenses, administers, or gives away marihuana shall within fifteen days after the effective date of this Act . . . pay the following special taxes respectively:

(1)   Importers, manufacturers, and compounders of marihuana, $24 per year.

(2) Producers of . . . $1 per year
(3) Physicians, dentists, veterinary surgeons, and other practitioners who distribute, dispense, administer, or prescribe . . . $1 per year

Sec. 12 Any person who is convicted of a violation of any provision of the Act shall be fined not more than $2,000 or imprisoned not more than five years, or both, in the discretion of the court.

Source: Marijuana Tax Act of 1937, Pub. L. 238, Chap. 553, 50 Stat. 551, 75th Congress, 1937, pp. 551–557.

The Single Convention on Narcotic Drugs of 1961

Intending to regulate the production, trade, and use of narcotic drugs, cocaine, and marijuana in one fell swoop, the Single Convention on Narcotics Drugs of 1961 was considered at its time the most comprehensive international drug control agreement. It consolidated all the current drug-control treaties into a single agreement. Almost doubling the number of 73 who originally signed it, by 1993 144 countries had signed the agreement. The following excerpts are from Articles 35 and 36:

Article 35. Action against the Illicit Traffic

The parties shall . . .

a) Make arrangements at the national level for coordination of preventive and repressive action against the illicit drug trade. . . .
b) Assist each other in the campaign against the illicit traffic in narcotic drugs;
c) Cooperate closely with each other and with the competent international organizations of which they are members with a view to maintaining a coordinated campaign against the illicit traffic;
d) Ensure that international cooperation between the appropriate agencies be conducted in an expeditious manner.

Article 36. Penal Provisions

1. a) Subject to its constitutional limitations, each Party shall adopt measures as will ensure that cultivation, production, manufacture, extraction, preparation, possession, offering, offering for sale, distribution, purchase, sale, delivery on any terms whatsoever, brokerage, dispatch in transit, transport, importation and exportation of drugs contrary to the provisions of the Convention. . . . shall be punishable offenses when committed inten-

tionally, and that serious offenses shall be liable to adequate punishment particularly by imprisonment or other penalties of deprivation of liberty

Source: http://www.incb.org/pdf/e/conv/convention_1961_en.pdf.

The Merida Initiative, 2008

On June 30, 2008, President George W. Bush signed the Merida Initiative (better known as Plan Mexico) into law. It passed Congress as part of the Iraq supplemental funding bill. Its passage was controversial as it had to be rewritten several times to be approved by Congress as legislators parried the Bush administration over human rights conditions under Mexican President Felipe Calderon's government. It was hoped that the final aid package of $400 million signaled a new era in bilateral cooperation in the fighting transnational organized crime on the border with Mexico. But many feared that Mexico's use of a military strategy to fight the narcotics trade would only increase drug-related violence and human rights abuses. Following is a joint statement issued by the Secretary of State, the Secretary of Defense, the Attorney General, the Deputy Secretary of Homeland Security, and the Director of National Drug Control Policy of the United States and the Secretary of Foreign Affairs, the Secretary of National Defense, the Attorney General, the Secretary of Public Security, and the Under Secretary of the Navy of Mexico, who, together with other senior government officials, met December 19, 2008, as the Merida Initiative High-Level Consultative Group.

Joint Statement of the Merida Initiative High Level Consultative Group

Presidents Felipe Calderon and George Bush met in Merida, Mexico in March 2007 and reviewed the broad range of issues affecting our two countries. The Joint U.S.–Mexico Communiqué issued on March 14, 2007 recognized the threat posed by organized crime and drug trafficking to both nations and our shared responsibility to address this threat. Moreover, the Presidents reaffirmed the commitment of our two countries to establish a lasting partnership to expand and intensify cooperation in what we have come to call the Merida Initiative. The Merida Initiative High-Level Consultative Group held its inaugural meeting today to discuss progress to date on these critical issues, and to chart a course for future cooperation.

Since the 2007 Summit in Merida, the Government of Mexico has taken bold and unprecedented steps to confront organized crime and violence, often at great cost. As his administration enters into its third year, President Felipe Calderon has reiterated and clearly demonstrated his commitment to combat, head-on, drug-trafficking and organized crime. The Government of the United States has supported this effort by increasing the provision of information and technical assistance and by complementary steps to stop the trafficking of illegal weapons from the United States, impede bulk currency smuggling across our border, reduce the domestic demand for illicit drugs, and combat drug trafficking and organized crime in the United States.

To provide resources for an enhanced security cooperation partnership as set forth in the 2007 Summit, President Bush sought funding from Congress for the "Merida Initiative." The Supplemental Appropriations Act of 2008, signed by President Bush on June 30, provided $400 million to fund training, equipment and other assistance under the Merida Initiative in Mexico, an initial installment of a multi-year, $1.4 billion program of support. On December 3, Mexico and the United States signed a Letter of Agreement (LOA) making available the first $197 million of this package.

Even before the signing of the LOA, Mexico and the United States have taken steps to strengthen our law enforcement and security cooperation by accelerating existing efforts and by focusing previously agreed upon assistance in areas that will advance the objectives of the Merida Initiative. In this regard, we have already:

> enhanced forensic capabilities, including the inauguration of a new forensics lab in Mexico;
> strengthened ties to investigate cross-border financial flows and combat money laundering;
> expanded collaboration to trace weapons and stop the illegal export of arms used by drug organizations;
> developed technical requirements for the transfer of counter-drug aviation assets;
> increased the number of fugitive apprehensions and extraditions;
> deployed X-ray equipped vans and radiation monitoring technology; and
> increased intelligence sharing on transnational drug trafficking organizations.

The breadth and depth of the cooperation between the United States and Mexico in confronting transnational organized crime and security threats requires new institutional mechanisms to ensure effective coordination, the timely use of operational intelli-
gence, and the efficient use of resources. Our governments intend therefore to establish before the end of 2009, a bilateral follow-up and implementation mechanism in Mexico City where officials of the United States and Mexico will work together to carry out mutually agreed assistance projects, monitor results, and revise and update cooperative activities under the Merida Initiative . . .

We also recognize the importance of close engagement with the countries of Central America and the Caribbean in addressing the common threats emanating from organized crime. A successful Merida Initiative must have a strong regional and hemispheric component, and we intend to explore ways to ensure that our bilateral U.S.–Mexico partnership addresses this dimension.

Source: U.S. Department of State, Joint Statement of the Merida Initiative High Level Consultative Group, http://www.state.gov/r/pa/prs/ ps/2008/dec/113368.html, Dec. 18, 2008.

Weapons Trafficking

Thanks to an increased demand for weapons resulting from the expansion of ethnic and regional conflict since the late 1980s in places such as Africa, Central America, the former Yugoslavia, and the former Soviet Union, the illegal trafficking in weapons has become a huge international business mostly controlled by organized criminal syndicates and networks. Their success, however, would be rather limited if not for the collusion of institutions and individuals outside the criminal organizations such as national defense ministries, national security agencies, legitimate arms dealers, and others. Among the following excerpts is a relatively new document, or End User Certificate—an attempt to restrict the illicit sales of weapons. Its requirement is intended to guarantee the destination of weapons shipments. However, the attempt to stem the flow of weapons is quixotic in a world awash in wars, weapons, and civil conflict. More recently the United States has been targeted as a major source for the weapons now wreaking havoc and taking thousands of lives south of the U.S.–Mexican border. Among the documents that follow are portions of the landmark Inter-American Convention against Illicit Manufacturing of and Trafficking in Firearms of 1997, which has yet to be ratified by the American government, more than a decade after signing it.

Inter-American Convention against the Illicit Manufacturing of and Trafficking in Firearms, Ammunition, Explosives and Other Related Materials, 1997

These excerpts are from a regional agreement from the Organization of American States (OAS). On November 14, 1997, the OAS adopted the Inter-American Convention against the Illicit Manufacturing of and

Trafficking in Firearms, Ammunition, Explosives, and Other Related Materials. This is the first multilateral convention designed to prevent, combat, and eradicate illegal transnational trafficking in firearms, ammunition, and explosives. The purpose of this Convention is to prevent, combat, and eradicate the illicit manufacturing of and trafficking in firearms, ammunition, explosives, and other related materials; to promote and facilitate cooperation and exchange of information and experience among States Parties to prevent, combat, and eradicate the illicit manufacturing of and trafficking in firearms, ammunition, explosives, and other related materials. In the statement by Senator Richard Lugar, he insists it is time for the United States to finally ratify the treaty in 2009, despite having signed on in 1997.

THE STATES PARTIES,

AWARE of the urgent need to prevent, combat, and eradicate the illicit manufacturing of and trafficking in firearms, ammunition, explosives, and other related materials, due to the harmful effects of these activities on the security of each state and the region as a whole, endangering the well-being of peoples, their social and economic development, and their right to live in peace;

CONCERNED by the increase, at the international level, in the illicit manufacturing of and trafficking in firearms, ammunition, explosives, and other related materials and by the serious problems resulting there from;

REAFFIRMING that States Parties give priority to preventing, combating, and eradicating the illicit manufacturing of and trafficking in firearms, ammunition, explosives, and other related materials because of the links of such activities with drug trafficking, terrorism, transnational organized crime, and mercenary and other criminal activities;

CONCERNED about the illicit manufacture of explosives from substances and articles that in and of themselves are not explosives—and that are not addressed by this Convention due to their other lawful uses—for activities related to drug trafficking, terrorism, transnational organized crime and mercenary and other criminal activities;

CONSIDERING the urgent need for all states, and especially those states that produce, export, and import arms, to take the necessary measures to prevent, combat, and eradicate the illicit manufacturing of and trafficking in firearms, ammunition, explosives, and other related materials;

CONVINCED that combating the illicit manufacturing of and trafficking in firearms, ammunition, explosives, and other related materials calls for international cooperation, exchange of information, and other appropriate measures at the national, regional, and international levels, and desiring to set a precedent for the international community in this regard;

STRESSING the need, in peace processes and post-conflict situations, to achieve effective control of firearms, ammunition, explosives, and other related materials in order to prevent their entry into the illicit market;

MINDFUL of the pertinent resolutions of the United Nations General Assembly on measures to eradicate the illicit transfer of conventional weapons and on the need for all states to guarantee their security, and of the efforts carried out in the framework of the Inter-American Drug Abuse Control Commission (CICAD);

RECOGNIZING the importance of strengthening existing international law enforcement support mechanisms such as the International Weapons and Explosives Tracking System (IWETS) of the International Criminal Police Organization (INTERPOL), to prevent, combat, and eradicate the illicit manufacturing of and trafficking in firearms, ammunition, explosives, and other related materials . . .

HAVE DECIDED TO ADOPT THIS INTER-AMERICAN CONVENTION AGAINST THE ILLICIT MANUFACTURING OF AND TRAFFICKING IN FIREARMS, AMMUNITION, EXPLOSIVES, AND OTHER RELATED MATERIALS:

Article I
Definitions

For the purposes of this Convention, the following definitions shall apply:

1. "Illicit manufacturing": the manufacture or assembly of firearms, ammunition, explosives, and other related materials:
    a. from components or parts illicitly trafficked; or
    b. without a license from a competent governmental authority of the State Party where the manufacture or assembly takes place; or
    c. without marking the firearms that require marking at the time of manufacturing.

2. "Illicit trafficking": the import, export, acquisition, sale, delivery, movement, or transfer of firearms, ammunition, explosives, and other related materials from or across the territory of one State Party to that of another State Party, if any one of the States Parties concerned does not authorize it.

3. "Firearms":
    a. any barreled weapon which will or is designed to or may be readily converted to expel a bullet or projectile by the action of an explosive, except antique firearms manufactured before the 20th Century or their replicas; or
    b. any other weapon or destructive device such as any explosive, incendiary or gas bomb, grenade, rocket, rocket launcher, missile, missile system, or mine.

4. "Ammunition": the complete round or its components, including cartridge cases, primers, propellant powder, bullets, or projectiles that are used in any firearm.

5. "Explosives": any substance or article that is made, manufactured, or used to produce an explosion, detonation, or propulsive or pyrotechnic effect, except:
   a. substances and articles that are not in and of themselves explosive; or
   b. substances and articles listed in the Annex to this Convention.

6. "Other related materials": any component, part, or replacement part of a firearm, or an accessory which can be attached to a firearm.

7. "Controlled delivery": the technique of allowing illicit or suspect consignments of firearms, ammunition, explosives, and other related materials to pass out of, through, or into the territory of one or more states, with the knowledge and under the supervision of their competent authorities, with a view to identifying persons involved in the commission of offenses referred to in Article IV of this Convention.

Source: U.S. Department of State, Inter-American Convention against the Illicit Manufacturing of and Trafficking in Firearms, Ammunition, Explosives, and Other Related Materials, www.state.gov/p/wha/rls/49907. htm, January 1, 1997.

U.S. Senator Richard Lugar on Weapons Trafficking, 2009

The following excerpt is from a statement submitted for the record by U.S. Senate Foreign Relations Committee Ranking Member Richard Lugar on March 30, 2009 at a field hearing in El Paso, Texas on U.S.–Mexico border violence. It is most notable for taking the United States to task for not ratifying the 1997 OAS initiative on weapons control.

Since entering office in December 2006, President Felipe Calderon has moved to improve security in his country and has recast U.S.–Mexico relations on the basis of equality and mutual respect. The Mexican government has committed billions of dollars to combat drug trafficking. . . . In addition, the Calderon government has strengthened law enforcement cooperation with the United States, extradited drug suspects to the U.S. and made record seizures of cocaine, methamphetamine precursors, cash and other assets. The Merida Initiative signed into law by the Administration of President George W. Bush is an attempt to seize the opportunity created by Mexico's invigorated anti-crime campaign by funding key programs and building stronger cooperation between Mexico and the United States. It recognizes that 90 percent of the cocaine entering the United States transits Mexico and that our efforts to combat this drug flow and associated criminal activities depend on a partnership with the Mexican government. . . . One area that requires more cooperation is arms trafficking. As much as 90 percent of the assault weapons and other guns used by Mexican drug cartels are coming from the United States, fueling drug-related violence that is believed to have killed more than 7,000 people since January 2008. . . . the Mexican government officials I met with consistently relayed their concerns about the flow of guns and explosives from the United States into Mexico. American Embassy officials confirmed that the U.S. was a major source of weapons for Mexican gangs and drug runners, as well. . . . In addition to supporting efforts to manage firearms under the Merida Initiative, we should consider ratifying, during this Congress, the Inter-American Convention against the Illicit Manufacturing of and Trafficking in Firearms, Ammunition, Explosives and other Related Materials (CIFTA) . . . signed by 33 countries in the Western Hemisphere and ratified by 29. The U.S. was an original signer in 1997, but ratification is still pending.

Source: Statement by Senator Lugar for field hearing on "U.S.–Mexico Border Violence," http://lugar.senate.gov/press/record.cfm?id=310624, March 27, 2009.

End User Certificate (EUC)

In an attempt to restrict the sale of weapons, documentation, called the End User Certificate, is required that purportedly guarantees the destination of weapons. A certificate must accompany every shipment, but most reports indicate these can be easily purchased from corrupt countries for a percentage of the eventual profit. The following is an excerpt from the instructions on filling out the form (DSP-83).

Instructions
The Department of State, United States of America, requires that this completed form (DSP-83) be included as a part of an application for authorization to export Significant Military Equipment (SME) and classified equipment or data (22 CFR §§ 123,10 (d) and 125.21). Failure to submit may result in the application being "Returned Without Action" (RWA). The form (DSP-83) must be completed by the appropriate foreign persons

(e.g., consignee, end-user, government) and forwarded to the Department of State through the U.S. person making the application.

1. The Applicant, when submitting the form with an application, should provide a reference to the application (e.g. transaction ID number on the application). The Department of State will enter the application number when the form (DSP-83) is submitted with the application. The U.S. applicant **must** provide the application/agreement number when the form (DSP-83) is submitted separately from the application.
2. Show the name of the U.S. person submitting the application to the Department of State.
3. Show the foreign person that will receive the articles/data for end use. A bank, freight forwarding agent, or other intermediary is not acceptable as an end-user.
4. Show the country in which the articles/data shall ultimately receive end-use.
5. Show precise quantities of the articles/data. List each article/data clearly, giving type, model number, make and (if known) U.S. military designation or national stock number. When components and spare parts are involved, fully identify the minor component, major component and end item in which they will be used (e.g. turbine blades for C-34 jet engine for F24B aircraft). Give a separate value for each major component. Values must represent only the selling price and not include supplementary costs such as packing and freight. For additional articles/data use an attachment sheet that includes "quantity, description and value" and make the last line in the description block "See attachment. The attachment should include the DTC case number or a company identifier (e.g. transaction ID number).
6. To be completed by the foreign person who has entered into the export transaction with the applicant to purchase the articles/data for delivery to the end-user. This item shall be completed only if the foreign consignee is not the same as the foreign end-user.
7. To be completed by the foreign person, in the country of ultimate destination, who will make final use of the articles/data.
8. When requested by the Department of State, this item is to be completed by an official of the country of ultimate destination having the authority to so commit the government of that country.

Source: End User Certificate Instructions, http://www.pmddtc.state.gov/licensing/documents/DSP_83.pdf.

Human Smuggling and Trafficking Legislation and Statistics

The smuggling and trafficking of human beings generates enormous profits for international organized crime. The distinctions between the two are often difficult to ascertain for law enforcement. Internationally accepted definitions are excerpted here.

Because subterfuge is the hallmark of smuggling and trafficking networks, accurate figures on the human trade are hard to come by. Like prostitution, drugs, and gambling, the illegal movement of humans is a victim-participant crime in which secrecy is preferred by both victim and perpetrator.

Human Trafficking and Smuggling Definitions

The following definitions are excerpted from several Conventions against human trafficking and smuggling between 1951 and 2005. Definitions cover a range of related activities. Because there is often overlapping in an individual's status, however, law enforcement is often confused as to where to relegate individuals according to various international and national statutes.

United Nations Convention Relating to the Status of Refugees, 1951

Asylum is not legally defined, but is generally regarded to mean the protection provided by a country to refugees in its territory. It means at the least, not forcibly returning people *[asylum seekers]* to territories where their lives or freedom would be threatened. Not all people seeking asylum meet the definition of a refugee. *Refugees,* are persons who, owing to a well-founded fear of being persecuted for their race, religion, nationality, membership in a particular social group, or political opinion, are outside their country of nationality and unable or unwilling (because of fear) to seek protection from that country.

Source: United Nations, http://www.unhcr.org/protect/PROTECTION/3b66c2aa10.pdf.

Protocol to Prevent, Suppress and Punish Trafficking in Persons, Article 3, Supplementing the UN Convention against Transnational Organized Crime, 2000

People Trafficking is recruiting, transporting, transferring, harboring or receiving persons for the purpose of exploitation; by using or threatening force, coercion, abduction, fraud, deception, or abuse of power against them; or by giving or receiving payment or benefit to those who control them.

Source: Adapted from Article 3, *Use of Terms*, http://www.uncjin.org/ Documents/Conventions/dcatoc/final_documents_2/convention_%20 traff_eng.pdf.

Protocol against the Smuggling of Migrants by Land, Sea and Air, Article 3, Supplementing the UN Convention against Transnational Organized Crime, 2000

This protocol refers to human smuggling as the "Smuggling of migrants." It defines it as "the procurement, in order to obtain, directly or indirectly, a financial or other material benefit, of the illegal entry of a person into a State Party of which the person is not a national or a permanent resident."

Source: Article 3, *Use of Terms*, http://www.uncjin.org/Documents/ Conventions/dcatoc/final_documents_2/convention_smug_eng.pdf.

The Council of Europe Convention on Action against Trafficking Human Beings, 2005

At the Third Summit of Heads of State and Government, the Council of Europe Convention on Action against Trafficking Human beings defined **trafficking in human beings** *as* the recruitment, transportation, transfer, harboring or receipt of persons, by means of the threat or use of force or other forms of coercion, of abduction, of fraud, of deception, of the abuse of power or of a position of vulnerability or of the giving or receiving payments or benefits to achieve the consent of a person having control over another person, for the purpose of exploitation. Exploitation shall include, at a minimum, the exploitation of the prostitution of others or other forms of sexual exploitation, forced labor or services, slavery or practices similar to slavery, servitude or the removal of organs.

Source: Quoted in Council of Europe. 2005. *Organised Crime Situation Report 2005: Focus on the Threat of Economic Crime.* Strasbourg, France: Council of Europe, p. 32.

Crackdown on Human Trafficking in 2005

This table reflects the fact that no region in the world is immune to human trafficking in the 21st century. Despite gaudy numbers reflecting prosecutions and convictions, most human trafficking is unreported and goes unnoticed, in part because of the initial acquiescence of the victims and their ultimate powerlessness once they reach a destination.

Selected Average Costs for Human Smuggling, 2005

The following costs charged by human smugglers demonstrate the allure that Western Europe has for those seeking to migrate from China, South Asia, North Africa, and Eastern Europe. Both Western Europe and North America remain at the top of the destination lists for most people seeking better opportunities and a better life. Unfortunately, once many arrive at their destinations they find that one's dreams are often trumped by reality.

TABLE 6.7
Crackdown on Human Trafficking in 2005

Region	Prosecutions	Convictions	New laws against human trafficking
Africa	194	58	12
East Asia And Pacific	2580	2347	5
Europe and Eurasia	2598	1984	12
Middle East	112	104	3
South Asia	964	214	0
North and South America	170	59	9

Source: U.S. Department of State, 2006 Trafficking in Persons Report, http://www.thefreelibrary.com/ Analyze+the+chart.a0161855548.

North Africa to Spain: 4,000 euros (2000 more for false identity papers)
Hungary/Russia to Western Europe: 8,000–10,000 euros
Slovakia to Italy: 3000 to 4000 euros
Serbia and Montenegro to Western Europe: $1,000USD
Croatia to Western Europe: 500 euros
China to Italy: $13,000USD
South Asia to Spain: 6,000 euros; double that with false identity papers

Source: Adapted from Council of Europe. 2005. *Organised Crime Situation Report 2005: Focus on the Threat of Economic Crime.* Strasbourg, France: Council of Europe.

Services Required by Successful Trafficking Operations

Successful trafficking operations require the assistance of numerous individuals with various skills, much like a typical transnational organized crime group. It is easier to understand why those being smuggled are required to pay such high prices when the logistics and humanpower required by an organization is broken down into the various services that the smugglers provide.

- Arranging transportation and proper documents
- Providing transport or counterfeit documents
- Acting as a guide to people crossing borders
- Serving as a chaperone on the journey
- Providing information at various stages of the border, such as, "How do you cross the border?"
- Arranging logistics such as bribing guards and officials
- Supervising victims at destination
- Providing accommodations and food
- Acting as security or bodyguard to intimidate victims

Source: Adapted from Rebecca Surtees. 2008. "Traffickers and Trafficking in Southern and Eastern Europe: Considering the Other Side of Human Trafficking." *European Journal of Criminology* 5 (1): 47; also adapted from International Labour Organization—International Programme on the Elimination of Child Labour. 2005. *Child Trafficking—The People Involved: A Synthesis of Findings from Albania, Moldova, Romania and Ukraine.* Geneva: ILO-IPEC, ix–x.

Organized Crime Groups in the European Union (2005)

The following list of organized crime groups exemplifies how once local or regional organized crime groups have morphed into global organized crime networks thanks to the opportunities provided by 21st century globalization. This is particularly true for exemplars from North Africa, China, and the world of outlaw motorcycle gangs.

- Indigenous organized crime groups still pose threat to EU.
- Italian Mafia-type OC groups are particularly dangerous for their ability in infiltrating the public and economic sectors.
- Lithuanian groups forge alliances with international OC and rapidly expanding all over the EU; extremely skilled in currency counterfeiting.
- Dutch OC groups are specialized in drug production and trafficking.
- German OC groups are involved in types of crimes that require a vast network of international connections.
- Russian and other former Soviet Union OC groups are involved in all types of crime; highly sophisticated in area of financial crime, fraud and money laundering.
- Turkish OC is mainly involved in heroin production and trafficking in EU.
- Chinese OC groups are well established in EU, and are involved in illegal migration, trafficking of human beings, and non-cash payment fraud.
- Moroccan groups are major provider of cannabis to EU drug market and are also involved in human trafficking and illegal migration.
- Outlaw motorcycle gangs are present in Nordic countries, Germany and Belgium and are expanding activities into other EU member states.

Source: Adapted from Council of Europe. 2005. *Organised Crime Situation Report 2005: Focus on the Threat of Economic Crime.* Strasbourg, France: Council of Europe, 49–50.

Council of Europe Convention on Action against Trafficking in Human Beings (2005)

The Council of Europe has been at the forefront in the battle against human trafficking. As Western Europe became the destination of choice for illegal and legal migrants from around the world, it was incumbent on the European community taking the lead in establishing ground rules to suppress the problem. What's more, it has become clear that many victims of sex trafficking come from Council of Europe members States. During the first years of the 21st century, members of the EU reported an increase in organized crime involvement in the smuggling of persons.

Article 1 — Purposes of the Convention

1. The purposes of this Convention are:
   a. to prevent and combat trafficking in human beings, while guaranteeing gender equality;
   b. to protect the human rights of the victims of trafficking, design a comprehensive framework for the protection and assistance of victims and witnesses, while guaranteeing gender equality, as well as to ensure effective investigation and prosecution;
   c. to promote international cooperation on action against trafficking in human beings.
2. In order to ensure effective implementation of its provisions by the Parties, this Convention sets up a specific monitoring mechanism.

Article 2 — Scope

This Convention shall apply to all forms of trafficking in human beings, whether national or transnational, whether or not connected with organized crime.

Article 3 — Non-discrimination Principle

The implementation of the provisions of this Convention by Parties, in particular the enjoyment of measures to protect and promote the rights of victims, shall be secured without discrimination on any ground such as sex, race, color, language, religion, political or other opinion, national or social origin, association with a national minority, property, birth or other status.

Article 4 — Definitions

For the purposes of this Convention:

   c. The recruitment, transportation, transfer, harboring or receipt of a child for the purpose of exploitation shall be considered

"trafficking in human beings" even if this does not involve any
of the means set forth in subparagraph (a) of this article;
d. "Child" shall mean any person under eighteen years of age;
e. "Victim" shall mean any natural person who is subject to trafficking in human beings as defined in this article.

Chapter II—Prevention, co-operation and other measures

Article 5—Prevention of Trafficking in Human Beings

1. Each Party shall take measures to establish or strengthen national co-ordination between the various bodies responsible for
   preventing and combating trafficking in human beings.
2. Each Party shall establish and/or strengthen effective policies
   and programmes to prevent trafficking in human beings, by such
   means as: research, information, awareness raising and education campaigns, social and economic initiatives and training programmes, in particular for persons vulnerable to trafficking and
   for professionals concerned with trafficking in human beings.
3. Each Party shall promote a Human Rights-based approach and
   shall use gender mainstreaming and a child-sensitive approach
   in the development, implementation and assessment of all the
   policies and programmes referred to in paragraph 2.
4. Each Party shall take appropriate measures, as may be necessary, to enable migration to take place legally, in particular
   through dissemination of accurate information by relevant offices, on the conditions enabling the legal entry in and stay on
   its territory.
5. Each Party shall take specific measures to reduce children's
   vulnerability to trafficking, notably by creating a protective environment for them.
6. Measures established in accordance with this article shall involve, where appropriate, nongovernmental organizations,
   other relevant organizations and other elements of civil society
   committed to the prevention of trafficking in human beings and
   victim protection or assistance.

Article 8—Security and Control of Documents

Each Party shall adopt such measures as may be necessary:

a. To ensure that travel or identity documents issued by it are of
   such quality that they cannot easily be misused and cannot readily be falsified or unlawfully altered, replicated or issued; and

b. To ensure the integrity and security of travel or identity documents issued by or on behalf of the Party and to prevent their unlawful creation and issuance.

Article 9 — Legitimacy and Validity of Documents

At the request of another Party, a Party shall, in accordance with its internal law, verify within a reasonable time the legitimacy and validity of travel or identity documents issued or purported to have been issued in its name and suspected of being used for trafficking in human beings.

Source: Council of Europe, http://conventions.coe.int/Treaty/EN/Treaties/Html/197.htm.

Other Types of Organized Crime

Kimberley Process Certification Scheme, 2003

Diamond smuggling has plagued Africa since they were first mined in the 19th century. In the 1880s, a Select Committee in South Africa was appointed to investigate the illegal diamond trade, resulting in the Diamond Trade Act in 1882, which offered punitive measures and doubled the police force to suppress impulses toward illicit trafficking. More recently, in 2003, African governments accepted the Kimberley (South Africa) Process Certification Scheme, which was geared toward preventing the trade in diamonds to fund conflict, hence references to conflict or blood diamonds. Recent research, however, suggests that although it makes it more difficult to smuggle diamonds from rebel-held regions to international markets, the trade continues due in no small part to weak diamond controls in some diamond-producing countries. Experts estimate that the illicit trade in diamonds in Sierra Leone represents almost 20 percent of the total trade. As a result the illegal diamond trade continues to fund terrorist groups and facilitate the laundering of money by criminal syndicates. The following are several excerpts from the Kimberley legislation including parts of the preamble and definitions:

PREAMBLE PARTICIPANTS, RECOGNISING that the trade in conflict diamonds is a matter of serious international concern, which can be directly linked to the fuelling of armed conflict, the activities of rebel movements aimed at undermining or overthrowing legitimate governments, and the illicit traffic in, and proliferation of, armaments, especially small arms and light weapons; *FURTHER RECOGNISING* the devastating impact of conflicts fuelled by the trade in conflict diamonds on the peace, safety and security of people in affected countries and the systematic and gross human rights violations that have been perpetrated in such conflicts; *NOTING* the negative impact of such conflicts on regional stability and the obligations placed upon states by the United Nations Charter regarding the maintenance of international peace and security; *BEARING IN MIND* that urgent international action is imperative to prevent the problem of conflict diamonds from negatively affecting the trade in legitimate diamonds, which makes a critical contribution to the economies of many of the producing, processing, exporting and importing states, especially developing states;

CONVINCED that the opportunity for conflict diamonds to play a role in fuelling armed conflict can be seriously reduced by introducing a certification scheme for rough diamonds designed to exclude conflict diamonds from the legitimate trade; *RECALLING* that the Kimberley Process considered that an international certification scheme for rough diamonds, based on national laws and practices and meeting internationally agreed minimum standards, will be the most effective system by which the problem of conflict diamonds could be addressed; ACKNOWLEDGING the important initiatives already taken to address this problem, in particular by the governments of Angola, the Democratic Republic of Congo, Guinea and Sierra Leone and by other key producing, exporting and importing countries, as well as by the diamond industry, in particular by the World Diamond Council, and by civil society; WELCOMING voluntary self-regulation initiatives announced by the diamond industry and recognizing that a system of such voluntary self-regulation contributes to ensuring an effective internal control system of rough diamonds based upon the international certification scheme for rough diamonds; RECOGNISING that an international certification scheme for rough diamonds will only be credible if all Participants have established internal systems of control designed to eliminate the presence of conflict diamonds in the chain of producing, exporting and importing rough diamonds within their own territories, while taking into account that differences in production methods and trading practices as well as differences in institutional controls thereof may require different approaches to meet minimum standards . . .

Recommend the Following Provisions:

SECTION I Definitions For the purposes of the international certification scheme for rough diamonds the following definitions apply:

> CONFLICT DIAMONDS means rough diamonds used by rebel movements or their allies to finance conflict aimed at undermining legitimate governments . . .

COUNTRY OF ORIGIN means the country where a shipment of rough diamonds has been mined or extracted;

COUNTRY OF PROVENANCE means the last Participant from where a shipment of rough diamonds was exported, as recorded on import documentation;

DIAMOND means a natural mineral consisting essentially of pure crystallised carbon in the isometric system, with a hardness on the Mohs (scratch) scale of 10, a specific gravity of approximately 3.52 and a refractive index of 2.42;

EXPORT means the physical leaving/taking out of any part of the geographical territory of a Participant;

EXPORTING AUTHORITY means the authority(ies) or body(ies) designated by a Participant from whose territory a shipment of rough diamonds is leaving, and which are authorized to validate the Kimberley Process Certificate;

FREE TRADE ZONE means a part of the territory of a Participant where any goods introduced are generally regarded, insofar as import duties and taxes are concerned, as being outside the customs territory;

IMPORT means the physical entering/bringing into any part of the geographical territory of a Participant;

Source: Kimberley Process Web site, http://www.state.gov/e/eeb/diamonds/c19974.htm.

Gambling Prohibition and Enforcement Act, 2006

Law enforcement has given illegal (and legal) gambling a low priority in recent years. But with the boom in televised gambling, mostly in the form of poker and its popularity on the Internet, U.S. authorities have begun to target gambling for the first time in a generation. The Gambling Prohibition Act forces U.S. banks and credit card companies to block electronic transactions to Internet gambling sites. Building on legislation introduced but rejected in 1999, this Act aims to prevent the use of certain payment instruments, credit cards, and fund transfers for unlawful Internet gambling, and for other purposes. The following excerpt pertains to the additional prohibitions.

Title I—Modernization of the Wire Act of 1961

Sec. 102. Modification of Existing Prohibition   Section 1084 of title 18, United States Code, is amended to read as follows:

Sec. 1084. Use of a communication facility to transmit bets or wagers; criminal penalties

(a) Except as otherwise provided in this section, whoever, being engaged in a gambling business, knowingly—

(1) uses a communication facility for the transmission in interstate or foreign commerce, within the special maritime and territorial jurisdiction of the United States, or to or from any place outside the jurisdiction of any nation with respect to any transmission to or from the United States, of—

  (A) bets or wagers;
  (B) information assisting in the placing of bets or wagers; or
  (C) a communication, which entitles the recipient to receive money or credit as a result of bets or wagers, or for information assisting in the placing of bets or wagers; or

(2) accepts, in connection with the transmission of a communication in interstate or foreign commerce, within the special maritime and territorial jurisdiction of the United States, or to or from any place outside the jurisdiction of any nation with respect to any transmission to or from the United States of bets or wagers or information assisting in the placing of bets or wagers—

  (A) credit, or the proceeds of credit, extended to or on behalf of another (including credit extended through the use of a credit card);
  (B) an electronic fund transfer or funds transmitted by or through a money transmitting business, or the proceeds of an electronic fund transfer or money transmitting service, from or on behalf of the other person;
  (C) any check, draft, or similar instrument which is drawn by or on behalf of the other person and is drawn on or payable through any financial institution; or
  (D) the proceeds of any other form of financial transaction as the Secretary of the Treasury and the Board of Governors of the Federal Reserve System may prescribe by regulation which involves a financial institution as a payor or financial intermediary on behalf of or for the benefit of the other person, shall be fined under this title or imprisoned not more than five years, or both.

Source: 109th Congress, 2nd Sess., H.R. 4411, July 13, 2006.

Money Laundering

The roots of modern money laundering can be discerned as early as the Prohibition Era (1920–1933) when American bootleggers found it necessary *to disguise their vast profits from the tax services. Meyer Lansky report-edly opened his first secret Swiss bank account in 1934, taking advan-tage of Swiss banking laws that ensured anonymity for clients. Today money laundering is used by every form of criminality, from white collar criminals and mobsters to terrorist groups. Some use cash businesses and others traffic in diamonds. But until relatively recently, offshore banks and shell corporations in the Caribbean were among the major components of schemes to launder vast amounts of cash. In 2001, New York's Federal Reserve Bank estimated that more than $800 billion was sitting in Grand Cayman banks. The creation of the Financial Action Task Force (FATF) by the G-7 group of industrialized nations in 1989, however, has closed some of the loopholes formerly enjoyed by money launderers.*

Bank Secrecy Act of 1970

In 1970, the U.S. Congress passed the Bank Secrecy Act (BSA), which is considered the first legislation in the United States specifically targeting money laundering. According to the BSA, all business are expected to keep up-to-date records and to file reports, thus guaranteeing tax en-forcement officers an important source of information for domestic and international law enforcement agencies targeting money laundering and tax evasion by criminal and terrorist groups. The following excerpt de-fines money laundering and the three steps typically used in the money laundering process.

Money laundering is the criminal practice of filtering ill-gotten gains or "dirty" money through a maze or series of transactions, so the funds are "cleaned" to look like proceeds from legal activities. Money laundering does not have to involve cash at every stage of the laundering process. Any transaction conducted with a bank might constitute money laundering. Although money laundering is a diverse and often complex process, it basically involves three independent steps that can occur si-multaneously:

Placement: The process of placing, through deposits or other means, unlawful cash proceeds into traditional financial institutions.

Layering: The process of separating the proceeds of criminal activity from their origin through the use of layers of complex financial transac-tions, such as converting cash into travelers' checks, money orders, wire transfers, letters of credit, stocks, bonds, or purchasing valuable assets, such as art or jewelry.

Integration: The process of using an apparently legitimate trans-action to disguise the illicit proceeds, allowing the laundered funds to be disbursed back to the criminal, such as sham loans or false import/excise invoices can be used.

Source: Bank Secrecy Act, *Comptroller's Handbook*, p. 17, http://www.occ.treas.gov/handbook/bsa.pdf.

Amounts of Money Reported Laundered in the Tri-Border Area (TBA), 1992–2001 (USD)

The border frontier between Argentina, Brazil, and Paraguay has long been a haven for organized crime activity and an active corridor for the smuggling of weapons, drugs, and now counterfeit goods. As the figures below indicate in 2000 alone it was estimated that $12 billion was being laundered each year. Porous borders have made it relatively easy to transport stolen cars from Brazil and Argentina into Paraguay via the TBA. Besides the indigenous groups, there is an increasing presence of international crime syndicates from Chile, Colombia, Corsica, Ghana, Italy, Ivory Coast, Japan, Korea, Lebanon, Libya, and Taiwan. Most of the criminal activity is centered in three closely connected population centers at Puerto Iguaçu, Argentina, Foz de Iguacu, Brazil, an Ciudad del Este, Paraguay. Testament to the region's growing diversity and impact of globalization was the 2001 census in Foz de Iguacu which determined there were 65 different nationalities living there.

TABLE 6.8

Amounts of Money Reported Laundered in the Tri-Border Area (TBA), 1992–2001 (USD)

Period	Amount	TBA location of activity
2000–2001	$12 billion per year	TBA in general
2000	$25 billion	TBA in general
2000	$5 billion annual average	Ciudad del Este
1998–1999	$12 billion total	Foz do Iguacu
1996–1997	$18 billion total	Foz do Iguacu
1992–1998	$70 billion total	Foz do Iguacu
1992–1998	$30 billion total	Foz do Iguacu

Source: Rex Hudson, "Terrorist and Organized Crime Groups in the Tri-Border Area (TBA) of South America," Federal Research Division, Library of Congress, July 2003, 52, http://www.state.gov/documents/organization/66086.pdf.

Combating Organized Crime in the United States

Organized Crime Drug Enforcement Task Force (OCDETF)

The Organized Crime Drug Enforcement Task Force Program was authorized in 1982 as federal drug enforcement program under the U.S. Attorney General and the Department of Justice. Its main tasks are disrupting major drug trafficking networks and solving related crimes including money laundering, tax and weapons violations, and violent crimes. Today, almost 2,500 agents work for the force. Structurally it combines resources and skills of other federal agencies including the FBI, ICE, BATF, the U.S. Marshals Service, the IRS, and the U.S. Coast Guard. The program's stated purpose is to focus its resources "on coordinated, nationwide investigations, targeting the entire infrastructure of major drug trafficking networks." Since its inception, its operations as of 2006 have led to more than 44,000 drug-related convictions and the seizure of more than $3 billion in cash and property. All of the country's 93 judicial districts are attached to one of the 9 OCDETF regions depending on its geographical location. Organizationally, within each region a hub city is selected.

TABLE 6.9
OCDETF Regions

Task force region	Core city
New England	Boston
New York/New Jersey	New York City
Mid-Atlantic	Baltimore
Great Lakes	Chicago
Southeast	Atlanta
West Central	St. Louis
Florida/Caribbean	Miami
Southwest	Houston
Pacific	San Francisco

Source: DEA Programs, Organized Crime Drug Enforcement Task Force, http://www.justice.gov/dea/programs/ocdetf.htm.

U.S. Patriot Act, 2001

In the aftermath of the September 11, 2001, terrorist attacks on the United States Congress, wide bipartisan support passed Public Law 107-56, The Uniting and Strengthening America by Providing Appropriate Tools Required to Intercept and Obstruct terrorism Act of 2001, better known either as the USA PATRIOT ACT or simply the Patriot Act. Although it clearly targets terrorists, there are a number of provisions outlining various investigative techniques and methods law enforcement can use against organized crime activity. The following excerpts focus on wiretapping and money laundering activities. Although the FBI already had a broad authority to scrutinize telephone and Internet communications, the Patriot Act further limited judicial oversight of electronic surveillance by:

(i) Subjecting private Internet communications to a minimal standard of review;

(ii) Permitting law enforcement to obtain what would be the equivalent of a 'blank warrant' in the physical world;

(iii) Authorizing scattershot intelligence wiretap orders that need not specify the place to be searched or require that only the target's conversations be eavesdropped upon; and

(iv) Allowing the FBI to use its 'intelligence' authority to circumvent the judicial review of the probable cause requirement of the Fourth Amendment.

The Patriot Act created several new money laundering crimes while increasing the penalties for some already established money laundering violations. Among the new provisions are the following:

- Prohibits the laundering of any proceeds from foreign crimes of violence or political corruption.
- Prohibits the laundering of proceeds of cybercrime and offenses relating to the support of a terrorist organization
- Prohibits bulk cash smuggling (concealed on the person, in a container, or a conveyance) and sets out procedures for the forfeiture of smuggled bulk cash shipments
- Revises the language of 18 U.S.C. 1960 relating to the operation of illegal money transmitting businesses by eliminating the old requirement that the government had to show that the defendant knew the business was operating illegally. Now any person who "knowingly conducts, controls, manages, supervises, directs, or owns all or part of an unlicensed money transmitting business" is subject to criminal sanctions.

The Patriot Act also contains a number of other provisions related to money laundering including:

- 31 U.S.C. 5318 (j); Act Section 313: Prohibition on U.S. Correspondent Accounts with Shell Banks
- 31 U.S.C 5318 (i); Act Section 312: Due Diligence for Private Banking and Correspondent Accounts
- 31 U.S.C. 5318A; Act Section 311: "Special Measures" for Certain Jurisdictions, Financial Institutions, and Accounts
- 31 U.S.C. 5318 (l); Act section 326: Standards for verification of Customer Identification
- 31 U.S.C. 5331, Act Section 365: Suspicious Activity Reporting
- 18 U.S.C 981 (k); Act Section 319: Forfeiture of Funds in U.S. Interbank Accounts
- 31 U.S.C. 5318 (g); Act Section 352: Anti-Money Laundering Program Requirement

Source: U.S. Patriot Act, 2001, http://frwebgate.access.gpo.gov/cgi-bin/getdoc.cgi?dbname=107_cong_public_laws&docid=f:publ056.107.pdf.

U.S. Attorney General Michael Mukasey, 2008

On April 30, 2008, Attorney General Michael Mukasey made a speech entitled "Combating the Growing Threat of International Organized Crime," at the Center for Strategic and International Studies (CSIS). The following is an excerpt from that speech.

Perhaps we are victims of our own success because it seems that there is a widespread belief around the country that organized crime is no longer a serious threat. Most Americans think of organized crime only as a part of America's past, its modern role merely the subject of popular movies or television dramas. I can assure you that organized crime is different in source and different in scope, but unfortunately this phenomenon, in a different institutional costume, is alive and well.

That is why, earlier this year, the Organized Crime Council met for the first time in 15 years. It did so because the United States faces a new and more modern threat, from international organized crime. We can't ignore criminal syndicates in other countries on the naïve assumption that they are a danger only in their homeland, whether it is located in Eurasia, Africa, or anywhere else.

International organized crime poses a greater challenge to law enforcement than did the traditional mafia in many respects. And the geographical source of the threat is not the only difference. The degree of sophistication is also markedly different, markedly higher. Some of the most significant international organized criminals are also infiltrating our own strategic industries and those of our allies, are providing logistical support to terrorist organizations and foreign intelligence agencies, and are capable of creating havoc in our economic infrastructure. These international criminals pose real natural security threats to this country. . . . International organized criminals are not motivated by ideology; they are motivated by the same thing that has motivated traditional organized criminals over history: money. International organized crime is a hybrid criminal problem that implicates three of the department's national priorities: national security, violent crime, and public corruption. . . . Therefore, the department and other federal agencies recently conducted a comprehensive review and assessment of international organized crime.

First, we learned that organized crime, in addition to being as varied and as dangerous as ever, has a remarkable ability to adapt to changing conditions. . . . They are more sophisticated; they are richer; they have greater influence over government and political institutions worldwide; and they are savvier about using the latest technology first to perpetrate and then to cover up their crimes . . .

A second threat we identified was the logistical and other support that organized crime provides to terrorists, foreign intelligence services, and foreign governments that may be targeting the United States or otherwise acting against our interests . . .

Another set of recent cases highlights yet a third threat—from international organized criminals who smuggle and traffic people and contraband into the country . . .

Another threat involves the ways organized crime exploits the U.S. and international financial systems to move illegal funds . . .

Yet another threat is the way international organized criminals use cyberspace to target U.S. victims and infrastructure . . .

Other threats identified in our assessment include manipulation of securities markets, corrupting public officials globally, [and] using violence as a basis for power (Mukasey 2008).

Source: Center for Strategic and International Studies, http://www.csis.org.

Quotations

All we can give you is a fragmentary picture of any great criminal enterprise. We can give you a fairly full picture of what happens at the bottom, a smaller picture of what happens at the next stratum . . . and very little up at the top.

Thomas Dewey, 1935 (quoted in Mary M. Stolberg, *Fighting Organized Crime: Politics, Justice, and the Legacy of Thomas E. Dewey* (Boston: Northeastern University Press, 1995), 95.

Organized crime stems from various forms of vice operations, gambling, prostitution, and the illegal sale of narcotics and liquor. . . . Vice activities are now and always have been the seedbed of organized crime.

McClellan Committee Report, Hearings before the Permanent Subcommittee on Investigations of the Committee on Government Operations, U.S. Senate, 88th Congress, 1st and 2nd Sess., Pt. 3, Oct. 10, 11, 15, 16, 1963.

There exists . . . today a criminal organization that is directly descended from and is patterned upon the centuries-old Sicilian terrorist society, the Mafia. This organization, also known as the La Cosa Nostra, operates vast illegal enterprises that produce an annual income of many billions of dollars. This combine has so much power and influence that it may be described as a private government of organized crime.

McClellan Committee Report, Hearings before the Permanent Subcommittee on Investigations of the Committee on Government Operations, U.S. Senate, 88th Congress, 1st and 2nd Sess., Pt. 3, Oct. 10, 11, 15, 16, 1963.

It is a malignant parasite, which fattens on human weakness. It survives on fear and corruption. . . . It is totalitarian in its organization. A way of life, it imposes rigid discipline on underlings who do the dirty work while the top men of organized crime are generally insulated from the criminal act and the consequent danger of prosecution.

Combating Organized Crime. A Report on the 1965 Oyster Bay Conference, New York, Conferences on Combating Organized Crime (Albany, New York: Office of the Counsel of the Governor, 1966), 19.

Since there is no organization, no secret society called mafia, one cannot write the history of such an institution. All that can be traced is the behavior pattern of Mafiosi in various historical situations, the role they played in the history of Sicily.

Henner Hess, *Mafia and Mafiosi: The Structure of Power* (Lexington, MA: Lexington Books, 1971), 155.

Up to the early 1980s a major branch of the scientific and popular discourse understood the term mafia as an attitude and behavior typical of Sicilians, denying a corporate dimension. Since then however, thanks to judicial in-

vestigations, it has become clear that organized crime groups lie at the core of the mafia phenomenon.

Letizia Paoli, "The Future of Sicilian and Calabrian Organized Crime." In Stanley Einstein and Menachem Amir, Eds., *Organized Crime: Uncertainties and Dilemmas* (Chicago: OICJ, 1999), 186.

Organized crime is a society that seeks to operate outside the control of the American people and their governments. It involves thousands of criminals, working within structures as complex as those of any large corporation, subject to laws more rigidly enforced than those of legitimate governments. Its actions are not impulsive but rather the result of intricate conspiracies carried on over many years and aimed at gaining control over whole fields of activity.

President's Commission on Law Enforcement and the Administration of Justice, *The Challenge of Crime in a Free Society*, 3rd ed. (New York: Avon, 1972), 437.

Transnational Organized Crime is crime committed by an organized criminal group, which is planned or committed in more than one state, or has substantial effects on more than one state, or is committed by a group which commits crimes in more than one state.

UN Convention against Transnational Organized Crime, 2000, http://www.uncjin.org/Documents/Conventions/dcatoc/final_ documents_2/convention_eng.pdf.

An organized criminal group is a structured group existing for a period of time and acting in concert, with the aim of committing one or more crimes for financial or other material benefit.

UN Convention against Transnational Organized Crime, 2000, http://www.uncjin.org/Documents/Conventions/dcatoc/final_ documents_2/convention_eng.pdf.

the FBI could get a wiretap to investigate the mafia, but they could not get one to investigate terrorists. To put it bluntly, that was crazy! What's good for the mob should be good for terrorists.

Sen. Joe Biden, Cong. Rec., Oct. 25, 2001, http://www.usdoj.gov/ archive/ll/subs/support/senbiden102501_1.pdf.

On Russian Organized Crime

An organized community of criminals ranging in size from 50 to 1,000 persons, which is engaged in systematic criminal business and protects itself from the law with the help of corruption.

Russian Ministry of the Interior, 1999, http://www.russianlaw. org/roc_csis.pdf.

was really a hodgepodge of criminal groups that were highly flexible and mobile.

Joseph D. Serio, *Investigating the Russian Mafia* (Durham, NC: Carolina Academic Press, 2008).

On Latin America and Mexican Drug Networks

Throughout Latin America, organized criminal networks exercise a significant degree of influence over the state.

Washington Office on Latin America, *The Captive State: Organized Crime and Human Rights in Latin America*, Oct. 28, 2007, 28 pp.

Colombian organized crime is quite different from the other organized crime groups because it operates as a cartel . . .

Louise I. Shelley, "Transnational Organized Crime: An Imminent Threat to the Nation State," *Journal of International Affairs* 48 (1995):479.

there was no group or association that was the cartel of Medellin. . . . I never heard any of us say the 'cartel of Medellin' or the 'cartel of Cali.'

Former Medellin member Juan David Ochoa, Frontline interview (n.d.), *Drug Wars*, http://www.pbs.org/wgbh/pages/frontline/shows/drugs/interviews/och.

The cartel myth achieved remarkable staying power in American popular culture, in part because of the vivid imagery it conveyed was plausible— and useful—to politicians eager to pass drug control legislation, law enforcement hoping for greater drug war resources, investigative journalists searching for profitable copy, and citizens fearful of the harmful effects of drug abuse and addiction . . . . The cartels never existed until they were created by the media and the U.S. government.

Michael Kenney, *From Pablo to Osama: Trafficking and Terrorist Networks, Government Bureaucracies, and Competitive Adaptations* (University Park: Pennsylvania State University Press, 2007) 25.

Our countries are working together to fight transnational gangs. And the President (of Guatemala) was right—I suggested we think about this issue regionally. You've got to understand that these gangs are able to move throughout Central America and up through Mexico into our own country.

President George W. Bush, Guatemala City, March 12, 2007, http://merln.ndu.edu/archivepdf/ARA/State/93800.pdf.

On Drug Trafficking

European criminals played crucial roles in the years of the greatest structural change in the production and trafficking of narcotics.

Alan Block, "European Drug Trafficking: Between the World Wars," in Alan Block, Ed., *Space, Time and Organized Crime* (New Brunswick: Transaction, 1994), 93–125, 94.

It's like being a good trucker. You don't want to travel the return leg with an empty truck. If you use this sort of analogy, you have drugs coming out one way and that produces money and that buys the weapons and the weapons go back in.

Quoted in Glen E. Curtis and Tara Karacan, "The Nexus Among Terrorists, Narcotics Traffickers, Weapons Proliferators, and Organized Crime Networks in Western Europe," Washington, D.C. Federal Research Division, Library of Congress, December 2002 (2–3), 1–30.

Methamphetamine is the most widely used illicit drug after marijuana.

World Health Organization, 2003, http://www.cbc.ca/fifth/dark-crystal/canada.html.

Drug prohibition is also a failure that causes more harm than the drug use it is purportedly intended to control.

Bar Association of the City of New York, 1986 (quoted in William F. Buckley, "Reefer Madness at the bar on the Rights," September 27, 1994, http://www.drugsense.org/tfyl/buck_bar.htm).

Drug prohibition in Bolivia and Afghanistan has done exactly what alcohol prohibition did in America: it has financed organized crime. . . . The Saudis can fight alcoholism by forbidding the sale of Jack Daniels, but we'd think they were crazy if they ordered us to eradicate fields of barley in Tennessee.

John Tierney, "Reading the Coca Leaves," *New York Times*, September 26, 2006, A23.

Street gangs, prison gangs, and outlaw motorcycle gangs have long been and continue to be the predominant organized retail drug distributors; their level of organization is the key factor that renders gangs a significant threat that gangs pose to the nation, their influence with respect to drug smuggling, transportation, and wholesale distribution has increased sharply.

National Drug Intelligence Center, "National Drug Threat Assessment 2006: Organized Gangs and Drug Trafficking," January 2006, http://www.usdoj.gov/ndic/pubs11/18862/gangs.htm.

7

Directory of Organizations

Academic and Research-Oriented Organizations

Academy of Criminal Justice Sciences

Web site: http://www.acjs.org

Founded in 1963, the Academy of Criminal Justice Science (CJS) is an international organization created to promote criminal justice education, research, and policy analysis within the discipline of criminal justice for both practitioners and educators. Membership is international in scope and multidisciplinary in orientation. Annual membership dues are $75 and include subscriptions to *Justice Quarterly*, the *Journal of Criminal Justice Education*, and *ACJS Now*.

American Society of Criminology (Division of International Criminology)

Web site: http://www.asc41.com
DIC Web site: http://www.internationalcriminology.com/dic_home

Despite its parochial-sounding title, the American Society of Criminology is an international organization with membership from around the world. Its annual meeting offers hundreds of papers and presentations revolving around international crime issues, many of them related to global trafficking issues and transnational organized crime. Nothing reflects the international dimensions of this organization, however, more than its Division of International

Criminology (DIC), which meets at the ASC's annual meeting. Its stated goals include fostering research and the exchange of information related to international criminology. To join the DIC, one must be a member of the American Society of Criminology. Dues for the DIC are $90 per year and include subscriptions to *Criminology, Criminology and Public Policy,* and the *Criminologist.* DIC membership dues are $20 annually. Members receive the peer-reviewed *International Journal of Comparative and Applied Criminal Justice* four times a year. This journal can be subscribed to without membership for $75 for members in the United States and $120 to international members.

The Centre for Information and Research on Organised Crime

Web site: http://www.ciroc.org/

Founded by the criminology departments at the Erasmus University Rotterdam and the Vrije Universiteit Amsterdam in 2001 and the Research and Documentation Center of the Dutch Ministry of Justice (WODC), the Centre for Information and Research on Organised Crime (CIROC) is an international center for information and research on organized crime and the fight against it. According to the CIROC, it intends to build rapport between criminologists and the practice of investigation, prosecution, and trial. From a global perspective, the CIROC works for and with such groups as research institutions, government bodies, nongovernmental bodies, the European Commission, the United Nations, and other agencies.

The European Institute for Crime Prevention and Control

Web site: http://www.heuni.fi

The European Institute for Crime Prevention and Control (HEUNI) was created on December 23, 1981. Established by an agreement between the United Nations and the Government of Finland, the organization works to promote the international exchange of strategies on crime prevention and control between countries in Europe. Its main contributions have been research oriented, providing technical assistance to countries when requested and offering workshops and meetings. Its current focus has been on topics related to organized crime, human trafficking, and violence against women. In addition it analyzes UN surveys on crime trends and the working of criminal justice systems and corrections, as well as publishing profiles of various European criminal justice systems.

Hong Kong Society of Criminology

Web site: http://www.crime.hku.hk/hksoccrim.htm

The Hong Kong Society of Criminology was established in 1983. Its founders included criminal justice practitioners, academics, and lay members—all interested in the study of crime in Hong Kong. The Society's objectives include promoting the discussion and dissemination of the latest international research on topics germane to law enforcement, crime, and criminal justice. The society collaborates with similar organizations locally and internationally and recently sponsored a symposium on organized crime, human smuggling, art crime, crime prevention, crime and the elderly, and other topics. Society membership, which includes police officers, lawyers, medical practitioners, social workers, correctional officers, academic criminologists, and many other types of practitioners, reflects its interdisciplinary nature.

International Association for the Study of Organized Crime

E-mail: iasoc_office@yahoo.com

Founded in 1984, the International Association for the Study of Organized Crime (IASOC) is a professional association made up of criminologists, researchers, working professionals, teachers, and students. Its stated purpose is to promote a greater understanding of all the facets of organized crime. Meetings are held at the annual meetings of the American Society of Criminology in November each year. The organization offers a Web site listing the expertise of members. Membership is $25 per year and includes a free online subscription to the quarterly *Trends in Organized Crime,* which features articles based on current research in organized crime activities, as well as the response by the criminal justice system.

Nathanson Centre on Transnational Human Rights, Crime and Security (Formerly Nathanson Centre for the Study of Organized Crime and Corruption)

Web site: http://www.osgoode.yorku.ca

The Jack and Mae Nathanson Centre for the Study of Organized Crime and Corruption was established in 1997. Over the ensuing decade the Nathanson Centre became a prominent base for the study of global organized crime issues, money laundering, and police strategies. It has also sponsored a number of conferences, books, symposia, and other research. In 2006, after a series of discussions, it was decided to expand its mandate to include other issues germane to the study of 21st-century organized crime by including terrorism, human rights accountability of transnational economic actors, and security intelligence activity. That same year the name was changed to reflect the new mandate. The Centre continues to support interdisciplinary research on transnational crime.

STRATFOR Global Intelligence

Web site: www.stratfor.com

STRATFOR was founded in 1996 by the futurologist George Friedman. It has earned a reputation as one of the world's leaders in collecting and analyzing global intelligence. Although it focuses on political, economic, and military forecasts, it features a number of reports detailing and forecasting global organized crime issues, particularly the confluence of terrorism and organized crime and the persistence of human trafficking and piracy. Although it is an open site, a membership fee is required to receive all geopolitical monographs, assessments, and situational reports (SITREPS). Free articles, however, can be downloaded and a free trial subscription is available.

Terrorism, Transnational Crime and Corruption Center (Headquarters)

Web site: http://policy-traccc.gmu.edu

The Terrorism, Transnational Crime and Corruption Center (TraCCC) was established in 1998. Most of its research and policy-building projects over the past decade have been devoted to the former states of the Soviet Union and Turkey. TraCCC is the first center in the United States dedicated to unraveling the links between terrorism, transnational crime, and corruption, while at the same time offering classes, training, research, and help in formulating policy related to these issues. Every year TraCCC hosts and supports visiting scholars and international leaders through such programs as Fulbright, IREX, and the Open World Leadership Program. Research topics have included human smuggling, nuclear proliferation issues, the convergence of terrorism and organized crime, money laundering, and other global crime issues.

Transnational Institute

Web site: http://www.tni.org

The Transnational Institute (TNI), established in 1974, is an international network made up of primarily activist-scholars who are committed to the critical examination of various global problems. Among its projects related to organized crime is the Crime and Globalisation project, which analyzes the relationship between globalization and crime. It takes into account the criminogenic effects of globalization and the concomitant development of what it calls an "underground axis of evil" made up of drug trafficking, transnational organized crime, and international terrorism. This project is devoted to opening a discussion on the criminogenic effects of globalization and to developing a new global security strategy that would entail a body of multilateral agreements. The TNI's Drugs and Democracy program likewise analyzes global trends in drug policy while promoting a more realistic approach to suppressing the illegal drug trade based on harm reduction principles. This program focuses on drugs and conflict in the Andean/Amazon region, Afghanistan, and Burma and ties it to wider issues such as demilitarization, democratization, and poverty reduction.

Governmental Organizations

Australian Crime Commission

Web site: http://www.crimecommission.gov.au

The Australian Crime Commission (ACC) was established on January 1, 2003, specifically to target national crime threats and organized criminal activity. Its creation merged the National Crime Authority, which was established in 1984 to handle organized crime, with the Australian Bureau of Criminal Intelligence and the Office of Strategic Assessments. It was hoped that a streamlined single-agency approach would be more effective. The ACC is led by a CEO, who is selected by the governor-general of Australia and is responsible for the organization's corporate management and the coordination and control of its operations and investigations. Day-to-day activities are the responsibility of directors and managers. The ACC is imbued with coercive powers that are not available to the Australian and state and territorial police forces. These nontraditional methods, however, must be first authorized by the ACC Board, which comprises the commissioner of the Australian Federal Police (chair of board), the secretary of the department, the chief executive officer of the Australian Customs service, the director-general of the Australian Security Intelligence Organization, the commissioner from each state and territory police force, and several others.

Borderpol European Secretariat c/o Hungarian National Police Service

Borderpol was officially established in March 2003 as a nonprofit international association dedicated to bringing together the international community to promote safe and secure borders. Its stated goal is to facilitate cooperation between progressive border services and related agencies in furtherance of establishing and operating border system that more effectively connect the global community. It devotes much of its resources consulting governments that are interested in improving the enforcement of transnational criminal activities such as smuggling humans, drugs, and weapons, as well as protecting against terrorism. Borderpol has access to more than 100 professionals in more than 12 countries that can provide services and advice at short notice.

Borderpol International Association

Web site: http://borderpol.org

Borderpol was officially established in March 2003 as a nonprofit international association dedicated to bringing together the international community in order promote safe and secure borders. Its stated goal is to facilitate cooperation between progressive border services and related agencies in furtherance of establishing and operating border system that more effectively connect the global community. It devotes much of its resources consulting governments that are interested in improving the enforcement of transnational criminal activities such as smuggling humans, drugs, and weapons as well as protecting against terrorism. Borderpol has access to more than 100 professionals in over 12 countries that can respond quickly on short notice to requests for advice.

Bureau for International Narcotics and Law Enforcement Affairs

Web site: http://www.state.gov/g/inl

The Bureau for International Narcotics and Law Enforcement Affairs (INL) is positioned within the undersecretary for political affairs for the U.S. State Department and is tasked with combating the global drug trade and other major crimes through programs involving other federal agencies and national governments. It is not a true law enforcement agency but functions as a source of funding to assist law enforcement personnel in the United States and other countries. The drug trade remains its primary mission, but in recent years it has moved toward working on other transnational criminal operations such as human trafficking. With an annual budget approaching a billion dollars, almost $14 million goes toward supporting efforts to suppress money laundering, intellectual property theft, and cybercrime. It also contributes to border security programs geared toward supporting counterterrorism training for port and airport police, as well as private security officials.

Caribbean Financial Action Task Force

Web site: http://www.cfatf.org

The Caribbean Financial Action Task Force (CFATF) was established in 1992 as a way of addressing criminal money laundering in the region. Today it is an organization of 30 states representing the Caribbean basin. Its main objective is to attain effective implementation of, and conformity with, its recommendations to prevent and control money laundering and the financing of terrorism through international finance markets.

Central Intelligence Agency

Web site: http://www.cia.gov

The Central Intelligence Agency (CIA) was created by the National Security Act of 1947. It mandated that the CIA would be responsible for coordinating the country's intelligence activities and with correlating and disseminating intelligence affecting national security. For most of its history, it focused on the machinations and threats of the Cold War era. Senior U.S. policymakers rely on the

CIA to provide timely national security intelligence. The Director of the Central Intelligence Agency (D/CIA) is selected by the President of the United States; however, the appointee must first be approved with the advice and consent of the Senate. The director is responsible for operations, personnel, and the budget of the CIA. Since the agency has no domestic police powers, when the CIA uncovers information on organized crime activities it sends the analytical information to the Federal Bureau of Investigation, the Drug Enforcement Administration, and the Office of Foreign Assets Control. As the CIA has become increasingly involved in fighting terrorism and the accompanying organized crime activities that often fund it, it has played an important role providing analytical support to the Department of State on human trafficking and smuggling. In 2004, President George W. Bush signed legislation that restructured the CIA by abolishing the positions of director and deputy directors of central intelligence and merging them into the position of director of the Central Intelligence Agency. In addition the act inaugurated the new position of director of national intelligence, which is tasked with supervising the Intelligence Community and the Counterterrorism Center.

Centre for International Crime Prevention

Web site: http://www.uncjin.org/CICP/cicp.html

The Centre for International Crime Prevention (CICP) is an office in the United Nations dedicated toward crime prevention, criminal justice, and legal reform. It is especially active in countering transnational organized crime networks, corruption, and the illicit trafficking of humans. The CICP is located within the United Nations Office for Drug Control and Crime Prevention. It recognizes the impact of globalization on the internationalization of criminal syndicates and emphasizes the international cooperation between law enforcement agencies and governments. It often collaborates with the United Nations Interregional Criminal Justice and Research Institute in Rome and has played a prominent role in the development of three proposals aimed at global crime: the *Global Programme against Corruption,* the *Global Programme against the Trafficking in Human Beings,* and a program called *Assessing Transnational Organized Crime Groups.* Links to these programs are available on this site as well as the biennial World Organized Crime Report published by the United Nations.

The Egmont Group

Web site: http://www.egmontgroup.org

The Egmont Group is an organization made up of Financial Intelligence Units (FIU) representing about 85 countries around the world. FIUs have been created to collect and store information about suspicious financial transactions, money laundering activities, and terrorist financing. The Egmont Group has a major goal of creating a global network dedicated to increasing international cooperation between FIUs. A number of countries in the Egmont Group, however, have been associated with lax money laundering policies. The Egmont Group homepage has links to all FIUs.

Home Office

Web site: http://www.homeoffice.gov.uk

Great Britain's Home Office is one of the country's largest government departments. It is the lead government department for immigration and passports, drug policy, counterterrorism, and police. Home Office headquarters contains the Office for Security and Counter-Terrorism, the Crime and Policing Group, and other professional services. Agencies germane to transnational crime include the UK Border Agency, the Identity and Passports Service, and the Criminal Records Bureau. In 2009, the Home Office, together with the Cabinet Office, published a new strategy for fighting organized crime in an effort to ensure that the government, law enforcement, business, and the public have the requisite knowledge and tools needed to reduce the harm of organized crime. No unit of the Home Office plays a larger role in this effort than the Serious Organized Crime Agency (SOCA).

Inter-American Drug Abuse Control Commission

Web site: http://www.cicad.oas.org

Established by the General Assembly of the Organization of American States (OAS) in 1986, the Inter-American Drug Abuse Control Commission (CICAD) assists member states in the construction of strong teams of qualified individuals to lead the region's fight against the illegal drug trade. Each member government selects a high-ranking representative to the commission, which meets twice each year. CICAD not only serves as a policy forum on all aspects of the drug problem but also promotes coordination and cooperation among the 34 OAS member states through action programs directed at preventing and treating substance abuse, reducing the availability of illicit drugs, improving money laundering control laws, and developing alternate sources of income for growers of coca, poppy, and marijuana. In 2008, CICAD consolidated Central America's first training and certification process, which included a structure curriculum for drug treatment counselors in an effort to provide better quality care to drug users and their families. This concept has been taken to heart by Central American states that support the establishment of a government-sponsored mechanism for training counselors.

International AntiCounterfeiting Coalition

Web site: http://www.iacc.org

The International AntiCounterfeiting Coalition (IACC) bills itself as the "world's largest non-profit organization" dedicated to suppressing counterfeiting and protecting intellectual property. Headquartered in Washington, D.C., the IACC was created in 1979. Today it is made up of a range of members representing businesses and industries that include among others the automotive, apparel, luxury goods, food and entertainment, and pharmaceutical industries. The annual revenues produced by its membership approaches $700 billion. The IACC offers anticounterfeiting programs intended to help protect patents, trademarks, copyrights, service marks, and trade secrets. The organization supports governmental and law enforcement actions directed at global counterfeiting operations. From a global organized crime perspective, the IACC firmly upholds the notion that global organized crime groups are deeply involved in counterfeiting and piracy activities.

Office of Territorial and International Criminal Intelligence and Drug Enforcement

E-mail: interpolpago@usa.com

The Office of Territorial and International Criminal Intelligence and Drug Enforcement (OTICIDE) was created to fulfill the commitments of the American Samoa Government to the South Pacific

Chiefs of Police Organization in the Pacific region, as well as their counterparts in the U.S. State Department. In recent year OTICIDE has become increasingly involved in countering drug-trafficking operations and organized crime activities in the region. On March 12, 2004, Samoa's governor issued an executive order recognizing OTICIDE as the leading agency for investigating illegal drug and human trafficking.

Organization of American States (OAS Anti-Trafficking in Persons Section)

Web site: http://www.oas.org

The Organization of American States was chartered in 1948. It is composed of 35 countries in the Western Hemisphere. When it comes to transnational organized crime, the organization has been instrumental with varying degrees of success in creating strategies for fighting corruption, drug trafficking, and the trafficking in persons. In 1986, it created the Inter-American Drug Abuse Control Commission (CICAD) as a policy forum to handle various aspects of the drug problem, weapons trafficking, and related issues. Its major goals are to strengthen existing drug laws, improve prevention programs, and making strides toward reducing the flow of illegal drugs and firearms. Brazil has been tasked with creating a high-level working group to develop an effective antidrug strategy in the hemisphere in 2009. With the increase in human trafficking, the OAS created the Anti-Trafficking in Persons (TIP) Section in 2004. Its goal is to promote the exchange of information among country members, provide training, and implement broad antitrafficking policies that will suppress the trafficking in persons, especially children, women, and adolescents on a transnational basis.

United States Customs and Border Patrol

Web site: http://www.cbp.gov

The U.S. Customs and Border Patrol (CBP) is an agency within the Department of Homeland Security. It was established in 1924 with a contingent of 450 officers. Initially its task was to police American borders with Canada and Mexico. During the 1980s and 1990s, a surge in illegal migration into the United States led to an increase in staff and introduction of new technologies such as infrared night vision scopes, seismic sensors, and modern computer-processing equipment to help apprehend and process those caught crossing the borders illegally. After the terrorist attacks on September 11, 2001 border security became a primary concern in Washington, leading to the reorganization of the agency within the new Department of Homeland Security (DHS).

Today the CBP is tasked with policing almost 6,000 miles of Mexican and Canadian international land borders and more than 2,000 miles of coastal waters adjoining the Florida peninsula and Puerto Rico. Preventing illegal immigration is still the primary task of the CBP, but the ongoing battle with international terrorists and the increase in drug trafficking along the Southwest border have added to the jobs of this group. More than a million people enter the United States through 327 different land, air, and seaports each day.

United States Department of Homeland Security

Web site: http://www.dhs.gov

The Department of Homeland Security (DHS) was created by Executive Order 13228 soon after the September 11, 2001, terrorist attacks. The DHS was designed to oversee and coordinate a comprehensive national strategy to protect the United States from terrorists and to respond to future attacks. Eight years later, the DHS has 210,000 employees and is the third largest department in the federal government. Since its inception its mandate has expanded to include various threats posed by organized crime groups and gangs on the nation's borders. Today it is tasked with preventing and investigating all illegal border activity, including the smuggling of people, drugs, cash, and weapons. The DHS has been particularly active on the southwest border, working to disrupt the drug, cash, and weapon smuggling that fuels cartel violence in Mexico and increasingly on the American side of the border. Of the 22 component agencies that make up DHS, seven are immigration-related, including Immigration and Customs Enforcement (ICE), Customs and Border Patrol (CBP), and U.S. Citizenship and Immigration Services (USCIS). Other related agencies include the U.S. Coast Guard, the Secret Service, the Transportation Security Administration (TSA), and Federal Emergency Management Agency (FEMA). The Office of Counternarcotics Enforcement (CNE) coordinates the department's multiagency efforts with other units and agencies. The Border Enforcement Security Taskforces (BEST) investigate cases that often involve disrupting cross-border smuggling activities.

United States Department of Justice

Web site: http://www.usdoj.gov

The U.S. Department of Justice (DOJ) is charged with enforcing the law and defending the interests of the United States. From an international perspective, it is also expected to ensure public safety against foreign and domestic threats. Among its agencies most germane in the fight against international organized crime are the U.S. Marshals Service, the Federal Bureau of Investigation, and the Drug Enforcement Administration. The creation of the Department of Homeland Security in 2001, however, saw the shifting of the Bureau of Customs and Border Patrol and the Bureau of Immigration and Customs Enforcement from the DOJ to the new department.

United States Treasury Department (Financial Crimes Enforcement Network)

Web site: http://www.fincen.gov

The Financial Crimes Enforcement Network (FinCEN) was created within the U.S. Treasury Department in 1990. It is tasked with supporting federal, state, local, and international law enforcement by analyzing the information required under the 1970 Bank Secrecy Act (BSA), which is considered one of the country's greatest tools against money laundering. The BSA records information on financial transactions that helps establish a paper trail for investigators. FinCEN assists foreign governments by providing training, technological advice, and policy guidelines in order to develop effective use of antimoney laundering and counterterrorism financing strategies worldwide. Today FinCEN employs 300 full-time employees, including federal agents, analysts, regulatory experts, and technology specialists. They are supplemented by almost 40 others representing 20 different law enforcement and regulatory agencies. The passage of the USA PATRIOT Act in 2001 expanded the focus of FinCEN to include more responsibilities in fighting terrorism and financing and money laundering, and in 2004 it became a lead office in the new Office of Terrorism and Financial Intelligence, responsible for fighting the financial war against terrorists and enforcing economic sanctions against rogue states.

World Customs Organization

Web site: http://www.wcoomd.org

The World Customs Organization (WCO) was established in 1952 and was originally called the Customs Co-operation Council (CCC).

Its initial task as an independent intergovernmental body was to improve the effectiveness and efficiency of the world's customs administrations. Today it is the only intergovernmental organization focused exclusively on customs matters. The WCO fights global organized crime by lobbying and crusading for new anticounterfeiting and piracy initiatives. It currently represents 174 customs administrations around the world who are collectively responsible for almost 98 percent of the world's trade.

Law Enforcement Organizations

**The Asian Gang Investigators'
Association of California**

Web site: http://www.agiaconline.org

The Asian Investigators' Association of California (AGIAC) was established in 1989 as a nonprofit organization dedicated to networking between various law enforcement units investigating Asian crime and gangs in California. In recent years the organization has expanded its mandate as more international members join. Membership, however, is limited only to law enforcement personnel. It continues to interact with its counterparts across the United States in developing and coordinating strategies that can be used against organized crime, Asian gangs, and terrorist groups.

Criminal Intelligence Service of Canada

Web site: http://www.cisc.gc.ca/

The Criminal Intelligence Service of Canada (CISC) was created in 1970 as part of a national strategy to fight organized crime. Based in Ottawa, it currently involves more than 380 agencies representing law enforcement at every level of government. It maintains and manages the Automated Criminal Intelligence Information System (ACIIS), which provides Canadian law enforcement with the latest information and trends on organized crime. The CISC is governed by a National Executive Committee of 22 members from the law enforcement community and chaired by the Commissioner of the Royal Canadian Mounted Police. Among its best known reports are its *Annual Report on Organized Crime in Canada* and the *National Criminal Intelligence Estimate.*

Direzione Investigativa Antimafia

Web site: http://www.interno.it

The Direzione Investigativa Antimafia (DIA) was created within the Italian Department of Public Safety in December 1991. The following year it began its first investigations targeting Sicily's mafia crime families. Later in the decade, the DIA channeled its efforts toward other organized crime groups on the mainland of Italy such as Sacra Corona Unita, 'Ndrangheta, and the Camorra, as well as other European syndicates. At the international level the DIA has established cooperative structures through multilateral projects with other international police forces. Operationally the DIA conducts its activities within the Public Security Department of the Italian Ministry of Interior. The organization has a staff approaching 1,500 individuals including investigators from the national security forces. The minister of the interior is responsible for disseminating the activities of the DIA to the Italian parliament twice a year. Structurally the DIA is headed by a director selected in rotation from among senior officials of the Carbinieri Corps and the Guardia di Finanza. Under him are two deputy directors. At the central level, the DIA is made up of a cabinet division and seven units subdivided into three branches (Preventive Investigations, Criminal Investigations Activities, and International Investigation Relations). The DIA plays a leading role in the fight against Mafia-related offenses in Italy and abroad. More recently it has participated in the G-8 Expert Working Group against Eastern European organized crime alongside police forces from the United States, Germany, Russia, Canada, Great Britain, France, and Japan.

European Police Office (Europol)

Web site: http://www.europol.eu.int

The European Police Office, more commonly known as Europol, was established by the Maastricht Treaty on European Union in 1992. Based on the Interpol model, its focus is on problems involving European transnational crime. Although it initially went after the illegal drug trade, in 1994 its mandate was expanded to include preventing trafficking in nuclear and radioactive substances, money laundering, immigrant smuggling and trafficking, and motor vehicle theft. In July 1996, European member states ratified Europol with the main objective of improving cooperation between members states in order to more effectively counter serious forms of international crimes and terrorism. Similar to Interpol, its agents have no arrest powers, although they are permitted to participate in operations along with members of other police agencies.

International Association of Asian Crime Investigators

Web site: http://www.iaaci.com/

The International Association of Asian Crime Investigators (IAACI) is a professional organization of law enforcement personnel responsible for the investigation of Asian organized crime and gangs. The IAACI was formed in Falls Church, Virginia in 1987. Today the organization has expanded from a handful of Asian investigators to a larger circle of Asian crime specialists. It continues to sponsor training seminars and the publication of research through the *Center for Asian Crime Studies (CACS)*.

International Association of Chiefs of Police (IACP) Organized Crime Committee

Web site: http://www.iacp.org

The International Chiefs of Police (IACP) was founded in 1893. Its initial goals were directed toward advancing the science of police services; developing and disseminating better administrative, technical, and operational practices and integrating these into everyday police work; and enhancing professional standards of performance and conduct. More important from an international standpoint was its attempts to foster police cooperation, especially the exchange of information. The IACP played an important role in spearheading a variety of professionally recognized programs in the United States and elsewhere. The FBI Identification Division and the Uniform Crime Records system can trace their origins back to the IACP. Over the past decades international policing has become more relevant than in times past as a result of the increasing complexity of transnational crime, terrorism activities, cybercrime, and the international trafficking of humans, drugs, weapons, and other contraband. A major step was taken toward this end with the creation of the Organized Crime Committee (OCC) of the IACP. Its stated mission is to fight global organized crime by strengthening cooperation and coordination among law enforcement agencies around the world. To this end every attempt is being made to establish best practices relative toward this goal by bringing together members of the international law enforcement community to share innovative strategies and analyze the nexus between organized crime and other disciplines. To accomplish this, the OCC of the IACP has established closer bonds with Interpol and partnered with the International Organized Crime Policy Coordinating Committee (IOCPCC) to remain abreast of the latest organized crime threats.

International Criminal Police Organization

Web site: http://www.interpol.int

Better known as Interpol, the International Criminal Police Organization was founded in Vienna in 1923. It was disbanded in 1938 and then resuscitated after World War II in 1946. It adopted Interpol as its formal name only in 1956 and have since become synonymous with international police cooperation. With more than 185 members today, it is second only to the United Nations as an international organization. Its main job is facilitating the introduction, coordination, and cooperation between law enforcement from different nations and cultures. More recently its focus has been directed toward fighting terrorism, organized crime, human trafficking, drug trafficking, money laundering, corruption, financial, and high-tech crime. It reportedly also has the world largest international criminal database. Today Interpol is active in various major projects targeting global organized crime. For example, Project Millennium focuses on Eurasian crime syndicates, Project AOC targeting Asian criminal groups, Project Pink Panthers focuses on armed jewelry robberies by gang members from the former Yugoslavia, and Project Bada targets maritime piracy.

International Latino Gang Investigators Association

Web site: http://www.ilgia.org

The International Latino Gang Investigators Association (ILGIA) was created on January 1, 2002. This organization of law enforcement personnel is dedicated to seeking information on the international drug trade linked to Latino gangs in the United States and Mexico. The ILGIA endeavors to inform policymakers on the need to confront the Mexican drug cartels and the associated gangs. The association hopes to assist federal, state, local, and tribal governments improve policies and resources to more efficiently gang-related organized crime. Membership costs $25 per year and is only open to law enforcement and correctional officers.

International Narcotic Enforcement Officers Association

Web site: http://www.ineoa.org

The International Narcotic Enforcement Officers Association (INEOA) was formally chartered as an association under the laws of New York in November 1960 as the International Narcotic Enforcement Officers Association. It is a nonprofit membership association with membership from law enforcement agencies around the globe. Its stated mission is to promote and foster mutual cooperation, discussion, and interest in the problems of dug abuse and the global drug trade. INEOA publishes the *Narc Officer* magazine. Among its valuable services it provides is assistance to families of law enforcement officers killed in the line of duty. It also recognizes officers who have distinguished themselves in drug enforcement operations during an annual awards ceremony. During its almost half-century history, the INEOA has provided training and education to more than 15,000 individuals. Its mission is not just directed toward narcotics officers at every level of government and internationally, but has also been directed toward a number of personnel from the medical, scientific, and educational disciplines. The INEOA boasts a diverse membership that includes members from the FBI, DEA, ATF, U.S. Customs and Border Protection, every branch of the U.S. Armed Forces, and other agencies within the U.S. Department of Justice and the U.S. Department of Homeland Security, as well as many state agencies and international organizations and agencies.

International Organization of Asian Crime Investigators and Specialists

Web site: http://www.ioacis.com

The International Association of Asian Crime Investigators and Specialists (IOACIS) is dedicated to providing a forum for international and American law enforcement personnel interested in strengthening global cooperation and coordination through teaching, education, and training. It hosts an annual conference called the International Conference on Asian Organized Crime and Terrorism (ICAOCT), formerly known as the International Asian Organized Crime Conference. The IOACIS has broadened its mandate in the 21st century by expanding its focus from mainly Asian gangs and organized crime to terrorism and other convergent issues. Membership costs $30 annually.

Serious Organised Crime Agency

Web site: http://www.soca.gov.uk

The Serious Organised Crime Agency (SOCA) was created on April 1, 2006 after the passage of the Serious Organised Crime and Police Act of 2005. Its creation merged the National Crime Squad, the National Criminal Intelligence Service, the National Hi-Tech Crime Unit, and investigators from the HM Revenue and Customs Service and the immigration service. It is Great Britain's first non-police law-enforcement agency. It has more investigative powers in England and Wales than in Northern Ireland and Scotland. Thus it often works in cooperation with the Northern Ireland Organized Crime Task Force and the Scottish Crime and Drug Enforcement Agency. The SOCA has sometimes been referred to as the "British FBI" by the media (but its tasks are closer to the U.S. Immigration and Customs Enforcement). The SOCA is tasked with investigating organized crime, including drug trafficking, money laundering, fraud, global pedophilia networks, and human smuggling. It currently has more than 4,200 employees and a budget of more than 400 million pounds. The government, however, has been criticized for investing so much more on counter-terrorism—2.5 billion pounds, leading critics to suggest the government does not take organized crime seriously. SOCA is led by a board consisting of 11 members and is divided into four directorates. Strategies are decided by the board, which has invested 40 percent of its efforts toward fighting the drug trade, 25 percent toward human trafficking and smuggling, 10 percent to fraud, 10 percent supporting other agencies and 15 percent on other forms of organized crime.

South Pacific Islands Criminal Intelligence Network

Web site: http://americansamoa.gov/departments/dhs/spicin.htm

The South Pacific Islands Criminal Intelligence Network (SPICIN) was established in October 1987. A rise in crime in this region led its 17 police executives to sign a regional cooperation agreement in an effort to improve information sharing between the countries of this region. The stated mission of the SPICIN is to support the police forces of the South Pacific Chiefs of Police Conference (SPCPC) in gathering information and developing and disseminating crime-related intelligence on a timely basis. In addition it was expected to help identify criminal organizations and facilitate successful prosecutions by providing necessary intelligence to the SPICIN Control Center and then to law enforcement organizations in member countries.

United States Drug Enforcement Administration

Web site: http://www.dea.gov

With the passage of an Executive Order in July 1973, President Richard Nixon created the Drug Enforcement Administration (DEA) with the intent of mounting "an all-out global war on the drug menace." It is tasked with enforcing all controlled substances laws and regulations and targeting organizations involved in the growing, manufacture, and distribution of controlled substances in the United States (or destined for here). In one of its most high-profile cases, DEA agent Enrique "Kiki" Camarena was tortured and murdered by Mexican drug kingpin Rafael Caro Quintero. This launched "Operation Leyenda" as the DEA launched a massive dragnet that resulted in nearly two dozen indictments including three drug lords now serving life sentences in the United States for the crime. Today it has 19 field offices across the United States and 87 foreign offices in 63 countries. Its staff had grown from 1,470 at its inception to more than 5,000 today. Its expanded responsibilities have led the DEA into investigations involving money laundering, terrorism, and other crimes. From a global perspective, the DEA is the U.S. liaison to the United Nations, Interpol, and other international antidrug trafficking efforts.

**United States Federal Bureau of Investigation
(Organized Crime Section)**

Web site: http://www.fbi.gov/hq/cid/orgcrime/ocshome.htm

The Federal Bureau of Investigation (FBI) was created on July 26, 1908 as the Bureau of Investigation (BOI). It grew gradually over its first decades. World War I, the Russian Revolution, and the Mann Act of 1910 (targeting sex trafficking) saw the expansion of the bureau's role in federal law enforcement. Concerns about rising crime during the 1930s led the U.S. Congress to enact a wave of legislation that vastly increased the power of the FBI. The official FBI stance on organized crime before 1957, however, was that it was mostly a local police problem committed by local gangsters and decentralized hoodlums and was not the FBI's responsibility. The discovery of the Apalachin meeting in upstate New York by New York state troopers and the high level of publicity accorded the high-level meeting of national Mafia figures forced J. Edgar Hoover to commit more resources to fighting organized crime. In one of its most lengthy global organized crime investigations, dubbed the "Pizza Connection" in 1984, the FBI documented the international connections between Italian American and Sicilian crime syndicates that were using pizza parlors as fronts for laundering heroin money. Today the FBI's Organized Crime Section is divided into three units focused on La Cosa Nostra, Italian organized crime, and racketeering; Eurasian/Middle Eastern organized crime; and Asian and African criminal syndicates. Each of the agency's 56 field offices investigates organized crime in its own territory. The FBI also participates in joint task forces in conjunction with other federal, state, and local law enforcement agencies. In 2005, the FBI had 651 pending investigations related to labor racketeering and Italian organized crime, with another 468 cases related to Asian and African criminal organizations. After opening its first international office in Moscow, FBI agents frequently work together with their counterparts in Italy, Hungary, and other countries.

United States Marshals Service

Web site: http://www.usmarshals.gov

Founded in 1789, the U.S. Marshals Service is America's oldest federal law enforcement agency. It is considered the enforcement wing of the federal courts and is therefore involved in every federal law enforcement initiative. Domestically, it is charged with apprehending federal fugitives, protecting the federal judiciary, operating the Witness Security Program, transporting federal prisoners, and seizing property acquired by criminals during their illegal activities. Today the purview of the U.S. Marshals has been expanded by the Department of Justice to include being responsible for the apprehension of fugitives from foreign countries and thought to be hiding in the United States. In addition the marshals are responsible for tracking and extraditing fugitives who are captured in foreign countries and wanted for prosecution in the United States. In essence U.S. Marshals have a statutory responsibility for all international, federal, and state extraditions. They often network with their counterparts in other countries. In 2003, the U.S. Marshals Service opened field offices in Mexico City, Mexico, Kingston, Jamaica, and Santo Domingo, Dominican Republic and have also established liaison programs on the borders of Canada and Mexico. In 1995, the Marshals and the Bureau of Immigration and Customs Service merged their air fleets to form the Justice Prisoner and Alien Transportation System (JPATS). It is considered an effective system for transporting prisoners and criminal aliens and is now one of the largest transporters of prisoners in the world. In 2008, the marshals coordinated more than 850 extraditions and deportations involving 60 countries.

Nongovernmental Organizations

Amnesty International

Web site: http://www.amnesty.org

Amnesty International was founded in 1961 by British lawyer Peter Berenson. During its early years it focused on the rights of political prisoners and other human rights issues. Over the following decades this international nongovernmental organization expanded its mission to concentrate on all categories of human rights violations. It was awarded the Nobel Peace Prize for its efforts in 1977. Currently there are more than 7,500 Amnesty International groups with almost 1 million members operating in 162 countries and territories. More recently it has become embroiled in the fight against the unregulated global arms trade. Together with Oxfam and the International Action Network on Small Arms (IANSA), Amnesty International set up the Control Arms campaign, which calls for an international and legally binding Arms Trade Treaty. In 2006, the UN General Assembly saw 152 governments vote for a resolution that would start the process toward a global Arms Trade Treaty.

Anti-Slavery International

Web site: http://www.antislavery.org

Created in 1839, this organization is the world's oldest international human rights organization. It also claims to be the only charity in the United Kingdom working exclusively against slavery and slavery-related crimes. Although headquartered in London, Anti-Slavery International works through local partnerships around the world in countries in Africa, South and East Asia, Latin America, Europe, and the Gulf region. Since it does not have any overseas offices, it seeks to work together with local organizations at the grassroots level. The organization issues a newsletter called the *Reporter* four times a year.

Coalition against Trafficking in Women

Web site: http://www.catwinternational.org

The Coalition against Trafficking in Women (CATW) was founded in 1988 and is considered the first nongovernmental organization to focus on human trafficking. Its goal is to promote women's rights by working on a global stage to end sexual exploitation, and especially the sex trafficking of women and girls. The CATW is made up of a coalition of regional networks and affiliated groups and individuals that endeavor to bring international attention to all forms of sexual exploitation including prostitution, pornography, sex tourism, and the selling of mail-order brides. CATW members testify before national congresses, parliaments, law reform commissions, regional and United Nations committees and commission and often serve as consultants to various governmental commissions seeking to draft new legislation on sex trafficking.

The Council of Europe

Web site: http://www.coe.int

The Council of Europe is made up of representatives of 47 European countries (virtually every European country). It is headquartered in Strasbourg (France). It was established on May 5, 1949 by an original nucleus of 10 countries. Its stated purpose is to develop throughout Europe common and democratic principles based on the European Convention on Human Rights and related documents on the protection of individuals and human rights. It is on behalf of these goals that the countries of the European Council cooperate to find shared solutions to major issues such as terrorism, organized crime and corruption, cybercrime, and the trafficking in human beings.

Global Alliance against Traffic in Women

Web site: http://www.gaatw.org

Created in Chiang Mai, Thailand in 1994, the Global Alliance against Traffic in Women (GAATW), coordinates, organizes, and facilitates strategies related to suppressing the trafficking of women and improving conditions for the labor migration of women throughout the world. A nongovernmental human rights organization, it continues to campaign for the inclusion of legal protection of the human rights of trafficking victims. Comprising an alliance of 100 nongovernmental organizations around the globe, its International Secretariat is now based in Bangkok, where it coordinates its activities and collects and disseminates information. The GAATW also has a special consultative status on the Economic and Social Council (ECOSOC) of the United Nations.

**International Organization for Migration
(Counter-Trafficking Service)**

Web site: http://www.iom.int

The International Organization for Migration (IOM) was established in 1951 and is considered one of the leading intergovernmental organizations in the arena of migration. It has 127 member states with 17 others holding observer status and offices in more than 100 countries. Its focus remains on promoting international migration law and protecting migrants' rights, migration health, and the gender dimension of migration. Among its current concerns are the rise in fraudulent offers of migration assistance from human smugglers and the rise in forced labor.

Investigative Roundtable
on Organized Crime

**La Strada International European Network
against Trafficking in Human Beings**

Web site: http://lastradainternational.org/?main=home

La Strada International is an association of nine independent human rights nongovernmental organizations. The countries making up this network are Belarus, Bosnia and Herzegovina, Bulgaria, the Czech Republic, Macedonia, Moldova, the Netherlands, Poland, and Ukraine. Its goal is to prevent human trafficking (as defined in Art.3 (a) of the UN Protocol to Prevent, Suppress and Punish Trafficking in persons), with particular focus on women in Central and Eastern Europe. Among its stated goals is to improve the position of women as well as their universal rights, which includes the freedom to choose to immigrate to other countries and to protect them from violence and abuse. According to La Strada most of the trafficked individuals who it has helped over the past decade are young women 18 to 30 years old who were trafficked into the sex trade. The organization runs hotlines, often 24/7. Consultants are available to provide information on destination countries, safety tips, and information about legislation in these countries. Several offices provide consultations for potential migrants.

Transparency International

Web site: http://www.transparency-usa.org/

Founded in 1993, Transparency International (TI) is a global society devoted to fighting corruption and helping its victims. Its global network is made up of more than 90 locally established national chapters (and chapters-in-formation). Together these bodies fight international corruption by bringing together representatives from government, the media, civil society, and business in an effort to promote transparency in elections, business, procurement, and public administration. IT also uses this network to lobby governments to introduce anticorruption campaigns. It is not involved in undertaking investigations of alleged corruption or exposing individual cases, but it will work with organizations that will.

United Nations Interregional Crime and Justice Research Institute

Web site: http://www.unicrit.it

The United Nations Interregional Crime and Justice Research Institute (UNICRI) was established in 1968. It is located on the United Nations campus in Turin, Italy. Its stated mission is to help intergovernmental, governmental, and nongovernmental organizations in developing and putting into practice new and improved policies related to crime prevention and criminal justice. Its work is organized into four areas. The one related to global organized crime is called "Emerging Crimes and Anti-Human Trafficking," which is dedicated to suppressing the trafficking of humans for commercial and sexual exploitation. It has also become more involved in designing antiorganized crime programs involving money laundering, counterfeiting, environmental crime, illegal trade in cultural artifacts, and cybercrime. The institute recently produced a report culled from data from governments and international organizations that offers recommendations for countering the growing problem of counterfeiting. The UNICRI carries out its projects in Africa, Southeast Asia, Central America, Eastern Europe, and the Balkans.

United Nations (United Nations Office on Drugs and Crime)

Web site: http://www.unodc.org

The United Nations officially came into existence on October 24, 1945. Since then it has become a global leader in the struggle against international organized crime. In 1997, it established the United Nations Office on Drugs and Crime (UNODC), which is now among the most prominent organizations combating international crime and the illicit drug trade. It was created through a merger of the United Nations Drug Control Program and the Centre for International Crime Prevention. The UNODC is active in every region of the world offering an extensive network of field offices. Ninety percent of its budget is funded by voluntary contributions, mostly from governments around the globe. The UNDOC mandate includes assisting member states in the fight against illegal drugs, crime, and terrorism. More recently the ratification of the Millennium Declaration asserted the resolution of member states to put more efforts into the struggle against global organized crime activity and to concerted actions against international terrorism. The UNODC work program requires field-based technical cooperation among member states to enhance their abilities to counteract global crime syndicates and terrorist activities. Among the UNODC's various counter-drug trafficking efforts are the Illicit Crop Monitoring Program (ICMP), the Alternative Development Program (ICMP), and the Global Program against Money Laundering (GPML). It has also created the Global Program against Trafficking in Human Beings (GPAT) in its ongoing effort to counter human trafficking networks around the world.

8

Resources

Print Resources

African Organized Crime
Periodicals and Publications
United Nations Office on Drugs and Crime. 2005. *Transnational Organized Crime in the West African Region.* New York: United Nations. 38 pages.

This United Nations report examines the development of transnational organized crime in five West African countries: Cote de Ivoire, Ghana, Nigeria, Senegal, and Sierra Leone. It highlights the numerous challenges facing the countries as well as the variety of operational structures used by organized crime groups, which range from very loose to networked structures. The report concludes that one must first take into account the historical development of organized crime and the socioeconomic and political factors that have made this region so vulnerable. Particular attention is paid to crimes such as oil bunkering, arms and drug trafficking, human trafficking, money laundering, cigarette smuggling, advance fee and Internet fraud, and diamond smuggling. Associations are also made with the looming terrorism threat in this region.

Asian Organized Crime
Books
Booth, Martin. 2001. *The Dragon Syndicates: The Global Phenomenon of the Triads.* New York: Carroll and Graff. 368 pages

This book examines the history of the Chinese Triads, or Dragon Syndicates. Booth demonstrates how these gangs have infiltrated legitimate business in Hong Kong and other parts of Asia. Furthermore, he draws a number of interesting parallels between the Triads and the Italian American crime syndicates, particularly dictates about maintaining secrecy and the importance placed on maintaining respect at all costs.

Hill, Peter B. E. 2006. *The Japanese Mafia: Yakuza, Law, and the State.* New York: Oxford University Press. 336 pages.

Hill's book is essential reading for anyone wanting to understand the intersection of the Yakuza, law and politics in Japan since the end of the Cold War. Especially instructive is his examination of the conditions of post-World War II Japan that led to development of "mafia-style" gangs. According to Hill this can be traced in part to an economy in shambles, a weak police force, and the availability of large number of unemployed and homeless former soldiers, and the emergence of a black market run by neighborhood strongmen. This book examines the decline of Yakuza membership in the 1960s and the emergence of larger Yakuza groups that subsumed smaller and less powerful ones. He follows their activities in the 1970s as a national crackdown on gambling leads the Yakuza into the more profitable amphetamine trade. Finally, the author delves into the impact of various countermeasures by the government in the 1990s, as well as the economic downturn that has adversely affected Yakuza influence and power in the early 21st century.

Lintner, Bertil. 2003. *Blood Brothers: The Criminal Underworld of Asia.* New York: Palgrave Macmillan. 480 pages.

Lintner's two decades of reporting from Asia have given him vast insight into the world of Asian organized crime. The book gracefully chronicles the various criminal fraternities of the Far East, and the author's research skills have revealed an exhaustive amount of data on large-scale organized crime in the region. He discusses all of the familiar rackets such as drugs, prostitution, gambling, extortion, kidnapping, piracy, and so forth. More important, he discusses the expansion of Asian crime syndicates into Australia and North America. The Yakuza and various Triads such as the Green Gang are among the various gangs covered.

Morgan, W. P. 1960. *Triad Societies in Hong Kong.* **Hong Kong: Government Press. 306 pages.**

Although written in 1960, this book by Hong Kong police inspector W. P. Morgan was considered the standard work on the subject for decades. Morgan's intent was to illustrate the growth (and deterioration) of the Hong Kong Triads in the 1950s. The book contains a rare account of the early elaborate Triad rituals compiled from his own experiences, as well as various interviews with Triad members in prison. The book is divided into a 60-page history of the Triads and almost 200 pages on the Triad societies, secret signs, and ceremonies. At the end of the book are appendices on the principal Hong Kong Triads between 1946 and 1958 and an Anglo-Chinese glossary.

Scholarly Journals
Asian Journal of Criminology
Social Science Research Centre, University of Hong Kong
Pokfulam Road, Hong Kong
Web site: http://www.ssrc.hku.hk

This journal is peer reviewed and is published 12 times a year. It promotes comparative studies about crime, crime prevention, and criminal justice in Asia. Articles are often multidisciplinary in scope, including those based on quantitative, qualitative, historical, and comparative methodologies. It encourages manuscripts from a broad range of disciplines. More recently it devoted two issues (Dec. 2007 and June 2008) to organized crime in Asia.

Asia Pacific Journal of Police & Criminal Justice
Appalachian State University
P.O. Box 32107
Boone, North Carolina 26808-2107
Web site: http://www.aaps.or.kr

Formerly known as *Asian Policing,* the *Asia Pacific Journal of Police and Criminal Justice* is a peer-reviewed journal published twice a year by the Asian Association of Police Studies. The regional focus of the journal is on the Asia-Pacific region, and most articles are related to criminal justice issues among the countries of Asia, North America, South America, and Oceania.

Canadian Organized Crime
Books
Schneider, Stephen. 2009. *Iced: The Story of Organized Crime in Canada*. Toronto, Ontario: John Wiley and Sons. 608 pages.

This book chronicles 400 years of organized crime in Canada. It is far ranging, covering Atlantic coast pirates, prohibition bootleggers, and international organized crime groups such as Chinese triads, Colombian "cocaine cowboys," the Italian mafia, outlaw motorcycle gangs, and others. The book also examines the often overlooked fact that Canada has long served as an important transit point for international smuggling syndicates.

Reference Books
Edwards, Peter, and Michael Auger. 2004. *The Encyclopedia of Canadian Organized Crime: From Captain Kidd to Mom Boucher*. McClelland and Stewart. 280 pages.

This encyclopedia on Canadian organized crime was written by two veteran crime reporters. It contains 300 entries arranged alphabetically and accompanied by more than 150 illustrations. Although the authors never define organized crime and many of the entries are clearly not related to organized crime, there is enough to edify those interested in learning about the impact of global crime groups on Canada, including such topics as early sea piracy, the Sicilian Mafia and the Calabrian 'Ndrangheta, American and Colombian drug syndicates, Russian mobsters, and the emergence of powerful outlaw motorcycle gangs.

Periodicals and Publications
Drug Enforcement Administration, the Federal Bureau of Investigation and the Royal Mounted Police. 2006. *Canada/U.S. Organized Crime Threat Assessment*. 16 pages.

This joint Canadian-American report examines transnational organized crime between these two countries. It looks at legal and illegal immigration, drug and contraband smuggling, and financial crimes. What seems most daunting to the authorities is the sheer challenge of policing such a large border between the countries, let alone coastal areas. The report found that both countries are plagued by Albanian, African, Russian, Italian, Latin American, and Asian organized crime syndicates.

European Organized Crime

Books

Fijnaut, Cyrille, and Letizia Paoli, eds. 2004. *Organised Crime in Europe: Concepts, Patterns and Control Policies in the European Union and Beyond.* Dordrecht, Netherlands: Springer. 1,074 pages.

This volume is one of the first attempts to compare systematically organized crime concepts, as well as concrete historical and contemporary patterns and control polices in 13 European countries. These include the original seven European Union states of Denmark, France, Germany, Italy, the Netherlands, Spain, and the United Kingdom, as well as new members, the Czech Republic and Poland, and the countries of Albania, Russia, and Switzerland, which had yet to join by 2004. Experts from a variety of legal and social disciplines offer detailed country reports in each chapter.

Van Duyne, Petrus C., Almir Maljevic, Maarten van Dijck, Klaus von Lampe, and Jackie Harvey, eds. 2006. *Crime Business and Crime Money in Europe: The Dirty Linen of Illicit Enterprise.* Nijmegan, Netherlands: Wolf Legal Publishers. 267 pages.

This book is based on the presentations of leading international organized (economic) crime scholars at the eighth Cross-Border Crime Colloquium conducted in May 2006. Among the topics covered in the 12 chapters are cigarette black markets in Estonia and the Netherlands, corruption in the Ukraine, human trafficking, money laundering, and recent criminal law initiatives by the European Union (EU) in the wake of 9/11, including the third EU money laundering directive.

Van Duyne, Petrus C., Jackie Harvey, Almir Maljevic, Miroslav Scheinost, and Klaus von Lampe, eds. 2008. *European Crime-Markets at Crossroads: Extended and Extending Criminal Europe.* Nijmegan, Netherlands: Wolf Legal Publishers. 290 pages.

This book contains a number of articles delivered at the ninth Cross-Border Crime Colloquium in October 2007. Among those related to organized crime are several on human trafficking in Great Britain and Ukraine. Others papers examine Slovene and Serbian offenders as "organized criminals," police corruption in Bosnia and Herzegovina, cigarette smuggling in Greece, value-added tax (VAT) fraud in the European Union, and various aspects of money laundering in the region.

Van Duyne, Petrus C., Klaus von Lampe, Maarten van Dijck, and James L. Newell, eds. 2005. *The Organised Crime Economy: Managing Crime Markets in Europe*. Nijmegan, Netherlands: Wolf Legal Publishers. 290 pages.

This edited volume of papers from the 2004 Cross Border Crime Colloquium includes articles on the ecstasy industry in the Netherlands in a global perspective; Norwegian organized crime; cigarette smuggling in Germany; economic crime in the Czech Republic, Russia, and the Baltic States; money laundering; cross border crime in Estonia; as well as drug trafficking in Bulgaria and women trafficking in Bosnia and Herzegovina.

Periodicals and Publications

Council of Europe. 2005, December. *Organised Crime Situation Report 2005: Focus on the Threat of Economic Crime*. Strasbourg: Department of Crime Problems. 134 pages.

This document was produced after the meeting of European heads of states and governments at the 3rd Summit of the Council of Europe in Warsaw, Poland. It is a major assessment of Europe's overall organized crime problem and aims to address new threats and major issues of concern and to help form anticrime policies. It is richly documented, with an emphasis on the threat of economic crime. Its first section examines the concept of organized crime and the purpose of the report. The second part chronicles various trafficking issues, cybercrime, money laundering, and various organized crime networks and groups. The third section offers case studies based in Western and Eastern Europe.

Europol. 2007, June. *The Organised Crime Threat Assessment (OCTA)*. The Hague: Europol. 28 pages.

Although the report's main focus is Europe, it also examines nonindigenous international organized crime groups in the region. This report marked a new proactive approach to fighting crime. The OCTA, which was first endorsed in 2006, replaced the Organised Crime Report (OCR) because of the need for a more future-oriented assessment of organized crime in Europe by highlighting strategic priorities in different regions in Europe.

Surtees, Rebecca. 2008. "Traffickers and Trafficking in Southern and Eastern Europe: Considering the Other Side of Human Trafficking." *European Journal of Criminology* 5 (1): 39–68.

This article examines human trafficking patterns from and within Southeastern Europe. Most research has been directed at victims of trafficking, but this article makes a valuable contribution by investigating the traffickers and their operations. In her effort to develop a profile of the typical trafficker in the region, Surtees finds them to be much more diverse than portrayed in the media. Unlike in Southeast Asia, where most trafficking is informally conducted through personal connections, in Southeastern Europe it is conducted by organized criminal syndicates. Especially valuable is information on methods traffickers use to recruit victims, relationships between the trafficker and the victim, and how they move victims across borders. Surtees reveals how transportation routes have changed in recent years, how travel arrangements are made, and in what type of configurations victims are moved (individually and groups). The treatment of victims and the behaviors of traffickers vary according to what is necessary to control victims. The article also examines the different types of sex trafficking, living and working conditions, payment and salary, and the control and use of abuse and violence. Finally, Surtees asserts that this type of research can help determine more effective methods of suppressing these activities through the criminal justice system.

Globalization and Organized Crime
Books
Chanda, Nayan. 2007. *Bound Together: How Traders, Preachers, Adventurers, and Warriors Shaped Globalization.* New Haven, CT: Yale University Press. 391 pages.

Chanda traces the roots of globalization to a process of interconnectedness and interdependence that began centuries ago. Especially illuminating is his accounts of how the British established the "first" global drug trade, when, in the 1840s, it went to war with China over the right to enforce the opium trade there. One of Chanda's most important assertions is that modern globalization has had the negative consequence of decreasing the ability of many national governments to prevent transnational crime and terrorism from flourishing in their countries.

Galeotti, Mark. 2005. *Global Crime Today: The Changing Face of Organised Crime.* London: Routledge. 166 pages.

This book offers 10 essays by various scholars on the modern manifestations of global organized crime. Chapters are devoted to the globalization of organized crime in North America, Latin America and the Caribbean, and East Central Europe, as well as the North Korean drug trade, the terrorism-organized crime nexus, the global dimension of cybercrime, and the changing nature of the Japanese Yakuza and Chinese organized crime.

Glenny, Misha. 2008. *McMafia: A Journey Through the Global Criminal Underworld.* **New York: Knopf. 375 pages.**

Investigative journalist Misha Glenny takes the reader through the global underworld in the wake of the fall of the Soviet Union. According to the author, organized crime should be regarded as one of the fundamental political narratives of the modern era. To get to the root of the matter, he traveled widely, interviewing police, crime victims, officials, and crime syndicate members from Eastern Europe, North and South America, Africa, the Middle East, China, Japan, and India. What he makes clear is that the world's organized crime groups have reaped the benefits of globalization, taking advantage of new technologies and the widespread poverty that still impacts much of the world.

Hagedorn, John M. 2008. *A World of Gangs: Armed Young Men and Gangsta Culture.* **Minneapolis: University of Minnesota Press. 198 pages.**

Written by a respected scholar on the international range of youth gangs, the book focuses on the conditions that create gangs in cities ranging from Chicago to Rio de Janeiro, Brazil, and Capetown, South Africa. Hagedorn observes how globalization has contributed to the development of urban gangs in societies throughout the world. He has found that a number of these gangs now play an important role in a variety of criminal activities ranging from drug trafficking and extortion to religious and political violence.

Madsen, Frank. 2009. *Transnational Organized Crime.* **London: Routledge. 144 pages.**

This book examines key issues related to organized crime including the war on drugs, antimoney laundering strategies, the relationship between terrorism and organized crime, the development of cyber-related crime, and international responses to transnational organized crime. The author brings a wealth of experience from his role as a police officer with Interpol and with the Danish police.

This book will be of interest to anyone looking for an introduction to the current crime problems related to globalization.

Naim, Moises. 2005 edition. *Illicit: How Smugglers, Traffickers, and Copycats are Hijacking the Global Economy.* **New York: Anchor Books edition. 340 pages.**

Moises Naim was among the first observers to identify the real consequences of transnational crime in the globalized world. This thought-provoking book demonstrates how small and illicit players are using the tools of globalization to weaken nations and economies around the world. Naim illuminates the underside of globalization, revealing the struggle between traffickers and the restricted bureaucracies trying to control them. Chapters focus on illegal migrants, drugs, weapons, counterfeit goods, and money laundering and on the black markets used by terrorists and new businesses.

Nicaso, Antonio, and Lee Lamothe. 2005. *Angels, Mobsters & Narco-Terrorists: The Rising Menace of Global Crime Empires.* **Toronto, Ontario: John Wiley and Sons Canada. 292 pages.**

Nicaso and Lamothe examine the changing tactics and strategies of global organized crime groups. They investigate a wide range of groups and activities ranging from outlaw motorcycle gangs to narcoterrorists. They find that criminal syndicates are expanding their activities worldwide and are cooperating with each other more than ever, citing such groups as the Italian Mafia and Chinese Triads, Albanian gangs, and Russian and Mexican trafficking networks. Finally, the authors delve into the world of investigators and crime victims.

Reichel, Philip, ed. 2005. *Handbook of Transnational Crime and Justice.* **Thousand Oaks, CA: Sage Publications. 512 pages.**

This book offers a variety of perspectives providing global coverage of the increasingly transnational nature of crime and the attempts to provide cooperative cross-national responses. Besides a comprehensive introduction to the topic of transnational crime, the book it provides chapters specifically focused on related issues including international terrorism, drug trafficking, and money laundering to illustrate the expansion of global organized crime activity.

Siegel, Dina, and Hans Nelen, eds. 2007. *Organized Crime: Culture, Markets and Policies.* **Dordrecht, Netherlands: Springer. 230 pages.**

This book offers 15 essays on various aspects of organized crime including drugs, diamonds, human trafficking, ecocrime, conflict resolution, and underground banking. The general consensus of the distinguished scholars represented in this book is that there is a dire need for more empirically funded research on specific situational contexts instead of merely concentrating on why organized crime develops throughout the world. Studies were conducted on Sicily, the Sinai, the United States, Quebec, Amsterdam, Antwerp, Sub-Saharan Africa, and Asia. What is most notable is the interdisciplinary nature of the research that includes sociology, history, criminology, political science, and anthropology.

Thachuk, Kimberly L., ed. 2007. *Transnational Threats: Smuggling and Trafficking in Arms, Drugs, and Human Life.* Westport, CT: Praeger. 256 pages.

This book of essays focuses on the unforeseen aspects of globalization. The essays document the challenges to law enforcement and unstable countries and regions by transnational criminal activity, featuring articles on the interconnectedness between terrorists and organized crime groups, narcotrafficking, human trafficking, and the illegal weapons trade. Some chapters focus on specific countries, regions, and international and security issues. Contributors represent a wide range of organizations from the FBI and the CIA to the Rand Corporation and the Congressional Research Service.

Williams, Phil, and Dimitri Vlassis, eds. 2001. *Combating Transnational Crime: Concepts, Activities and Responses.* London: Frank Cass. 272 pages.

This book is divided into three sections containing 20 articles by some of the leading academics on transnational organized crime. The first section examines conceptual issues and features seven chapters on issues such as emerging trends in Chinese transnational organized crime and organized crime and ethnic minorities. The second part focuses on criminal activities and markets and is made up of four chapters featuring weapons trafficking, sex trafficking, cybercrime, and maritime fraud and piracy. The final section contains nine articles focused on responses to transnational organized crime. Particularly useful is a section at the end containing all of the article abstracts.

Periodicals and Publications
United Nations Office on Drugs and Crime. 2002, September. *Global Programme against Transnational Organized Crime: Results of a Pilot Survey of Forty Selected Organized Criminal Groups in Sixteen Countries.* New York: United Nations.

This project report assesses transnational organized crime based on the results of a pilot survey of 40 selected organized criminal groups in 16 countries undertaken by the United Nations center for international crime prevention is presented. The objective of the report was to collect and present data on different criminal groups spread globally, as well as to develop a method by which it can be analyzed and monitored to help policymakers and law enforcement officials working on the phenomenon of organized crime groups around the world.

Italian Organized Crime
Books
Arlacchi, Pino. 1993. *Men of Dishonor: Inside the Sicilian Mafia.* New York: William Morrow. 285 pages.

Mafia expert Pino Arlacchi collaborated with former Sicilian crime boss Don Antonino Calderone on his autobiography to give the reader a rare first-hand glimpse into the hierarchy of a Sicilian crime family. Among his revelations was a detailed description of the Mafia initiation ceremonies. After his testimony in the 1980s, academics revisited the previously discredited testimony of American mafia turncoat Joseph Valachi and found a remarkable amount of substantiation of some of his testimony. Calderone had run the Catania "family" from the 1960s to the 1980s before his arrest and imprisonment. During this time he decided to cooperate with the authorities. His testimony led to the arrest of more than 200 individuals. Calderone then moved out of Italy under an assumed identity.

Behan, Tom. 1996. *The Camorra.* London: Routledge. 225 pages.

Behan chronicles the emergence of the Camorra as an international force in international organized crime by the 1990s. He traces its roots to the 19th century and chronicles how it expanded from a group of small-time cigarette smugglers in the 1960s into the savvy entrepreneurs of the 1990s. This book supplements the current research on the Camorra as exemplified by Saviano's *Gomorrah* (reviewed later). Especially informative is Behan's coverage of the organization's relationships with the region's politicians in the 1970s that allowed the Camorra to become more powerful, expanding its protection rackets, investing in the drug business, and laundering the proceeds in the construction business after the destructive 1980 earthquake.

Dickie, John. 2004. *Cosa Nostra: A History of the Sicilian Mafia*. London: Palgrave Macmillan. 400 pages.

This book is among the best and most readable accounts of the history of the Sicilian Mafia. With access to a vast amount of new research and information, Dickie has written a compelling and comprehensive account of the *Cosa Nostra*, the more common expression for Mafia among insiders. He traces it from its early roots in Sicilian society to its modern-day incarnation. More than half of the book is devoted to the post-World War II Mafia. Especially instructive is the coverage of its links to the highest levels of politics and the concomitant corruption that allowed the Cosa Nostra to move unimpeded through much of the 20th century.

Fiandaca, Giovanni, ed. 2007. *Women and the Mafia*. New York: Springer. 308 pages.

This book is a collection of essays devoted to chronicling women who participate in organized crime activity in Italy and other countries. Written by authors from a wide variety of disciplines, chapters are dedicated to women involved in organized crime activities in Argentina, Albania, Russia, Brazil, Germany, Japan, and the United States. The book also reveals the abuse and violence these women are often subjected to.

Jamieson, Alison. 2000. *The Antimafia: Italy's Fight against Organized Crime*. New York: St. Martin's Press. 257 pages.

This book chronicles the successes and failures of the Italian government's Antimafia campaign after the murders of magistrates Giovanni Falcone and Paolo Borsellino in 1992 and the bombings in Rome, Florence, and Milan in 1993. What sets this book apart is its use of primary sources, interviews with judges, police officers, and families of victims. It examines allegations of collusion between the Mafia and the seven-times elected Prime Minister Giulio Andreotti, as well as other criminal alliances between the upperworld and underworld.

Longrigg, Clare. 2009. *Boss of Bosses: How One Man Saved the Sicilian Mafia.* **London: John Murray. 300 pages.**

Investigative journalist Clare Longrigg offers the first detailed biography of Bernardo "The Tractor" Provenzano. After evading capture for 43 years, he was brought down in 2006. He had taken over the reins of the Mafia at its low point after the 1980s' Maxi Trial and the assassinations of prosecutors Giovanni Falcone and Paolo Borsellino. This book offers a wealth of information about Provenzano's family and the investigators who tracked him for decades. More important, it examines how after the arrest of the brutal Toto Riina, Provenzano took the Sicilian Mafia underground, eschewing former methods of high-profile killings and prospering in the new age of globalization.

Paoli, Letizia. 2003. *Mafia Brotherhoods: Organized Crime Italian Style.* **New York: Oxford University Press. 320 pages.**

Paoli's book is considered among the most important academic works on the 'Ndrangheta. Its sources include previously undisclosed confessions of former members who are now cooperating with police. This interdisciplinary work uses a host of methodologies to provide deep insight into mafia behavior, motivations, and structure in Italy.

Saviano, Robert. 2008. *Gomorrah: A Personal Journey into the Violent International Empire of Naples' Organized Crime System.* **London: Picador. 320 pages.**

Investigative journalist Robert Saviano risked life and limb to document the modern rise of Naples's Camorra crime families. These gangs have eclipsed the power of the Sicilian mafia in recent years as they expanded their activities into the construction and high fashion rackets, drug trafficking, and the movement of hazardous waste. Having witnessed his first gangland killing while barely in his teens, Saviano has written a compelling book that has led to renewed interest in this crime faction and resulted in the author having to live under full-time protection while avoiding contract killers hoping to collect a payoff for his murder.

Stille, Alexander. 1996. *Excellent Cadavers: The Mafia and the Death of the First Italian Republic.* **New York: Vintage Books. 480 pages.**

The "excellent cadavers" referred to in the book's title are Sicilian Mafia victims who are government officials. In this case Stille chronicles the antimafia crusade of the prosecutors Giovanni Falcone and Paolo Borsellino that ultimately led to their murders just two months apart in 1992. Before their untimely deaths, the two exposed mafia corruption in the highest corridors of power. Stille chronicles the rise and fall of Mafia fortunes after the assassinations, as well as the investigations that implicated the politicians Bettino Craxi and Guilio Andreotti.

Periodicals and Publications
Federal Bureau of Investigation. 1958, July 9. *Mafia Monograph.* Washington, D.C. Freedom of Information Act. 258 pages.

This document was prepared by the FBI's Central Research Section and for many years was a confidential file available only to federal law enforcement. It is now available under the Freedom of Information Act. The stated purpose of the monograph is to present evidence that the Mafia exists in the United States and to explain what it is. It examines the origins and activities of the Mafia and its transplantation to the New World through immigration. Although a product of the 1950s, it is richly documented with citations. Topics range from mafia practices of vendetta and *omerta*, to speculations about the existence (or nonexistence) of the Mafia, the Black Hand, and many others.

Varese, Federico. 2006. "How Mafias Migrate: The Case of 'Ndrangheta in Northern Italy." *Law & Society Review* 40 (2): 411–444.

In this article, one of the leading scholars on Italian organized crime tests several theories on the extent to which mafia groups migrate beyond their place of origin. Among the factors studied are migration from territories with high mafia density, the policy of forcing criminals to resettle outside their region of origin, the existence of mafia wars, different systems of recruitment into mafia families, the level of impersonal trust in the new territory, and the demand for criminal protection. The author concludes that contrary to the established theories of social capital and trust, a high degree of impersonal trust among the respectable residents is not sufficient to hinder mafia transplantation. Varese's conclusions are based on two case studies. One involves the transplantation of 'Ndrangheta members from Calabria to Bardonecchia in the Piedmont region; the other involves their movement into Verona in the Veneto region.

Law Enforcement
Books
Diaz, Tom. 2009. *No Boundaries: Transnational Latino Gangs and American law Enforcement.* Ann Arbor: University of Michigan Press. 341 pages.

Former journalist Tom Diaz explored the world of Latino gangs for this book. He uncovers the international dimensions of modern Latino gangs and chronicles their development into highly structured criminal organizations. He examines the life of the "first Latin godfather in the United States," Nelson Martinez Comandari, as well as influential gangs with international ties such as the Los Angeles-based Mara Salvatrucha (MS-13), the 18th Street Gang, and the Latin Kings, based in Chicago. Diaz also tells a parallel story focusing on complex American issues such as racial tensions and immigration policy, conflict in Latin America, and the forces of globalization.

Richards, James R. 1998. *Transnational Criminal Organizations, Cybercrime, and Money Laundering: A Handbook for Law Enforcement Officers, Auditors, and Financial Investigators.* Boca Raton, FL: CRC Press. 344 pages.

Although this book is written for a law enforcement audience and is more than a decade –old, it has much to recommend it to academics and practitioners. The book contains a section devoted to all of the usual suspects—from the Italian Mafia to the Colombian and Mexican drug trafficking organizations; it also includes case studies of international terrorist-cum-organized crime groups such as the Irish Republic Army and the Peruvian Shining Path and international figures immersed in the transnational crime such as Khun Sa and Manuel Noriega. Two-thirds of the book is devoted to well-organized chapters on money laundering, cyberbanking, investigative techniques, international treaties, law enforcement agencies, and asset forfeiture.

Periodicals and Publications
Levi, Michael, and Alaster Smith. 2002. *A Comparative Analysis of Organised Crime Conspiracy Legislation and Practice and Their*

Relevance to England and Wales. **Home Office Online Report 17/02. http://www.homeoffice.gov.uk/rds/pdfs2/rdsolr1702.pdf.**

This article examines and compares the operation of the Racketeer Influenced and Corrupt Organizations Act (RICO) in the United States and similar legislation geared toward countering organized crime in England and Wales. More than 30 investigators and prosecutors from the United States, Canada, New Zealand, the Netherlands, Italy, and Great Britain were interviewed on various aspects of legislation dealing with proof and organized crime activity.

Scholarly Journals
Policing: An International Journal of Police Strategies
College of Education
Department of Criminal Justice
University of Cincinnati
600 Dyer Hall
P.O. Box 210389
Cincinnati, Ohio 45221-0389
E-mail: Lawrence.Travis@uc.edu

This journal is published four times a year. Although most articles are related to various aspects of policing, it claims in its mission statement to welcome articles related to the intersection of organized crime and policing, particularly when it comes to new police strategies developed to suppress organized crime activities. The journal is peer reviewed and offers book reviews and debates and abstracts of articles published in related journals.

Maritime Piracy

Gottschalk, Jack A., Brian P. Flanagan, Lawrence J. Kahn, and Dennis M. Larochelle. 2000. *Jolly Roger with an Uzi: The Rise and Threat of Modern Piracy.* **Annapolis, MD: Naval Institute Press. 192 pages.**

Although written almost a decade ago, this book serves as an introduction to modern piracy at the end of the 20th century. It will be of interest to professional mariners as well as pleasure-boat sailors and government officials. The authors are both lawyers and have written the book for a general audience. They chronicle an 80 percent rise in pirate attacks and offer several case studies to illustrate pirate activities in the waters off the coasts of Indonesia, Brazil, Somalia, and the South China Sea. The authors also offer suggestions for reducing this crime such as redefining jurisdictions, policy reforms, and an expansion of the mandates of military and maritime enforcement agencies.

Langewiesche, William. 2004. *The Outlaw Sea: A World of Freedom, Chaos, and Crime.* **New York: North Point Press. 256 pages.**

In the wake of the recent spate of high-profile pirate attacks off the coast of Somalia, this book is all the more compelling for its discussion of the current state of maritime law and order. The book discusses the unforeseen consequences of globalization on the shipping industry. Langewiesche not only explores the rising crime of piracy and its potential connections to terrorism, but he turns a discerning eye toward the poor state of affairs in the shipping industry, plagued by poorly trained and paid seamen, dishonest ship owners, and overmatched regulators.

Mueller, G.O.W., and Freda Adler. 1985. *Outlaws of the Ocean: The Complete Book of Contemporary Crime on the High Seas.* **New York: Hearst Marine Books. 362 pages.**

The well-known criminologists Mueller and Adler were among the first to look at piracy from an academic perspective. In fact they begin the book noting how little research has been conducted by criminologists on crime in the oceans. Their findings are prescient, establishing links between sea piracy with the growing problems of international organized crime, terrorism, illegal immigration, and drug trafficking (almost 25 years ago). Anyone interested in analyzing modern piracy and homeland security would do well to begin with this book, as the authors combine empirical research with nautical minutia and real-life maritime experience.

Organized Crime and Related Issues
Books
Allum, Felia, and Renate Siebert, eds. 2003. *Organized Crime and the Challenge to Democracy.* **London: Routledge. 238 pages.**

This volume consists of 12 essays and a conclusion focusing on the impact and threat of organized crime to democratic institutions. The book is divided into four parts, with the first examining definitions and the myths and reality of transnational organized crime. The second part examines states under siege in Europe, Russia, and Colombia. The third part delves into the choices of civil society in responding to organized crime. The last focuses on the interconnectedness of politics and organized crime in France, Italy, and Japan.

Bovenkerk, Frank, and Michael Levi, eds. 2007. *The Organized Crime Community: Essays in Honor of Alan A. Block*. New York: Springer. 231 pages.

This book is a collection of essays on organized crime by students and friends of Penn State University's Professor Alan Block, a pioneer in the study of this phenomenon. The first chapter reprints Block's well-known study on the origins of the Iran Contra scandal and moves on to chapters on the social history of organized crime in the United States, corruption in the United Nations Oil-for-Food Program in Iraq, the fight against identity fraud, efforts to control international money laundering, the development of the illegal drug industry in Afghanistan and Colombia, and other issues.

Reference Books
Chepesiuk, Ron. 1999. *The War on Drugs: An International Encyclopedia*. Santa Barbara, CA: ABC-CLIO. 317 pages.

Although this book was published a decade ago, there is still much to recommend it. It is constructed alphabetically covering subjects including major drug cartels and kingpins, trafficking organizations, smuggling and counter-smuggling strategies, legal issues, case studies, and historical background germane to understanding drug prohibition and trafficking in the 21st century.

Newton, Michael. 2004. *The Encyclopedia of High-Tech Crime and Crime-Fighting: From Airport Security to the ZYX Computer Virus*. New York: Facts on File. 374 pages.

There are a number of references in this encyclopedia to global high-tech crime including the trafficking in synthetic narcotic and designer drugs; software, video, and satellite piracy; computer viruses and worms; as well as electronic crimes such as identification theft, cell phone cloning and fraud, bank fraud, and online gambling.

Newton, Michael. 2007. *The Encyclopedia of Gangsters: A Worldwide Guide to Organized Crime*. New York: Thunder's Mouth Press. 256 pages.

This reference book offers a comprehensive look at the world's leading crime syndicates past and present. It is arranged in chapters geographically, showing the history of organized crime in different parts of the world, chronicling prominent individuals and crimes. Chapters include the Sicilian mafia and its American incarnation, the gangsters of Marseilles and Paris, Jamaican Posses and Yardies, and legendary London gangsters such as the Kray brothers.

Shanty, Frank G., ed. 2008. *Organized Crime: From Trafficking to Terrorism*, 2 vols. Santa Barbara, CA: ABC-CLIO. 792 pages.

This two-volume reference is broken up into one volume detailing transnational organized crime issues around the world, describing the workings of crime syndicates around the world as well as international law enforcement efforts to suppress them. The second volume is a compilation of national and international laws and treaties aimed at organized crime enterprises in different corners of the world.

Periodicals and Publications

Finklea, Kristin M. 2009, April 16. *Organized Crime in the United States: Trends and Issues for Congress*. Washington, D.C.: Congressional Research Service. 28 pages.

This document was prepared by a domestic security analyst, especially for members of Congress. Its focus is on the increasingly transnational nature of organized crime in the United States. It examines current organized crime trends in the United States, focusing on Eurasian, Russian, Asian, Balkan, Italian, and other groups. Finklea also provides a definitional overview of organized crime, explaining various federal law enforcement efforts to combat organized crime, as well as recent statutes. The author also examines the domestic impact of money laundering, cigarette smuggling, piracy and counterfeiting, as well as the convergence of terrorism and organized crime. She also poses potential issues for Congress involving staffing organized crime units, setting budgetary resources, and multilateral crime fighting efforts.

Grabosky, Peter. 2007. "The Internet, Technology, and Organized Crime." *Asian Journal of Criminology: An Interdisciplinary Journal on Crime, Law and Deviance* **2 (2), http://www.springerlink. com/content/d361354j58h05u35/.**

This article examines how organized crime groups have exploited digital technology over the past decade while chronicling developments in communications and in information storage and retrieval. Grabosky demonstrates how organized crime groups are among the actors who have readily adapted their activities to a digital world. He also examines the criminal exploitation of digital technology using several case studies from Asia and other regions. One of the important questions taken up by the author is whether the activities of Asian organized crime groups have changed noticeably after adopting new technologies or whether it is just a case of becoming more efficient and effective through the use of technology in committing old crimes. Especially alarming is the transnational nature of organized crime today. The author offers several control strategies that may be used to confront high-tech criminals.

Shaw, Mark. 2002. "Typologies of Transnational Organized Crime Groups." Center for International Crime Prevention, UNODC. www.unodc.org/pdf/crime/training/typologies.pdf.

According to this study by Mark Shaw, a future analysis of trends in transnational organized crime could benefit by investigating several components, which he refers to as groups, clusters, and markets. At the lowest level, *groups* refer to the collecting of data on individual criminal organizations. *Clusters* refer to the collection of information around various clusters of criminal groups (often geographically defined). *Markets* refer to information on regional criminal markets. Shaw creates a profile of 40 selected organized crime groups in 16 different countries using this analysis.

United States Department of Justice. 2009. *National Drug Threat Assessment.* **Washington, D.C.: National Drug Intelligence Center. 81 pages.**

This report contains the strategic findings on the progress and emerging counter-drug challenges. It offers maps and recent figures related to the drug trade in the United States and on its borders. Among its most relevant summations are that Mexican drug trafficking organizations are the greatest organized crime threat to the United States. It also asserts that violent street gangs are an important cog in retail-level drug distribution, and that cocaine and methamphetamine remain the leading drug threats. Attention is devoted to how drug gangs acquire precursor chemicals for methamphetamine despite myriad state and federal restrictions. Also noteworthy is the Mexican participation in the heroin trade, the rising potency of marijuana, and the involvement of Asian drug trafficking groups in the production of drugs such as MDMA in Canadian superlabs. The report is divided into separate reports containing an overview, strategic findings, intelligence gaps, and outlooks for the future of the trafficking in cocaine, methamphetamine, marijuana, heroin, controlled prescription drugs, and MDMA. Attention is also given to drug threats on Indian reservations, various illicit finance systems, and drug trafficking organizations.

Scholarly Journals
Crime, Law and Social Change
Northeastern University
College of Criminal Justice
400 Churchill Hall
Boston, MA 02115-5000
Web site: http://www.wkap.nl/journals/cris

This peer-reviewed journal publishes articles and essays related to the political economy of organized crime, political corruption, environmental crime, and the expropriation of resources from developing nations. It is also dedicated to publishing scholarship in the realm of human rights, including genocide, and studies examining compensation and survivors of state-sponsored terrorism and mass murder. It also offers a large book review section.

Global Crime
Web site: http://www.tandf.co.uk/journals/titles/17440572.asp

Global Crime is a social science journal published four times a year. Interdisciplinary in scope, articles come from such disciplines as history, sociology, criminology, economics, political science, and other areas of research. The journal publishes peer-reviewed articles on any topic relating to crime, including organized criminality, its history, activities, relations with the state and its impact on global economies, as well as corruption, illegal migration, terrorism, illicit markets, violence, and police studies. Each issue features a substantial book review section. In most years one issue is edited by a guest editor (s). Personal subscriptions cost $95 per year.

International Journal of Comparative and Applied Criminal Justice
School of Criminal Justice
Michigan State University
East Lansing, Michigan 48824-1118
Web site: http://www.ijcacj.com

Published four times a year, the *International Journal of Comparative and Applied Criminal Justice* is the official journal for the American Society of Criminology Division of International Criminology. Individual subscriptions are $40 annually and $30 for students.

Journal of Gang Research
National Gang Crime Research Center
P.O. Box 990
Peotone, Illinois 604681-0990
Web site: http://www.ngrc.com

The *Journal of Gang Research* is published four times a year by the National Gang Crime Research Center. This professional interdisciplinary journal publishes original research on gangs, gang members, gang problems, gang crime patterns, gang prevention, and many other related issues. Some articles are international in scope, chronicling "cross-national gangs" that operate across national borders and that operate inside or pose a threat to the United States. It examines new types of gangs, new strategies for old gang problems, and recent developments in the purview of social policy on gangs.

Trends in Organized Crime
Springer, New York
23 Spring Street
New York 10013
E-mail: welmoed.spahr@springer.com

Trends in Organized Crime is a peer-reviewed journal published four times a year in association with the International Association of Organized Crime (IASOC). It publishes a wide range of original research including significant government reports. It also publishes book reviews of recent organized crime-related books and offers analysis and commentary on current organized crime-related topics. This journal has a readership that includes practitioners, scholars, and policymakers.

Organized Crime-Terrorism Nexus
Periodicals and Publications
Berry, LaVerle, Glenn E. Curtis, Tara Karacan, Nina Kollars, John N. Gibbs, Rex Hudson, and Ramon Miro. 2003, October. *Nations Hospitable to Organized Crime and Terrorism*. Washington, DC: Federal Research Division, Library of Congress.

This article is a must for anyone trying to get a handle on the convergence of organized crime and terrorism in the 21st century. The report examines conditions that attract transnational criminal and terrorist activity. It examines the years 1999–2002 using a variety of sources including periodicals, Western and regional sources, reliable Internet sites, selected monographs, and personal communications with experts in the regions. The report is divided geographically into Africa, the Former Soviet Union and Eastern Europe, South Asia, Southeast Asia, Western Europe, and the Western Hemisphere. Emphasis is on the countries with the most serious problems, although there are profiles on most countries and regions within the subheadings.

Makarenko, Tamara. 2004. "The Crime-Terror Continuum: Tracing the Interplay between Transnational Organized Crime and Terrorism." *Global Crime* 6 (1): 129–145.

Makarenko offers one of the best models for understanding the interconnectedness between terrorism and crime and pioneers an approach that is increasingly finding favor with theorists and practitioners. She asserts that beginning with the use of terror by Colombian drug organizations, often referred to as narcoterrorism, in the 1980s the use of crime has become a key factor in the growth of terrorism. What's more, both groups are learning from each other, by discovering what works or does not work before adapting a particular strategy from the other.

Shelley, Louise, and John T. Picarelli. 2005, Winter. "Methods and Motives: Exploring Links between Transnational Organized Crime and International Terrorism." *Trends in Organized Crime* 9 (2): 52–67.

The authors assert that the distinction has become blurred between organized crime and terrorist groups. Demonstrating how terrorist groups have adopted the same methods as criminals, this report identifies their points of convergence. Among the regions studied are Chechnya, the Black Sea region, and Latin America's Tri-Border area. The authors conclude that law enforcement should integrate crime analysis in the work of intelligence analysts and others addressing terrorism. What's more, it is no longer possible to rely on the once accepted divide that all terrorists are ideologically motivated while crime groups are all just profit-driven.

Sverdlick, Ana R. 2005. "Terrorists and Organized Crime Entrepreneurs in the 'Triple Frontier' among Argentina, Brazil, and Paraguay." *Trends in Organized Crime* 9 (2): 84–93.

This article examines the characteristics of the organized crime sanctuary along the Tri-Border region of Latin America where Argentina, Brazil, and Paraguay meet. She demonstrates how terrorists and organized crime groups often collaborate and cooperate in order to support their operations. Her research demonstrates that there is often a fine line, if there is one at all, separating the activities of both groups.

Outlaw Motorcycle Gangs
Books
Marsden, William, and Julian Sher. 2006. *Angels of Death: Inside the Bikers' Global Crime Empire*. Cambridge, MA: Da Capo Press. 480 pages.

Although this book focuses on the Hells Angeles outlaw motorcycle gang, it is also an examination of the globalization of the Hells Angels and several other major competitors. In rich detail the authors recount several specific cases to illustrate the brutal nature of this phenomenon. The story of the Angels and their leader Ralph "Sonny" Barger takes the reader on a tour of bikerdom and its associated organized crime activities in the Netherlands, Canada, United States, and Australia (where bikers are known as "bikies"). This book is both well researched and well written.

Russian and Soviet-Era Organized Crime

Books

Galeotti, Mark, ed. 2002. *Russian and Post Soviet Organized Crime*. Burlington, VT: Ashgate. 340 pages.

This volume edited by noted organized crime scholar Mark Galeotti contains 23 chapters on various aspects of Russian organized crime. It is divided into five sections. The first section offers five articles on the criminal foundations of Russian organized crime. The next section devotes six pieces to exploring what exactly is the Russian "Mafiya." The third section has four essays assessing Russian organized crime in the 1990s. The fourth section has four articles on the interconnectedness of Russian organized crime and the economy. The final section is composed of four chapters examining global Russian organized crime.

Orttung, Robert W., and Anthony Latta, eds. 2008. *Russia's Battle with Crime, Corruption and Terrorism*. New York: Routledge. 202 pages.

This book is a collection of essays examining Russia's response to post-Soviet threats such as rising crime, corruption, and terrorism. Combined together the articles demonstrate the inextricable links between a growing drug trade, organized crime, border problems, migration issues, corruption, and terrorism. Authors examine rampant corruption, ties between organized crime groups and law enforcement agencies, crime and migration in Siberia, drug trafficking along the Russian-Kazakh border, and the numerous challenges facing the government and law enforcement.

Satter, David. 2003. *Darkness at Dawn: The Rise of the Russian Criminal State*. New Haven, CT: Yale University Press. 314 pages.

This book looks at the evolution of organized crime in Russia in its various manifestations since the breakup of the Soviet Union. The author has the benefit of having observed life firsthand in Russia as he reported on the country for more than two decades. Among his most cogent assessments is that it was unexpected that after a decade of freedom and democracy the country was still marked by poverty and the existence of organized crime activity at virtually every level of life.

Serio, Joseph D. 2008. *Investigating the Russian Mafia*. Durham, NC: Carolina Academic Press. 324 pages.

This book is unique in that is based on the observations of an American who spent seven years in the Soviet Union before its collapse. During this time he served an internship in the Organized Crime Control Department of the Soviet police, and it was from this vantage point that he observed the evolution of organized crime activity in the region. It is especially valuable as a counterpoint to the avalanche of "Russian Mafia" books that have dominated much of the discussion on this misunderstood phenomenon. More important, Serio seeks to explain what the Russian "mafia" actually means. His close examination of official statistics and his analyses of the various nationalities and ethnic groups involved in organized crime in this region are especially useful.

Shelley, Louise, Erik R. Scott, and Anthony Latta, eds. 2007. *Organized Crime and Corruption in Georgia*. London: Routledge. 129 pages.

This collection of six essays focuses on organized crime in Georgia since the collapse of the Soviet Union. Chapters focus on the nation's so-called anti-corruption revolution and its aftermath, smuggling in the Abkhazia and Tskhinvali region in 2003–2004, the use of public service reform to overcome economic crime, and recent Georgian police reform efforts.

Trafficking and Criminal Networks

Books

Farah, Douglas. 2004. *Blood from Stones: The Secret Financial Network of Terror*. New York: Broadway Books. 225 pages.

Prize-winning investigative journalist Douglas Farah traveled into the heart of Africa to uncover the connections between corrupt politicians, diamond and weapons traffickers, and terrorist money laundering operations. Farah traces the global dimensions of the illicit diamond trade, which stretches from West Africa to Belgium and the Middle East. He reveals the interlocking links between underground financial systems, charities, and friendly bankers that allow such terrorist groups as al Qaeda to launder its cash through the illegal diamond trade.

Farah, Douglas, and Stephen Braun. 2007. *Merchant of Death: Money, Guns, Planes, and the Man Who Makes War Possible*. Hoboken, NJ: John Wiley. 320 pages.

Investigative journalists Farah and Braun have written a well-researched expose of the Russian arms trafficker Viktor Bout. The supposed inspiration for the movie *Lord of War,* Bout has been linked to the illegal weapons trade from the Cold War era until his recent arrest in Thailand. The authors chronicle the demise of the Soviet Union and the aftermath that left the weapons of a world power ripe for the taking and its weapons manufacturers looking for clients to sell them to. This book reveals the sordid story of how dictators, warlords, insurgent groups, and organized crime syndicates acquire weapons despite well-publicized UN embargoes. When it comes to the major activities of global organized crime networks, most focus has been devoted to human smuggling and drug trafficking. The weapons trade has yet to receive its magnum opus, but this is a welcome addition to the body of literature on international arms trafficking.

Kenney, Michael. 2007. *From Pablo to Osama: Trafficking and Terrorist Networks, Government Bureaucracies, and Competitive Adaptation.* **University Park: The Pennsylvania State University Press. 293 pages.**

This book is a comparative study of Colombian drug trafficking networks and terrorist networks, including al-Qaeda, and the myriad law enforcement organizations devoted to their destruction. Kenny interviews gang informants and former drug smugglers and many others to give a better-rounded picture of how the gangs and police officials operate. What's more he illustrates the uncanny abilities of terrorists and Colombian drug kingpins to adjust to the strategies of their adversaries.

Lee, Maggie, ed. 2007. *Human Trafficking.* **Devon, UK: Willan Publishing. 239 pages.**

This book offers an interdisciplinary examination of human trafficking over the centuries. Leading experts in criminology, sociology, social anthropology, politics, law, and human rights weigh forth on the continuum between the historical slave trade and modern human trafficking as they examine the changing nature, pattern, and process of human trafficking.

Lunde, Paul. 2004. *Organized Crime: A Guide to the World's Most Successful Industry.* **New York: DK Publishing. 192 pages.**

This book traces the evolution of organized crime activity from piracy and secret societies to the emergence of today's group. Lunde profiles the major syndicates, chronicling their origins and structure, methods, territories, codes of behavior, rites and rituals, and connections to the legitimate business world and governments.

Morselli, Carlo. 2009. *Inside Criminal Networks*. New York: Springer. 203 pages.

Morselli uses a social network perspective to examine a variety of criminal networks. What stands out is his analysis of how organizations and members adapt when key members are lost, the roles of key members and peripheral ones, and the use of legitimate actors in illegal situations, but the focus of the book is the flexibility of modern crime syndicates (flexible order). Morselli uses a wealth of communication data, electronic surveillance material, and other investigative sources, as well as case studies to demonstrate the flexible nature of modern syndicates. This book will be of interest to both organized crime researchers and social network theorists and analysts.

Nonprint Resources

Videos
American Organized Crime

American Gangster: Season One
Type: DVD
Date: 2007
Length: 246 minutes
Source: Black Entertainment Television

The inaugural season of this popular documentary series features two discs chronicling the stories of Stanley "Tookie" Williams, cofounder of the Crips; Harlem drug kingpin Leroy "Nicky" Barnes; crack kingpin "Freeway" Ricky Ross; jewel thieves Troy and Dino Smith; the Chambers Brothers; and Lorenzo "Fat Cat" Nichols.

American Gangster: Season Two
Type: DVD
Date: 2007
Length: 420 minutes
Source: Black Entertainment Network

This three-disc collection examines the Philly Black Mafia; Larry Hoover and the Gangster Disciples; Melvin Williams; Frank Lucas (the inspiration for the Denzel Washington film *American Gangster*); Felix Mitchell, Oakland California's first major heroin kingpin; Jeff Fort and the Blackstone Rangers; and others. Bonus features include extended interviews with Frank Lucas and others.

Busting the Mob
Type: DVD
Date: 2008
Length: 50 minutes
Source: A&E Television Networks

This documentary examines the various surveillance strategies used to incriminate some of America's leading organized crime figures in the early 1980s. Those interested in how undercover agents go about their investigations will enjoy the first-person accounts by agents describing how they placed various listening devices that led to the Pizza Connection trial and convictions. This case is significant, representing one of law enforcement's few major successes in the fight against Cosa Nostra, and leading to imprisonment of four of the five major Mafia bosses of New York City. The fifth, Paul Castellano of the Gambino family, was killed before he could be sentenced.

Gangland: Season One
Type: DVD
Date: 2007
Length: 10 hours, 11 minutes
Source: A&E Television Networks

Season one examines 13 gangs on four discs including La Nuestra Familia, MS-13, the Mexican Mafia, Hells Angels, the Almighty Black P. Stone, skinheads, and others. Several episodes reveal how gang members join the military to gain weapons expertise, battle each other over racial issues, and fight over the Harlem heroin trade.

Gangland: Season Two
Type: DVD
Date: 2008
Length: 9 hours, 24 minutes
Source: A&E Television Networks

Season two documents 12 different gangs on three DVDS, including the Maniac Latin Disciples, Chicago Gangster Disciples, the Texas Syndicate, the Los Angeles 18th Street Gang, the Mongols, the L. A. Crips and Bloods, the Chicago Vice Lords, the Outlaws, Hells Angels, and Asian Triads.

Gangland: Season Three
Type: DVD
Date: 2008
Length: 9 hours, 24 minutes
Source: A&T Television Networks

Season three examines 12 American gangs on three DVDs, including the Bandidos, Los Zetas, Warlocks, Gotti Boys, Los Solidos, Satan Disciples, Tiny Rascal Gangsters, La Gran Familia, as well as Zoe Pound (Haitians), Friends Stand United, and the Utah Crips.

Gangland: Season Four
Type: DVD
Date: 2009
Length: 9 hours, 24 minutes
Source: A&E Television Networks

Season four consists of three discs covering 12 American gangs and organized crime groups including the Pagans, Hells Angels, Aryan Brotherhood of Texas, Sons of Silence, Chicago's Latin Kings, the Avenues, the Best Friends, and others.

In Search of History: Five Points Gang
Type: DVD
Date: 1997
Length: 50 minutes
Source: A&E Television Networks

This film chronicles the evolution of New York City's first major gangs in the Five Points Section of New York. From a global perspective these gangs were primarily made up of Irish immigrants. Over time some of these gangs would morph into organized crime syndicates thanks to their corrupt overseers in city government. The story of gangs developing out of marginalized populations in American slums is an oft-repeated story in most other developing urban communities. By the end of the 19th century, German, Italian,

Jewish, and Chinese gangs would vie for turf in the area left by the assimilating Irish.

Asian Organized Crime

The Yakuza Papers
Type: DVD
Date: 2004
Length: 500+ minutes
Source: Home Vision Entertainment

This series came out the year after the Godfather. It offers a deromanticized portrait of the Japanese underworld. It is based on the memoirs of an actual Yakuza boss. A sixth disc supplements the five films in the series and features an interview with David Kaplan on the evolution of the Japanese underworld after World War II.

British Organized Crime

The Long Good Friday
Type: DVD
Date: 2006
Length: 109 minutes
Source: Anchor Bay Entertainment

This film has been compared to the *Godfather* and *Scarface*. Its portrayal of the London underworld is unsurpassed. Particularly interesting is that it was filmed in 1979 and offers an early glimpse of the convergence of terrorism and organized crime through the competition of the Irish Republican Army (IRA) and the London mob over criminal rackets.

Italian and Italian American Organized Crime

Excellent Cadavers: Fighting the Mafia in Sicily
Type: DVD
Date: 2005
Length: 92 minutes
Source: First Run Icarus Films

This documentary is based on the eponymous 1995 book by Alexander Stille. It focuses on the amoral relationship between corporate and political interests that has protected the Mafia for so long. The story is linked with the tragic campaigns of the ill-fated prosecutors Giovanni Falcone and Paolo Borsellino, both killed in 1992. The film features interviews with the photojournalist Letizia Battaglia, whose photos have chronicled the Mafia's violent legacy in Palermo for more than 20 years. Bonus materials include a photo gallery and biographies.

Godfathers Collection: The True History of the Mafia
Type: DVD
Date: 2003
Length: 5 hours
Source: A&E Television Networks

This two-disc collection is divided into five programs. Four are episodes from the BIOGRAPHY television series, featuring portraits of Lucky Luciano, Meyer Lansky, Bugsy Siegel, and the Genovese Family. The other section is a separate 100-minute disc featuring the history of American organized crime from the 19th century, using newly discovered footage from Italian archives and rare interviews with investigators and gangsters.

Mafia: The History of the Mob in America
Type: DVD
Date: 2001
Length: 250 minutes
Source: A&E Television Networks
Former title: American Justice: Target Mafia

This two-DVD set is divided into four sections covering The Prohibition Years/Birth of the American Mafia, The Kennedys and the Mob, Unions and the Mob, and the Empire of Crime, covering post-World War II activities. It also includes interactive menus. Its strength lies in its delineation of the origins of ethnic gangs in America.

Irish and Irish American Organized Crime

Paddy Whacked: The Irish Mob
Type: DVD

Date: 2007
Length: 100 minutes
Source: A&E Television Networks

Based in part on T. J. English's best-selling book of the same name, it covers the evolution of Irish organized crime in America from the "Westies" of New York to gangs in Boston, Chicago, and Philadelphia. It is especially strong in describing the horrific conditions that led to Irish immigration to the United States, as well as disease, vice, and other conditions that awaited them in America.

Global Organized Crime and Trafficking

Lords of the Mafia
Type: DVD
Date: 2000
Length: 780 minutes
Source: Koch Vision, Port Washington, NY 11050

Robert Stack narrates this 13-hour investigation of global organized crime. This seven-disc collection features examination of Japan and China, Britain and Sicily, New York and New Orleans, Los Angeles and Vietnam, Mexico and Colombia, Russia and Jamaica, and a final hour that ties in the relationships between various global organized crime groups. The DVD set also features extensive biographical and background information for the entire series, including profiles of crime bosses and charts of organization and much more.

Traffik
Type: DVD
Date: 2001
Length: 315 minutes
Source: Acorn Media

This miniseries, originally broadcast on *Masterpiece Theater* in 1989, is as timely today as it was then. Much of the film takes place in the opium fields of Pakistan and Afghanistan. The series revolves around a British drug addict, her drug czar father, and various functionaries in the drug-trafficking continuum. Their intertwined lives offer a microcosm of the continuing international drug trade and its victims.

The World History of Organized Crime
Type: DVD
Date: 2001
Length: 250 minutes
Source: A&E Television Networks

This two-disc set includes one that features China, India, and Co-lombia (150 minutes) and one that covers Sicily and Russia. Extra features includes a Timeline of Critical Events for each Featured Country and interactive menus.

Web Sites

Australian Institute of Criminology
The Australian Institute of Criminology is the country's lead-ing research center on crime and justice issues. It offers links to a number of documents and sites related to global organized crime networks, corruption, and various forms of illegal trafficking. http://www.aic.gov.au

Centre for Transnational Crime Prevention
(Faculty of Law: University of Wollongong)
Established in 2000, the center focuses on responding to organized crime activities that threaten global security, including cybercrime, terrorism, all forms of illegal trafficking, money laundering and other mainstays of organized crime. http://www.ctcp.uow.edu.au

Crime Magazine: An Encyclopedia of Crime
(Organized Crime)
This online magazine is devoted to all forms of criminal activ-ity. It offers links by topics, including organized crime. Most links are related to American and Italian organized crime, but it does offer a few related to transnational activities. http://www.crimemaga zine.com

Criminal Intelligence Service Canada
(Annual Reports on Organized Crime)
Available in both English and French, this site features annual re-ports on organized crime trends and activities in Canada based on intelligence and investigative reports. http://www.cisc.gc.ca

**Criminal Justice Resources: Organized Crime
(Michigan State University Library)**
This site offers dozens of links to resources devoted to organized crime, including reports, documents, articles, and references to global trafficking activities. http://staff.lib.msu.edu/harris23/crim just/orgcrime.htm

Drug Library (Online Library)
This site bills itself as the "World's Largest Online Library of Drug Policy." It might be right. Among the most useful links are the library resources available from the Schaffer Library of Drug Policy link. http://druglibrary.org

European Market Ecstasy Trafficking
This site offers links to everything ecstasy, including recent research on the drug, the rave party scene, and various law enforcement and public health attempts to suppress the drug. http://www.narcomafie.it/emet

**Italian Law Enforcement Agency
"Direzione Investigativa Antimafia" (DIA)**
The DIA is responsible only for mafia-related offenses. This site offers data on various Italian organized crime factions between 1992 and 2004. http://www.interno.it/dip_ps/dia/eng/compet.htm

**Klaus Von Lampe Home Page:
Topics on Organized Crime**
This site is especially helpful for anyone interested in the international definitions of organized crime. It lists samples from dozens of countries. It is also a great resource for book reviews on the subject. http://people.freenet.de/kvlampe/index.html

**The Mafia and Organised Crime in General
(The Influence of Criminal Organizations in
Banking and Finance)**
This site offers a variety of links to articles, reports, and resources dedicated to the influence of organized crime on banking and financial crimes. http://www.ex.ac.uk/~RDavies/arian/scandals/mafia.html

Mob Watcher: Antonio Nicaso's Homepage
This site has links to numerous book reviews on the latest organized crime-related books. Some are in Italian, but it is a helpful resource for hard-to-find European sources. http://www.nicaso.com

Newsfile: Time Archive on Organized Crime
This site offers an archive of hundreds of *Time* magazine articles on organized crime dating from the present back to more than 20 years ago. These can all be accessed by searching under the topic of organized crime. http://www.search.time.com

Rick Porrello's American Mafia.com
This site offers article-length reports on various aspects of the history of organized crime in America by some of the leading researchers in the field. http://americanmafia.com/

Royal Canadian Mounted Police
This is the homepage for the Royal Canadian Mounted Police and its strategies for fighting transnational organized crime. http://www.rcmp-grc.gc.ca

United Nations Convention against Transnational Organized Crime
The 2003 United Nations Convention against Transnational Organized Crime can be accessed here. http://www.odccp.org/palermo/convmain.html

United Nations Crime and Justice Information Network
This site is home to the Centre for International Crime Prevention, offering numerous links to research sources, statistics, documents, and organizations related to international organized crime and crime-fighting. http://www.uncjin.org

U.S. Department of State, International Information Programs
On the following links are international information programs dedicated to various forms of global organized crime and related law enforcement efforts.

The Fight against Bribery and Corruption   http://usinfo.state.gov/topi cal/econ/bribes

Chinese Alien Smuggling   http://usinfo.state.gov/regional/ea/chinaaliens/homepage.htm

Global Forum on Fighting Corruption   http://usinfo.state.gov/topical/econ/integrity

U.S. Treasury Department Financial Crimes Enforcement Network
The Global Fight against Money Laundering   This site is dedicated to fighting international financial crimes. Under International Programs are links to a number of financial crime fighting efforts and strategies. http://www.fincen.gov

Glossary

Activity appropriation   Process in which terrorists and organized crime actors borrow each other's methods.

Advance Fee Fraud   Also known as the 419 scam, this fraud is perpetrated typically by Nigerians. It involves sending mass e-mails to individuals soliciting help in transferring funds out of the country for a percentage of the profits by borrowing a victim's personal information.

African Connection   This refers to the involvement of Nigerians in the global heroin trade. Nigeria emerged as a major transshipment stop for Southeast Asian heroin heading to Europe and the United States in the 1990s.

Apartheid   This is a system of racial separation that existed in South Africa before it became a constitutional democracy in 1994.

Bank Secrecy Act   In 1970, this became the first important piece of legislation directed toward money laundering. It mandated a series of reporting and recordkeeping requirements to help track money launderers.

Boryokudan   Japanese police prefers to eschew the term *Yakuza* in favor of this word meaning "the violent ones."

Cacique   This is Mexico's version of a political boss who accepts bribes.

Camorra   This criminal society originated in the prisons of Naples, Italy in the early 1800s. Camorra gangs continue to flourish in the 21st century.

Capone, Al   He was America's public enemy number one during the 1920s and early 1930s.

Cartels   This term is used to describe many drug-trafficking networks in Latin America and Mexico. From an economic perspective, cartel members should have the ability to control prices, production, and the marketing of certain commodities.

Coronelismo   This is Brazil's version of a corrupt political boss.

Cosa Nostra   This expression, which means "our thing," is preferred over "Mafia" by the Italian criminal milieu in the United States and Sicily.

Coyotes These are Mexican human smugglers who participate in the illegal smuggling of immigrants, often from Mexico and Central America, into the southwestern United States.

Cybercrime Most authorities assert that computer-assisted crimes are changing the nature and shape of organized crime. The FBI ranks it as its third priority behind terrorism and espionage.

European Union Created in 1993, the EU is a treaty-based framework that defines and manages economic and political cooperation among its member states. This region is the most profitable for global drug-trafficking syndicates. The unintended consequences of EU policies allowing for the free movement of goods, services, people, and capital in the member countries have facilitated smuggling operations for transnational crime groups.

Export syndicates Recent scholarship presents this as an alternative perspective to the cartel. Rather than control raw material production and most distribution systems like a cartel, drug trafficking organizations are more like "export syndicates," in which trafficking networks are created to share risks and guarantee profits for each partner, a form of risk minimization..

Failed State This is a nation-state characterized by high levels of crime, corruption, and violence, a country in which areas are beyond government control and subsequently become havens for organized crime and terrorist groups.

FARC This acronym stands for the Revolutionary Armed Forces of Colombia, a leftist paramilitary organization that is also a major player in the region's cocaine traffic.

Financial Action Task Force The FATF was established by seven industrialized countries in 1989 to fight money laundering.

419 Scam This is the same as the advance fee fraud. The 419 refers to the Nigerian criminal statute that made this fraud illegal in 1980.

French Connection In the 1930s, Corsican gangsters in Marseilles, France worked together with French gangsters in the heroin business and established that city as the epicenter of the heroin trade, or the French Connection, until the 1960s.

Globalization This is a process that refers to the increasing integration and interdependence of the world's nation states.

Golden Age of Piracy Sea pirates were most active between 1650 and 1730. It is estimated that up to 4,000 pirates roamed the high seas. Modern organized crime scholars have been able to draw a number of parallels with this era and global organized crime activities in the 21st century.

Great Nordic Biker War Between 1994 and 1997, the Hells Angeles and Bandidos outlaw motorcycle gangs fought for supremacy over Denmark's criminal operations. The conflict left almost a dozen dead and at least 100 wounded.

Harrison Narcotics Act   This 1914 law criminalized the nonmedical use of opium, morphine, and coca derivatives in the United States and set the stage for the development of global drug-trafficking networks to supply the drugs.

Hawala   This informal underground banking system evolved in South Asia. It is used to exchange money for commodities without leaving a paper trail for investigators. Based on trust, it is used by criminal and terrorist networks to transmit funds, usually for illicit activities, on a global scale.

Hezbollah   This terrorist group was created in Lebanon by Revolutionary Guards from Iran shortly after the Israeli invasion of Lebanon. Although it receives funding from Iran and Syria, it also relies on funding through various organized crime activities.

Human smuggling   Unlike human trafficking, this form of smuggling usually involves the full participation of those being smuggled, with the assistance of individuals who facilitate the movement between national boundaries by avoiding the legitimate protocol for immigration.

Human trafficking   This refers to the movement of people through a variety of illegal practices such as coercion, abduction, and deception. It also sometimes results in sexual exploitation such as prostitution, as well as forced labor and other practices similar to slavery.

Hybrid groups   Over the decades certain groups such as FARC have taken on a "hybrid" appearance, blurring the distinction between terrorist and organized crime networks.

International Maritime Bureau   This agency is a clearinghouse for sea piracy data.

Interpol   The International Criminal Police Organization, more commonly known by its acronym, was created in 1923. Headquartered in Lyons, France, it helps global police forces coordinate and cooperate on transnational criminal issues.

Kosovo Liberation Army   The KLA emerged in 1996 out of the problems created by the Yugoslavian conflicts. Its goal was to win Kosovan independence from Serbia. Few organizations illustrate the nexus between organized crime and terrorism more than the relationship between the KLA and Albanian crime syndicates beginning in the 1990s.

Krysha   In Russian this means roof and refers to an organization or individual that can provide protection and patronage necessary to carry on business or government practices.

Mafia   First found in an Italian dictionary in the 1860s, this term has been used interchangeably with organized crime for so long its meaning has become obscured in a blizzard of stereotypes and clichés. Probably of Arabic origin, it has been used to refer to traditional organized crime groups that originated on the island of Sicily and then later saw some of its traditions imported to the United States during a wave of late 19th-century immigration. The American and Sicilian versions of the mafia remain distinct.

Mafiya   In the waning days of the Soviet Union, it became popular to brand different forms of corruption as *Mafiya*. Unlike its more recognizable counterpart in Italy, the Russian term referred to the daily inequities of life in the communist system rather than to any monolithic crime group. In the aftermath of the Soviet Union, journalists used this term to refer to emerging crime syndicates.

Mara Salvatrucha   Better known as MS-13, this gang was named after La Mara, a street in El Salvador as well as for Salvatrucha guerrillas who fought in the country's civil war in the 1980s. The gang is unique for having made the transition from street gang to transnational organized crime group in a rather short time, as well as for its influence in drug trafficking throughout Mexico, Central America, and the United States.

Money laundering   Organized crime groups from around the world use this process to conceal the existence and source of illicit income.

Mustache Petes   This refers to the Old World bosses from Sicily who ran operations in New York City and elsewhere in the United States before their demise in a series of slayings in 1931.

Narcoterrorism   This term was coined by Peruvian President Belaunde Terry in 1983 to describe the violent attacks on antinarcotics police by the Shining Path terrorist group. In the 1980s, however, it became more identified as a form of terrorism used by drug cartels such as Colombia's Medillin drug kingpin Carlos Escobar.

Navigation Acts   The English Parliament passed a series of acts between 1651 and 1696 meant to control the movement of certain commodities into the English colonies in North America. Organized gangs of smugglers, pirates, and black marketeers stepped in to supply the colonists with luxury goods prohibited from other countries.

'Ndrangheta   The "honored society" or "brotherhood" is well established in southern Italy's Calabria. This organization has apparently surpassed the power of the Sicilian Mafia in both clout and international contacts and has readily adapted to globalization.

Operation Jessica   This 2002 FBI operation revealed the existence of large-scale organized crime involvement in the counterfeiting of CDs in Italy, as well as the transnational operational structure that ran the enterprise.

Opium War The defeat of the Chinese by the British in this 1842 war forced China to accept the free trade of opium within its borders, inaugurating the global drug trade.

Outlaw Motorcycle Gangs (OMGs) OMGs are motorcycle gangs such as Hells Angels that have evolved into structured organized crime groups.

Pizza Connection Case This was one of the first organized crime investigations and prosecutions with international implications. Police agencies from at least five countries cooperated in the 1980s to shut down a major drug-trafficking and money-laundering operation using pizza restaurants as fronts for heroin traffic.

Plata o plomo The expression "silver or lead" refers to the choice given to Colombian judges by Medillin drug cartel members in Colombia of either taking financial bribes or a bullet.

Posses These are Jamaican gangs that developed in the poverty-stricken areas of Kingston, Jamaica, before emerging as an organized crime threat in the United States and Great Britain (where they are known as Yardies) in the 1980s. At their zenith, they played an important role in the expansion of the crack cocaine trade in the United States.

President's Commission on Organized Crime (PCOC) In 1986, this commission's findings forced scholars and public officials to reevaluate their understanding of organized crime by refocusing their attentions from traditional Italian organized crime to emerging groups such as Jamaican posses, Asian gangs, prison gangs, Russian mafiya, and others.

Smurfing In the 1980s, drug-trafficking groups used the tactic of breaking large sums of money into smaller amounts in order to conduct financial transactions at financial institutions and avoid certain reporting procedures.

Snakeheads These are Chinese human smugglers who facilitate the migration of individuals from China overseas. Almost 85 percent come from the Fujian province. The modern snakeheads emerged in the 1960s and 1970s when many mainland Chinese fled to Hong Kong for more freedom.

Triads These are Chinese secret societies, many of whom are engaged in various organized crime activities. They have been involved in global crime activities since around 1917. Triads are decentralized, lacking a central body capable of uniting all the groups or giving universally accepted commands.

Tribalism In certain regions of the world, particularly in Africa, a high premium is placed on one's tribal or ethnic background. It is not uncommon for criminal gangs and organized crime groups to be bound by these natural affinities.

United Nations Convention against Transnational Organized Crime
Signed into law in 2003, this Convention offered for the first time a singular legal definition of transnational organized crime that was acceptable to most countries.

Vory-v-zakone   Between the 1920s and the 1990s, the Soviet labor camps gave birth to this elite criminal fraternity, whose members lived according to a *thieves' law,* an unwritten system of rules and behavior.

Yakuza   This term originally referred to a losing hand of cards, hence its traditional association with gambling rackets. After the post-World War II economy recovered in the 1950s, Yakuza gangs flourished thanks to alliances with politicians at all levels of government, inadequate policing, and fear of extreme left-wing activity by labor unions and student groups. Groups have a fairly complex hierarchy. Members are unique for carrying business cards and maintaining identifiable headquarters. There are roughly 22 Yakuza syndicates today with about 85,000 members. A government crackdown, however, has shattered much of their former prestige.

Zetas   These are former members of the Mexican Army who deserted in the late 1990s and enlisted in the Gulf cartel as killers and enforcers. By 2006. they had become influential in their own right by trying to control their own drug routes.

Index

293

About the Author

Mitchel P. Roth is professor of criminal justice at Sam Houston State University in the College of Criminal Justice. He has also been a regular instructor at the International Law Enforcement Academy (ILEA) in Roswell, New Mexico, since 2001, where he has focused on organized crime issues. He is the author of numerous articles and book chapters and 10 books including *Organized Crime,* published by Pearson-Prentice Hall (2009); *Crime and Punishment: A History of the Criminal Justice System,* published by Cengage (2005); *Prisons and Prison Systems: A Global Encyclopedia,* Greenwood Press (2003); and *Historical Dictionary of Law Enforcement,* Greenwood Press (2001). He has taught numerous study-abroad classes including one, in the summer of 2009, focusing on the Sicilian Mafia.